PLENTY OF PEOPLE

The World's Population Pressures, Problems, and Policies, and How They Concern Us

By

WARREN S. THOMPSON

SCRIPPS FOUNDATION FOR RESEARCH
IN POPULATION PROBLEMS

REVISED EDITION

THE RONALD PRESS COMPANY · NEW YORK

2

11, 969

PREFACE

In the United States we have come to take for granted the "naturalness" of rapid population growth and we also have assumed that this rapid growth increased the general welfare. We have never had occasion to consider seriously the relation of numbers to food supply, nor have we needed hitherto to consider whether we were numerous enough to defend ourselves from our possible enemies. Moreover, we have never been made to feel inferior by seeing some of our neighbors overtake and pass us in numbers and industrial strength as has happened to several other nations.

It is not surprising, therefore, that we have paid little attention to the problems of population either at home or abroad. Since we have not needed to concern ourselves with our own numbers and with their increase it was quite natural to assume that matters of population growth were equally unimportant in other lands and in the world at large. After all, it is difficult to visualize conditions greatly different from those with which one is familiar.

However, several situations have arisen in recent years which have given us occasion to wonder whether there may not be some relation between numbers and welfare other than that we have so casually assumed. We had a depression during the 1930's which threw millions of men out of work for years at a time; our 1940 Census provided clear evidence to the public at large that we were no longer growing rapidly. We had less than half the rate of increase 1930-40 that we had in the preceding decade. In recent years we have also learned more about the increase of population in Japan, the Soviet Union, India, and elsewhere with the result that our current increase appears rather insignificant both proportionately and in absolute

iii

numbers. Naturally we are beginning to ask ourselves whether our numbers are and will be large enough to insure military security; whether there is a conflict between our military need and our desire to raise the level of living; whether it is desirable to have such a large proportion of our people living in dense city aggregations subject to instantaneous destruction; whether the depression of the 1930's is in any way related to the changes in our population growth; and whether it would be desirable to maintain the higher birth rate of the past few years.

No attempt has been made here to arrive at conclusive answers to these and to many other questions regarding population that are being raised, but clearly we can no longer take it for granted that all population changes are good. If population growth and distribution are closely related to welfare then it is not certain that what just "happens" in population matters will be for the "best." It is no more certain that the purely personal judgment of the individual as to what is best for him as regards the number of his children, the growth of his city, the expansion of the labor force, etc., is also best for the community and the nation—for the general welfare.

All these questions involving numbers and their relation to welfare make it incumbent on us to look into these matters more carefully than in the past—to try to understand how population changes are related to welfare and how they may be controlled to this end if it seems desirable to do so.

This book is an attempt to introduce the lay reader to the questions arising out of population growth and its distribution not only in our own country but in the world. The writer has, therefore, tried to avoid technical discussion and has ignored or glossed over many points which would be of interest to specialists.

In the interests of economy as well as of easy reading he has also used footnotes sparingly, and without doubt credit has not been given where it should have been. In addition, the reader is asked to take on faith many of the data presented.

Those who would like to explore any of these matters more fully will find much material at their disposal in the few works cited which will in turn lead him to other valuable materials.

The author wishes to acknowledge his great indebtedness to the work of many scholars both in this country and abroad. He also wishes to make special acknowledgment of the assistance of the members of the staff of the Scripps Foundation. He is particularly indebted to Ruth Wiley Smith who did a large part of the statistical work for the revision, who outlined the charts, compiled the index, and assumed the chief burden of seeing the book through the press.

WARREN S. THOMPSON

Oxford, Ohio
July, 1948

CONTENTS

ILLUSTRATIONS

xi

TABLES

xiii

PLENTY OF PEOPLE

CHAPTER 1

THE POPULATION GROWTH OF THE WORLD
SINCE 1800

The year 1800 was chosen as the point from which to start our survey of modern population growth for several reasons. In the first place, there is little exact information about the size of populations, to say nothing of their rates of growth, prior to that time. Indeed, reliable information was still very scanty at that date, but there was enough interest in numbers that several countries in the West took censuses at about that time. In the second place, 1800 is as good a point as any other from which to date the beginning of what amounts to a revolution in population growth in the West, although, like all dates given for the beginning of great social changes, it is only approximate. In the third place, Malthus published his essay on population in 1798 and although this in itself was not an epoch-making event it was proof of a growing interest in man's numbers and their increase as factors in human welfare. From that time on social scientists could not completely ignore population growth when considering human welfare although they might dismiss it as a factor of negligible importance. Finally, without the perspective of a considerable past it will be quite impossible to appreciate the unique features of population growth in modern times, and to project this experience into the future with reasonable hope of profiting by it.

MALTHUS ON POPULATION GROWTH

The central question with which Malthus concerned himself was the relation of population growth to human welfare. He was not by any means the first person to raise this question but he raised it so effectively that since his day the study of population growth has been considered a proper field of inquiry for social scientists although until quite recently it has been regarded by most of them, as well as by statesmen, as of little practical importance. From such data as Malthus could find, which were both scanty and often inaccurate, and from the accounts of travelers in Europe as well as in other continents, he came to the conclusion that the growth of population was determined almost entirely by the scarcity or abundance of the *means of subsistence*. By this he meant chiefly the food supply, although clothing and shelter were also included. He believed that where subsistence was abundant population grew rapidly because the death rate would be relatively low. His favorite example of rapid growth was the United States, where subsistence was plentiful. On the other hand, where subsistence was scarce population could grow slowly if at all. Malthus very frequently cited China and India as countries in which the death rate was high because of the lack of subsistence and in which population was either stationary or grew very slowly. He recognized that disease and war also affected population growth, particularly disease, but placed the major emphasis on subsistence (food) as the great controller of population growth.

The result was that Malthus held out little hope for any permanent improvement in human living conditions, since he believed that population always had a tendency to grow faster than food supply. He believed that even in a new country like America, where the food supply could be greatly and rapidly increased, population growth would about keep pace with it. Hence, once its new land was exhausted, America would be no better off than the older settled countries where there was always great want and poverty. This belief, of course, rested on the assumption that the birth rate was practically fixed at, or near, physiological capacity (see Chapter 2) while subsistence was not often capable of being expanded rapidly and then not for any long time. Actually, Malthus was not quite as pessimistic as this line of reasoning should have made him, for he believed that postponement of marriage and abstinence from marital relations, as well as certain customs and taboos, did reduce the birth rate a little. But when all these matters were taken into account he remained basically pessimistic because he did not see any way out of the dilemma created by a high birth rate in a world having a limited amount of tillable land. Malthus seems never to have appreciated the possibilities of birth control as an agent in adjusting population to the means of subsistence, although there was a fairly vigorous birth control campaign carried on in England during the decade before his death in 1834.

For almost a century following Malthus there was very little interest in his doctrines because every informed person in Western Europe and America knew that man's numbers were increasing at a very rapid rate in many Western countries, and also that most of the people in these lands were living better than their ancestors had lived.[1] These facts seemed to indicate that Malthus was wrong and that there was no practical need for man to concern himself with population growth as a factor limiting his welfare. Man was actually finding ways to avoid the pressure of population on subsistence. He was exploiting new lands and discovering more efficient ways of making things.

To the majority of thinking people in the West, this view seemed entirely reasonable throughout most of the nineteenth century. But after a century or more of indifference to population questions, we are again coming to realize that even though

---

[1] An exception must be made of a few advocates of birth control who believed that this was the solution of the Malthusian dilemma and a few Utopians who believed that it was the privileges of the upper classes which made it impossible to increase "subsistence" as fast as population could grow.

the Malthusian dilemma can be resolved, population growth and human welfare are intimately and intricately related. In the West, population questions are attracting the attention of people today, not because there is danger of increased poverty arising from a too-rapid growth of population, as Malthus held, but because there is now danger that population will soon cease to grow or even decline. In the East, on the other hand, there is much interest in Malthus' views because they seem to describe quite accurately the situation which exists in many of those countries.

THE POPULATION OF THE WORLD

Table 1 gives estimates of the population of the several continents at various times since 1800. For 1800 almost all popu-

TABLE 1

ESTIMATED POPULATION OF THE WORLD AND ITS DISTRIBUTION
BY CONTINENTS, 1800-1946 *

Continent	1800	1850	1900	1913	1939	1946
	Population (in millions)					
World	919	1,091	1,527	1,723	2,080	2,221
Asia	600	664	839	923	1,097	1,199
Europe	188	266	390	468	542	533
Africa	100	100	141	135	157	173
North and Central						
America	15	39	110	134	184	203
South America	14	20	41	56	89	101
Oceania	2	2	6	8	11	12
	Percentage Distribution					
World	100.0	100.0	100.0	100.0	100.0	100.0
Asia	65.3	60.9	54.9	53.6	52.7	54.0
Europe	20.5	24.4	25.5	27.2	26.1	24.0
Africa	10.9	9.2	9.2	7.8	7.5	7.8
North and Central						
America	1.6	3.6	7.2	7.8	8.8	9.1
South America	1.5	1.8	2.7	3.2	4.3	4.5
Oceania	0.2	0.2	0.4	0.5	0.5	0.5

* Data for 1800 and 1850 are from Walter F. Willcox, *Studies in American Demography*, Ithaca, N. Y.: Cornell University Press, 1940, p. 45; those for later years are from a number of official and semi-official year books. Other estimates for earlier years are available but the writer knows of none which would make any difference to the argument of this chapter.

lation figures are estimates, as only a few Western European countries and the United States had reasonably accurate censuses. By 1850 a few more European countries could be added to those whose numbers were known with reasonable accuracy. By 1900 students began to feel that they could speak of the population of the world with a modest amount of assurance although for most of the world informed guesses (estimates) still had to be relied upon. Today our knowledge of the world's population is considerably greater although there are still important gaps in our knowledge. However, in spite of these gaps, there is good reason to believe that the pattern of the changes in the population of the different parts of the world shown here is essentially correct.

Trends in Growth.—The most outstanding trend in population growth between 1800 and 1913 is the increase in the proportion of people of European descent in the world's population. Whereas Europeans probably constituted only about 22 percent of the world's population in 1800, they rose to about 35 percent in 1913, assuming that China's population was 357 million in the latter year (see Figure 1). In numbers the increase

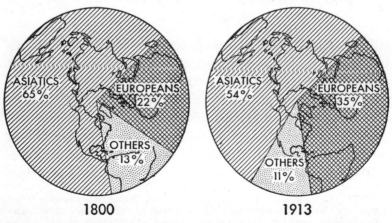

Figure 1. Proportions of Europeans, Asiatics, and Other Peoples in the World in 1800 and 1913

was from about 200 million to about 600 million, or an increase of about 200 percent.[2] The steady and rapid increase of Europeans for over a century is one of the most remarkable facts of human history. It is highly probable that no such continuous growth in a large population had ever before occurred in mankind's experience.

This great relative increase in Europeans was accompanied by an almost equally great relative decrease in Asiatics—from over 65 percent of the world's total in 1800 to about 54 percent in 1913. In absolute numbers the increase in Asiatics during this period was probably about 75 million less than that of people of European stock, if the smaller figure is used for China, although Asiatics were about three times as numerous as Europeans in 1800.

The importance of the several factors which led to this great difference in the rate of increase of Europeans and Asiatics can be more easily understood if we trace the growth of population during this period in several countries where the facts are well established.

REASONS FOR RAPID POPULATION GROWTH IN THE UNITED STATES

The United States had an extremely high rate of growth from the time of the first census (1790) down to the outbreak of World War I. In the 30 years between 1790 and 1820 the population grew by almost 150 percent and this rate was maintained during the succeeding 30 years. In the next 30 years (1850-80), however, the rate fell to about 116 percent and in the period 1880-1910 to about 80 percent. In the 30 years 1910-40, it grew by only 43 percent and only a little over one-

---

[2] The relative increase in Europeans is a little less impressive if it is assumed that China grew from 357 million in 1900 to 442 million in 1913. The writer believes, however, that the preponderance of evidence points to a relatively stationary population in China during the last four or five decades, except for the expansion of the Chinese into Manchuria.

fifth of this took place between 1930 and 1940. Since 1940 the rate of growth has risen and between 1940 and 1950 it appears probable that our rate of increase will be about 12 percent and will total between 15 and 16 million. The tremendous rate of growth maintained up to the outbreak of World War I was made possible by a variety of factors only a few of the more important of which can be discussed here.

Land Policy.—In the first place, throughout most of the nineteenth century the abundance of good land, coupled with our land policy, made it easy for almost anyone, native and immigrant alike, to become a landowner and farmer. It is doubtful whether the common man ever enjoyed such free opportunity to gain security anywhere else, for land ownership did mean security when 75 percent or more of the people were farmers and all farmers were largely self-sustaining. Such opportunity was highly favorable to early marriage and early marriage was favorable to a high birth rate.

Scattered Farmsteads and Disease.—Another factor of great importance was that a new land like this, thinly settled and with isolated self-sufficing farmsteads, did not suffer from the infectious and contagious diseases to the same extent as many of the older, more thickly settled countries. In Europe and Asia the farmers lived in villages in which a single source of infection, e.g., a contaminated well, was more likely to spread disease over the entire community than in our farm settlements. Then, too, most parts of Western Europe had a few large cities and better roads so that pestilence, once started, could be carried more readily to the entire country than in the United States. Daniel Defoe (author of *Robinson Crusoe*) describes how the great pestilence of 1665 started in London and was then spread all over England by people fleeing from the city to escape its ravages. There is no record of any catastrophe in our history at all comparable to this, although we have by no means been

free from serious local epidemics. It was not until the influenza
epidemic of 1918-19, which killed about 500,000, that we had
a well-recognized nation-wide epidemic of the pattern not uncommon in many older countries from time immemorial.

Rurality of the Population.—We were distinctly a rural people until quite recently. As late as 1870, 72 percent of our
white population (including immigrants) and 77 percent of our
native white population lived in places of less than 2,500 inhabitants, and the proportion of Negroes in such communities
was even higher (86 percent). This is of the greatest significance because until quite recently rural people as a class have
always had lower death rates than urban people. Even today
most rural communities have lower death rates than most cities
in spite of the fact that public health work is largely confined to
cities and that many rural communities have very scanty medical service. In addition, and of even more significance, rural
people have also had higher birth rates than city people ever
since we have had any information on this point. As is shown
in Chapter 2, the differences in their birth rates are still large.

Immigration.—Fourthly, the fact that a large part of our
immigrants have always been young adults of the ages when
reproduction is highest has no doubt exercised an important influence on our rate of population growth. The writer does not
subscribe to what may be called the "substitution theory" of immigration, viz., that the lower level of living among the immigrants and their higher birth rates create such severe economic
competition that the natives reduce their birth rate below what
it would be if there were no immigration.[3]

Famine.—Famine has never been a factor of any importance
in determining our death rate. This does not mean, of course,
that no one has died of hunger in this country, but rather that

[3] Warren S. Thompson and P. K. Whelpton, *Population Trends in the
United States,* New York: McGraw-Hill Book Co., Inc., 1933, pp. 304-305.

no considerable group has ever perished because of the lack of subsistence as was so common everywhere prior to the nineteenth century, and as is still the case in many lands.

POPULATION GROWTH IN WESTERN EUROPE

While the United States was a country in which all conditions—economic conditions, immigration, and rural living—were unusually favorable to a rapid increase of population we find that population also grew rapidly in most of Western Europe, although nowhere in Europe was the growth as rapid as in the United States. However, even in those countries which had long been settled and which sent forth large numbers of emigrants, the rate of growth was high throughout most of the nineteenth century and in the early part of the twentieth.

TABLE 2
GROWTH OF POPULATION IN SELECTED COUNTRIES, 1850-1946
(*In thousands*)

Year	United States	England and Wales	France	Japan	India (without Burma)
1850......	23,192	17,928	35,783		
1860......	31,443	20,119	37,390		
1870......	38,558	22,789	36,140	33,111	256,378
1880......	50,156	25,974	37,672	37,702	259,284
1890......	62,948	29,003	38,343	41,388	282,967
1900......	75,995	32,528	38,962	43,764	285,610
1910......	91,972	36,070	39,602	49,589	303,041
1920......	105,711	37,887	39,210	55,963	305,730
1930......	122,775	39,948	41,835	64,448	338,171
1940......	131,669	41,862*	41,200*	73,114	388,998
1946......	141,229*	41,690*	40,518*	73,114*	414,000*

* Estimated.

These countries did not have the abundance of land of the New World but they were learning how to control the death rate, they were steadily expanding employment opportunities by the establishment of new industry, they were improving their agriculture, and they were drawing great quantities of food and raw materials from the new lands through their development of cheap transportation. The tremendous emigration from Europe during this time attests to the relatively slower growth of opportunity in these older lands than in the New World, but their unusual population growth also attests the great increase in opportunity to make a better living arising out of the Industrial Revolution. The facts of population growth for several of these countries will abundantly support this position. Table 2 shows the growth of population in five important countries.

Population Growth in Great Britain.—England, Wales, and Scotland had a population of 10,500,000 in 1801 which rose to 20,800,000 by 1851, an increase of almost 100 percent. This is a very rapid growth but is considerably less than one-half as great as that of the United States during the same period. In the next 50 years the population of these countries increased by about 80 percent, to 37,000,000 in 1900. Besides, during this century many millions of people moved from the British Isles to new homes in America, Australasia, and South Africa, and other hundreds of thousands were scattered throughout the world, ruling the British Empire and carrying on British trade. The records of outbound passengers from the United Kingdom during the years 1815 to 1900 show that over 15 million persons departed.[4] These were by no means all emigrants, and the figures include the Irish as well as people from continental Europe who sailed from British ports; but the total from the United Kingdom was hardly less than 10 million, for almost 9 million[5] British and Irish left the British Isles between 1853 and the end of the century. If these emigrants and their children were added to the population of the British Isles there is not the least doubt that their numbers would have far more than doubled in each 50-year period.

---

[4] W. A. Carrothers, *Emigration from the British Isles,* London: P. S. King & Son, Ltd., 1929, p. 10.
[5] *Ibid.,* pp. 308-309.

Population Growth in Sweden.—The growth of Sweden's population shows the same general trend although it was not quite as rapid as that of the United Kingdom. It grew from 2,347,000 in 1800 to 3,483,000 in 1850, or by 48 percent; and to 5,136,000 in 1900, or by 47 percent, during the second half of the century. The Swedish records do not show the number of people emigrating until 1851, and do not show the number of immigrants until 1875, but the total number of emigrants in the second half of the century was 912,789 while the number of immigrants recorded during the period from 1875 to 1900 was 144,158. The net outward movement during the whole of the nineteenth century is estimated to amount to about 870,-000 [6], or equivalent to somewhat more than one third of the 1800 population. Swedish out-migration continued after 1900 but not at as rapid a rate as during the latter half of the nineteenth century. The net out-migration during the period from 1900 to 1940 amounted to 321,758. Clearly, if these emigrants and their children were added to the Swedish population its rate of growth would have been much higher assuming, of course, that they could have been provided for in Sweden.

Population Growth in France.—France is the one great Western power which showed a relatively slow rate of growth throughout the nineteenth century. Her population grew only from 27.5 million in 1801 to 35.8 million in 1851, or by 30 percent, and in the second half of the century, allowing for the loss of Alsace-Lorraine to Germany, the increase was less than 15 percent. The great losses France suffered during the Napoleonic wars undoubtedly affected her population growth during the first half of the century [7] and the Franco-Prussian War (1870-71) had a lesser effect in the second half, but the great difference between France and other Western nations during most of the century was in the birth rate as will be shown

---

[6] Gustav Sundbärg, *Bevölkerungsstatistik Schwedens, 1750-1900*, Stockholm: P. A. Norstedt & Söner, 1907, p. 71.

[7] See Chapter 5 for a discussion of War and Population Growth.

in Chapter 2 (Birth Rate). Unlike most of the other countries of Western Europe, France's population growth was not much affected by migration until after World War I. Since then she has received a considerable number of immigrants.

An examination of population growth in other European countries shows that the rate of growth in England and Sweden rather than in France was charactertistic of the continent. Europe had a population of about 188 million in 1800 which grew to about 266 million in 1850, a gain of 41 percent, and to about 390 million in 1900, a gain of 47 percent. By 1914 (outbreak of World War I) it had grown to approximately 468 million, or 20 percent in 14 years. This is a rapid increase.

Europe's Growth Since 1914

Europe's population has continued to grow since 1914, but at a considerably slower rate. Whereas its rate of increase was about 1.4 percent a year between 1900 and 1914, it was a little less than 0.6 percent a year between the outbreak of World War I and World War II. Much of this slower growth is due to losses connected with World War I and the Russian Revolution (see Chapter 5), for during the 20 years between wars it grew at the rate of about 1.0 percent a year, averaging about 4.5 million a year. The net result of this slower growth was to reduce Europe's share of the world's population in 1939 slightly below what it was in 1913—from about 27.2 percent to 26.1 percent. By 1946 this proportion was further reduced to 24.0 percent. This is a significant change (see Chapter 6).

The Eastward and Southward Shift.—But of more interest to us at this point than its slight proportional decline in recent years is the fact that Europe's gain in population has been coming more and more largely from Southern and Eastern Europe since sometime during the latter half of the nineteenth century. In 1850 slightly over half of the population of Europe lived in

Northern and Western Europe; by 1913 this proportion had fallen to 43 percent and by 1939 to 42 percent (see Figure 2). Throughout this period the annual rate of increase in Southern and Eastern Europe has been almost twice as great (1.1 percent

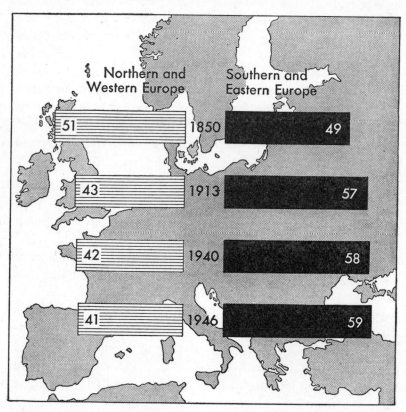

Figure 2. Growth of the Population of Europe by Major Geographic Divisions, 1850, 1913, 1940, and 1946

from 1850 to 1913 and 0.7 percent, 1913 to 1939) as in Western and Northern Europe (0.6 percent 1850 to 1913 and 0.4 percent 1913 to 1939).

From 1850 to 1913 the total increase in Europe was about 200 million. Of this increase about one third took place in

Northern and Western Europe although it had half the population in 1850 and about two thirds came from Southern and Eastern Europe. It seems highly probable that this shift in Europe's population growth from west to east and south will be accelerated in the future with consequences which will be of vast importance in world affairs (see Chapter 7).

POPULATION GROWTH IN JAPAN

Because it will further help in understanding the factors controlling population growth under different conditions, it will be of interest to examine the growth of population in the two Oriental countries about which we know most, viz., Japan and India.

Before 1900.—No true census was taken in Japan prior to 1920 but the estimates for earlier years are more reliable than for most other Asiatic lands. They may be used without going too far astray. In 1800 Japan is generally assumed to have had a population of about 27 million. The estimate for 1872 most frequently used gives her a population of about 33 million, but since the continuation of this series of estimates based on local population registers yielded a population about 2 million larger than enumerated in the census of 1920 the writer believes it reasonable to scale down the 1872 estimate by about a million and to assume a population of 32 million at that time. Thus there was probably an increase of little less than one fifth in the first three fourths of the nineteenth century, or about 0.25 percent annually. If the 1900 estimate is reduced from 44,826,000 to 44,000,000, for the reason just given, the increase during the last 28 years of the nineteenth century was approximately 12 million, or an average of 1.2 percent a year. This is between four and five times as great as in the first three fourths of the century and much the same rate as that of many European countries during a considerable part of the nineteenth century.

Since 1900.—Unlike most of the countries of Western Europe, Japan's rate of population growth did not decline after World War I. From 1900 to 1936 the annual rate of population increase in Japan averaged about 1.4 percent and did not vary greatly from year to year. This is not far from the rate achieved by England (1860-90) and Germany (1880-1910) at the periods of their most rapid growth. After the outbreak of her undeclared war with China, Japan's population growth showed a decided decline. Thus the general pattern of Japan's population growth since about 1875 is almost identical with that of England, Germany, and other Western European countries, three to five decades earlier. This seems a perfectly natural lag, if, as shown below, the recent changes in birth rates and death rates are closely associated with the development of modern industrialism, enlarged commercial activities, the rapid urbanization of the population, and the improvement of health conditions. Japan did not come in contact with modern industry until over a century after England began to use power machinery and was several decades behind most of the remainder of Western Europe. It would be expected, therefore, to lag in much the same measure in the control of its death rates and birth rates.

There is unmistakable evidence since 1920 that both of these rates have been declining, but since they appear to have moved almost apace until 1937 the rate of increase remained almost constant. Before Japan's attack on Pearl Harbor it appeared probable that if she did not become involved in war on a vast scale her birth rate could be expected to decline somewhat faster than her death rate and, hence, that the rate of natural increase would decline, thus following the pattern previously set by Western nations as industry expanded and more and more people crowded into cities. How the destruction wrought in Japan during the war, the reparations policies of the Allies, the Occupation, and the new economic conditions which Japan will have to face in attempting to rebuild her foreign trade, will affect her population growth no one can say. But it is far from impossible that poverty and disease will take a much heavier toll in Japan for some time to come than in recent decades, and that her population growth will for some time revert towards the subsistence basis described by Malthus.

POPULATION GROWTH IN INDIA

The first serious attempt to count the population of India was made in 1872. As would be expected, a first count in a country not well organized for such a huge administrative task was highly deficient. The count of that year was somewhat in excess of 203 million, not including Burma. Investigations made later led the Indian census authorities to believe that this count was deficient by 11 million on account of poor methods and incomplete enumeration, while additional territory included in the census area in 1881 had about 33 million persons in 1872, so that of the total increase of 47 million between 1872 and 1881 only 3 million were believed to represent actual increase. When allowance is made for these deficiencies and changes in area, the population of India in the area as enumerated in 1921, but not including Burma, actually grew by only about 49 million between 1872 and 1921 and amounted to about 306 million in the latter year. This is a growth of about 19 percent in the 49 years ending in 1921, or an average annual rate of slightly less than 0.4 percent. This is about half the rate that prevailed in Europe from 1850 to 1900 and about one third the rate of Japan in the period from 1872 to 1900. Since 1921, however, India's population has grown at a rate considerably in excess of that prevailing in Europe from about 1850 to the outbreak of World War I, the increase being from 306 million in 1921 to 389 million in 1941, a growth of over 27 percent in 20 years which gives an average annual rate of 1.2 percent.

Variability in India's Population Growth.—The most significant feature of India's population growth during the past 70 years is its great variability. It grew by only 1.5 percent or less in three of these seven decades and only since 1921 has it shown a consistently high rate of growth—about 11 percent in the decade 1921-31 and 15 percent from 1931-41. So far as the writer can find, no other country having fairly reliable census data and not engaged in a war has had such a high variability over as long a period.[8] The reasons for these great fluctuations in India's population growth are to be found in the slight control over the death rate exercised by a people having but a feeble health organization with little means at its disposal, and in the fact that the Indians live close to the subsistence level (see Chapter 4). India, more than any other country for which we have reliable census data, was until recently subject to the great fluctuations in death rates which have prevailed from time immemorial over most of the earth. In addition, famine has taken a heavy toll from time to time and as recently as 1943-44 a famine in Bengal, due chiefly to the inability to import the usual amounts of rice from Burma, is said to have killed as many as 2 or 3 million, possibly even more.

The unprecedented growth of India's population since 1921 may have made it even more vulnerable to famine than in the 20 years preceding. Certainly many Indians believe that this is the case. To use Malthus' language, India's population may have grown faster in recent years than its means of subsistence, thus putting pressure on a level of living already close to subsistence. In India, too, the regular malnutrition of a large part

---

[8] Russia undoubtedly lost population from 1913 to 1922 as a result of war, revolution, epidemics, and famine, and again in World War II, but these seem to have been the only periods in recent times during which there was not a substantial gain. For an excellent discussion of Russia's population growth see, Frank Lorimer, *The Population of the Soviet Union: History and Prospects,* League of Nations, 1946. For a more detailed discussion of population growth in Japan and India see the author's *Population and Peace in the Pacific,* Chicago: University of Chicago Press, 1946, Chs. 6 and 10.

of the population makes the people an easy prey to the many contagious and infectious diseases which are always present and may assume epidemic proportions at any time. Malaria is also very widespread.

Factors in India's Population Growth.—Our knowledge of the factors controlling India's population growth is so much more adequate than that regarding population growth in most other parts of the world where social and economic conditions are somewhat similar that it will be well to point out in more concrete terms the roles of pestilence and famine in this growth. In 1911 India (without Burma) had a population of somewhat over 303 million and in the preceding decade had grown by about 17 million (6.1 percent). The census of 1921 showed an increase of only 2.7 million or 0.9 percent. Why this great decline in growth? The chief factor appears to have been the influenza epidemic of 1918-19. This epidemic struck India with devastating force. In addition, the population had been considerably weakened in many areas as a result of short crops caused by the failure of the southwest monsoon in 1918. Thus the people were easy prey to influenza and other diseases during the latter part of 1918 and the first half of 1919. The exact toll taken by influenza will never be known, for the registration machinery broke down completely in many communities and diagnosis in many cases was highly questionable, but the recorded mortality from this cause amounted to about 8.5 million. Moreover, the deficit in population counted in 1921 as compared with the population "expected" if only 8.5 million died of the influenza was 4 million. From these figures it would appear quite probable that as many as 12-13 million persons died of the influenza at that time. But this is not all, the total may have been much larger, for many deaths from influenza are quite likely to have been reported merely as deaths from "fever" which is generally interpreted as malaria or other tropical fever and is always the greatest "cause" of deaths in India.

The 1918 Influenza Epidemic.—In addition, at the census of 1931 the *enumerated* population, exclusive of Burma, exceeded the number *expected* (which was based primarily on deaths subtracted from births) by 3.9 million, indicating that there was a much greater nonregistration of births than of deaths. This is quite the usual thing where registration is highly deficient because burials are more public than births and hence easier to register. In the decade 1911-21, however, the enumerated population, as noted above, was over 4 million short of the expected. It seems reasonable to assume, therefore, that recorded deaths during this decade were not merely 4 million short as the census suggests but perhaps twice that amount because of the greater underregistration of births. Thus the influenza epidemic, the accompanying famine and the other troubles of that decade may very easily have taken a toll amounting to 15-17 million. That such an estimate of excess deaths during this period, as compared with 1901-11 and 1921-31, is quite reasonable may be better appreciated by examining briefly population growth in these two decades. From 1901 to 1911 the increase, as just noted, was approximately 17 million. During this period the chief abnormal factor in the death rate appears to have been an epidemic of plague, 6.5 million deaths being recorded from this cause. In the decade 1921-31 the increase of population was about 32 million. During this decade there is no record of any *unusual* famine or epidemic and population growth rose to about one percent a year. The average numerical increase during these two decades, in spite of the fact that one of them had perhaps 3 or 4 million *unusual* deaths from plague, was about 25 million. If it be assumed that this would have been the increase for the decade 1911-21 with only slightly *unusual* mortality, then the influenza epidemic, the minor outbreak of plague (only half as deadly as the one in the preceding decade), the serious food shortage in considerable areas, and the heightened incidence of cholera, which almost always accompanies famine, must be presumed to have exacted an unusual toll of 22-23 million, since the actual increase was only 2.7 million.

That the growth of population was reduced through pestilence and famine by some such number during the decade 1911-21 appears all the more likely when we also take into account the increase during the last decade, 1931-41. In 1931 the population of India (without Burma) was approximately 338 million and in 1941 it was 389 million, an increase of over 50 million or 15 percent. In this decade there is no record of epidemics or famines of sufficient importance to attract attention. Thus since 1921 the growth of India's population has been of about the same order as the growth of Europe's in the half century preceding World War I and as that of Japan in recent decades.

India as an Example of Population Growth.—The author regards the population growth of India as particularly instructive because he believes that what happened in India prior to 1921 shows the general pattern of what has happened throughout most of human history up to the development of machine industry and modern sanitation, although he thinks it probable that even before 1921 conditions in India were somewhat more favorable for growth than was usual in ages past. The reasons for believing that even before 1921 conditions in India were more favorable for population growth than was usual may be noted briefly.

By the time of the first census (1872) the British had the government of India well enough organized to support the development of a unified transportation system, to undertake some expensive additions to the irrigated area, and to prevent wars between the several states, principalities and communities, which had been a more or less regular feature of Indian life in earlier periods. The government also had the means to organize famine relief, and was beginning to develop public health work. These measures should have had, and undoubtedly have had, an increasingly favorable effect on the death rate. But there is serious doubt whether the death rate can be brought under secure control until, perhaps one should say, unless, the per capita productivity of the Indian laborer, both agricultural and industrial, can be greatly increased. The moral of this brief description of India's population growth in recent decades is that such steady growth as the Western peoples have had since about 1800 is the *unusual,* while fluctuations in growth, as in India, are far more usual in the experience of mankind.

POPULATION GROWTH IN OTHER ASIATIC LANDS

Japan and India are not the only Asiatic countries which have had a rapid rate of growth in recent years. The Philippines have practically doubled in population since they became an American possession in 1898. The island of Java, the heart of the Netherlands Indies (47 million), is now believed to have over ten times the population it had in 1816. The Malay peninsula has also been growing at a rapid rate during the last two or three decades. The lowering of the death rate which is certainly taking place in Japan and India is also being achieved in other parts of the East. But we have no way of knowing how much of this lowering of death rates is due to improved sanitation, how much to a better level of living, e.g., to the increase in subsistence through the extension of irrigated areas, how much to the prevention of intertribal and interstate wars and forays, and how much to the ability of the colonial authorities to organize famine relief when local areas are stricken. But whatever the more decisive factors in any country at any given time, the important fact is that many of these Eastern lands have entered on a new phase of population growth within the last few decades comparable to that which began in Europe about a century earlier and that still others are almost certain to grow rapidly once they, too, start to industrialize, to gain control over the infectious diseases through the establishment of health service, to extend irrigation and improve agriculture and to exercise a more effective control over internal disturbances.

POPULATION GROWTH IN CHINA

Thus far in the discussion of the growth of population in Asia nothing has been said about China. This is, in part, because so little is known about it, but also, in part, because it deserves special attention. To begin with, it should be made clear that we do not know what China's population was at any given time in the past and we do not know what it is now. Moreover, we do not even know whether it is increasing or decreasing. During the last 20 or 30 years there has been a very common tendency among those speaking of China's population to assume that China has been growing in much the same way as India, or even Japan. When this is done and it is further assumed that China had 350-360 million in 1900, an estimate of 450-500 million at the present time is inevitable. There is no sound basis for either of these assumptions.

Differences Between China and India.—The chief reason for rejecting the assumption that China is now growing at about the same rate as India is the difference between the two countries in the effectiveness of their political and economic organization. India has had a strong central government for nearly a century which built, or fostered the building of, a reasonably good transportation system; which was primarily responsible for bringing 30 million acres or more under irrigation; which was able to organize a health service, inadequate to be sure, but one which is still probably better than any in Asia outside Japan and the Philippines; and, finally the government was also able to organize famine relief when needed.

China, on the other hand, lags far behind India in all of these respects. The writer believes that if China is to be compared in population growth with India the decades in which

India was very seriously afflicted with pestilence and famine (1872-81, 1891-1901, and 1911-21) are to be considered more typical of the China of today than those in which these checks to population growth were in some measure held in abeyance.

For almost a century China has had no central government capable of preventing great and devastating internal disturbances. In the middle of the nineteenth century there was the great Taiping Rebellion, which many people believe caused the death, directly and indirectly, of 50 million or more people. Moreover, since the Boxer disturbances (1900) there has been incessant internal strife in many parts of the country, and since 1931 China has suffered heavily from foreign aggression. For these reasons China has not been able to provide any of the conditions which have made possible India's population growth in the period since census-taking began there. Hence, the author does not believe that it is reasonable to assume that China's death rate has yet come under any significant degree of control even for short periods as is the case in India.

As regards the assumption that China had a population of about 350-360 million in 1900, it has long seemed to the writer that the preponderance of evidence casts serious doubt on whether China had such a large population at that time, although he has used this figure (357 million) for 1913.

China's Potential Growth.—There is little doubt, however, that China's potential rate of population growth is as great as India's, possibly even greater, for much of China is in the temperate zone, where it seems reasonable to expect somewhat lower death rates with less health effort than in the tropics. But it appears that China's actual population growth in the near future is likely to be small, and there may even be a significant decrease such as may very well have occurred during the Japanese occupation. At the moment, the civil war may be even more disruptive of the regular processes of agriculture and commerce than the Japanese invasion and occupation and may have a more deadly effect on population. Until China has peace and a government able and willing to undertake the development of transportation, the improvement of agriculture, the establishment of public health service, and to encourage the growth of machine industry, little growth of population is to be expected. In the future China's population may well grow at a rate of 10 to 15 percent in 10 years for several decades, but the writer very much doubts whether it has grown significantly in the recent past or whether it will attain a rate of growth equal to that of India until it has developed a relatively strong political organization which can assure the whole country those stable and improved social and economic conditions which have been shown to be essential to a declining death rate elsewhere in the modern world.

The Growth of Other Peoples

As for the populations of most of Africa and the industrially more backward parts of South America, they are still in the stage of development where what has just been said about China will apply almost equally well to them since most of these peoples also have high death rates and high birth rates. But experience has shown that where there is a relative abundance of land, as there still is in parts of South America and Africa, a reduction in death rates may proceed rapidly with a consequent rapid growth in numbers. We may, therefore, look for considerable population growth in certain of these industrially backward areas where population has remained relatively stable in the past.

At this point attention should be called to the great difficulty of maintaining a population increase of 10 to 15 percent each decade for 8 to 10 decades in countries like India and China, where population is already dense and there is relatively little new land to be brought into use. Better agricultural practices, the extension of irrigation, the improvement of transportation, the development of machine industry, the expansion of public health work, and many other improvements will increase the capacity of these lands to support people at any given level of living, but they are not new lands like those in the Americas and they are already densely peopled in relation to their resources. Hence, any large growth of population like that which has taken place in India since 1921 (83 million) can only be regarded as dangerous to the future welfare of the country and probably to the future peace of the world (see Chapter 7). Think of an India with 389 million in 1941 growing by 10 percent each decade until the end of this century! She would then have a population of about 689 million and I know of no one who really believes that India can support such a population, even at her present low level of living.

CHAPTER 2

THE BIRTH RATE

The preceding account of the growth of population in the world since 1800 takes much for granted. Birth rates and death rates are treated as though they were simple quantities with a precise and simple meaning. No attempt was made to indicate in any exact way the role they played in population growth. But if we are to understand the meaning of the changes in population growth now going on and their probable direction in the future we cannot rest content with this treatment. We must know more about the operation of these factors which at any given moment determine population growth. We must see how they change, and if possible, why they change.

It is, then, in the belief that changes in population will appear more meaningful and that the problems connected with them will be easier to understand, that the reader is asked to explore the significance of birth rates and death rates in more detail.

THE CRUDE BIRTH RATE

The birth rate of a community is usually given as the number of births per 1,000 of the population and this is known as the "crude" rate. If all communities had the same proportion of men and women and all had the same proportion of women at each age—15-19, 20-24, etc.—and if all the births were recorded, then the "crude" birth rate would be sufficient to enable us to make accurate birth comparisons between different groups. But, as we shall see, we still would not know enough to look ahead and see how the current birth rate would affect future growth, except in a very rough manner. Moreover, experience

28

has taught the demographer that complete likeness in age and sex is never attained and that, at times, there are large differences in the proportions of births registered in different communities.

Faulty Registration of Births.—To illustrate how nonregistration affects the birth rate we may use the 1942 figures for the United States. In that year there were 2,809,000 births recorded and the birth rate was 20.9 per 1,000 of the population. However, a careful study of the shortcomings of our birth registration leads to the conclusion that there actually were about 3,037,000 births and the birth rate was 22.7 instead of 20.9. Hence, if the birth rate of the United States were compared with that of a country having better registration, and no allowance was made for this difference, the comparison would be misleading. This is also true for different states, some of which have almost perfect registration (New York and Massachusetts) while others have extremely faulty registration (Oklahoma and Arkansas).

Crude Birth Rates as Affected by Age, Sex and Marriage. —In 1800 in the most distinctly pioneer regions of the United States there were 162 women aged 16-44 in each 1,000 of the population, while in the most industrialized states there were 202 such women in each 1,000. In any year, therefore, 162 pioneer women of these ages would have had to bear the same number of children as 202 women in the more industrial states if the two populations were to have the same crude birth rate. Where we find such differences in the proportions of women we also generally find differences in the age make-up of the women. Thus in the pioneer population just referred to, 54.4 percent of all the women 16-44 were aged 16-25 while in the more industrial states only 48.1 percent of the women 16-44 were aged 16-25. Since the years 16-25 are generally the most fertile years of a woman's life, especially when early marriage is the rule, it is clear that the pioneer women had a more favorable age composition from the standpoint of maintaining a high birth rate.

The differences in sex and age proportions just noted may be allowed for so that a rate showing real differences in birth rates is obtained. Thus the number of births, or number of children 0-4, per 1,000 women aged 15-44 allows for the fact that different populations have different proportions of women of childbearing age. In addition, when the data are available, differences in the proportions of women in the several age groups 15-19, 20-24, etc., may also be allowed for so that an adjusted birth rate or a standardized ratio of children to women can be calculated. Such a ratio or rate gives a much more accurate comparison between two populations than does the crude rate.

In the example of pioneer and industrial states used above the birth rate is not known but the ratio of children 0-4 to 1,000 women 16-44 is known. It was 1,215 children 0-4 per 1,000 women 16-44 in the pioneer states and 784 per 1,000 in the more industrial states. These ratios cannot be standardized because of lack of data, hence they do not take account of the age differences in these two groups of women. But even so they permit of no doubt that as long ago as 1800 the pioneer women had a much higher birth rate than the women in the more industrial states.

The proportion of women who are married will also affect the crude birth rates. Thus the proportion of women 15-44 in the United States who were married (1940) is 61 percent while in Sweden it was only 44 percent. It is apparent from these figures that the average married woman in Sweden would have to bear more children than in the United States to maintain the same crude birth rate unless the proportion of females (15-44) was much higher than in the United States, and/or the proportion of illegitimate births was much greater.

The points just noted should be borne in mind as the discussion proceeds, but they do not preclude the use of crude birth rates for many practical purposes. They are raised only to induce a measure of caution into the use of such rates.

EXTREMES OF THE BIRTH RATE

Throughout a large part of human history and among most peoples the birth rate has tended to approach the physiological maximum, i.e., most women have borne about as many children as they were physiologically capable of bearing, although the potential maximum has probably never been attained. Every people has some customs or mores which interfere more or less seriously with the attainment of the highest birth rate physiologically possible. As examples of such customs one may mention the prohibition of the remarriage of widows in India, the Jewish customs of purification of women after childbirth, and the taboos on marital relations prevailing among many primitive peoples.

The Maximum Birth Rate.—As a result of the widespread prevalence of these and similar customs we cannot say with any exactness what the maximum physiological birth rate is, but we have some facts which indicate that an attainable maximum crude rate probably is in the neighborhood of 50 or a little more per 1,000, where the age and sex make-up of the population are not abnormal. Thus there are data for the Ukraine (Russia) in 1866-70 which yield a crude rate of 48.9. Again, a critical study of birth rates in the provinces of India in 1921 led Mr. Acland to estimate the birth rate of Bengal as 46.7 and of the United Provinces as 46.5. In the United States an estimate of the birth rate for 1800 based on the number of children per 1,000 women 16-44 gave an estimated rate of 55.0. Records kept in the small Chinese community of Hsiao Chi from 1931-35 showed a rate of 45.1.[1] Finally, the highest crude

---

[1] C. M. Chiao and Warren S. Thompson, *An Experiment in the Registration of Vital Statistics in China*, Oxford, Ohio: Scripps Foundation for Research in Population Problems, 1938, p. 41.

rate the writer has been able to find for recent years is that of the Arabs in Palestine, 53.4 for the years 1943-45. It may be of interest to note that in the same years the birth rate of the Jews was only 29.8. However, actual recorded rates which exceed 45 are rare—probably because early records are defective and also because by the time any community is well enough organized to keep accurate records the birth rate has fallen below this point.

The Minimum Birth Rate.—At the other extreme it is theoretically possible to have a population in which there are no births, but in modern times no such population of any size is known. The lowest recorded crude rates are found in some of the larger cities. The birth rate in Vienna in 1937 was 5.4, that of Paris (1934) 12.3, London (1934) 13.4, New York (1938-40) 13.6 and San Francisco (1938-40) 12.2. Thus it seems probable that the crude birth rate for the entire United States in 1800 was about ten times the crude rate of Vienna in 1937. A birth rate based on childbearing women would probably show even greater differences than those given above because Vienna, like all large cities, had a larger proportion of childbearing women in its population in 1937 than the United States in 1800.

THE TREND OF THE BIRTH RATE

Figure 3 shows the crude birth rates for a few of the leading countries of the world for some decades past. Three conclusions can be drawn from these data: (1) in most of the countries for which the records run back several decades there has been a considerable decline in the birth rate during the last half century or more, (2) there is a larger proportional difference between the birth rates of the several countries in recent years than there was 50 or more years ago, to judge from such records as are available, and (3) the largest differences in birth rates between nations today are between highly industrialized nations, on the one hand, and nations largely agricultural on the other.

When Did the Birth Rate Begin to Decline in the West?— It is impossible to tell exactly when the birth rate began to decline in most of the countries where a decline is now clearly established because the organization for registering births (and deaths) generally functions rather badly when first set up but becomes more efficient with time, so that often what appears to be an increase in the birth rate over several decades may be, and probably is in most cases, only evidence of more complete registration. But it makes no great difference to our discussion whether the birth rate began to decline in England and Wales in 1868 or in 1878. The point of importance is that since the latter date there can be no reasonable doubt that the birth rate has declined almost continuously, if the annual fluctuations are eliminated by using five-year averages. In Sweden the decline in the birth rate began about 15 years earlier and continued up to 1936. In Germany the decline set in a little later than in England and Wales. But since the decline in Germany started from a somewhat higher level and took place rather slowly at first, the birth rate remained considerably higher than that of England and Wales—30.0 compared with 25.2 (1908-12)— up to World War I. France has had an almost steadily declining birth rate from the early years of the nineteenth century, and even in 1800 her rate was low when compared with the birth rates of Sweden and Finland (see Figure 3).

The United States has had birth registration in all the states only since 1933. However, it is possible to estimate a birth rate from 1800 on by using the number of women and children in the population at the several censuses. These data indicate that our birth rate, like that of France, has been declining since 1800. But because it was much higher at the beginning of the nineteenth century than in the European countries for which there are records the birth rate could decline in much the same

Births per 1,000 population

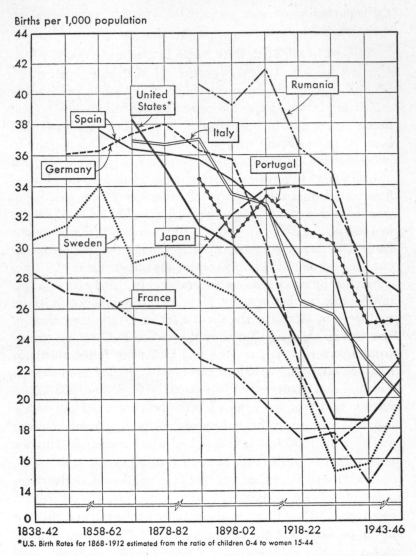

*U.S. Birth Rates for 1868-1912 estimated from the ratio of children 0-4 to women 15-44

Figure 3. Crude Birth Rates (births per 1,000 population) in Selected Countries, 1838-1946. Five-year averages, except 1943-46

way it did in these countries and still remain somewhat above
them up to the present time.

Such data as are available indicate that in Russia the birth
rate has long been well above 40 per 1,000 and that it probably
still was near that level at the outbreak of World War II.
Poland, Rumania, Bulgaria, and Yugoslavia have also had birth
rates of 40 or more in the not distant past, although none of
them had rates above 30 at last reports.

Birth Rates in Other Lands.—Outside of Europe several
countries still report rates of 40, or rates so near to 40 that, in
view of the incompleteness of registration, we can be reasonably
sure they are 40 or above. Thus Egypt reports rates well
above 40, while Chile and Guatemala report rates close to 40.
There can be little doubt that several other South and Central
American countries also fall in the over-40 group.

In Asia, only Japan has recorded birth rates which are fairly
reliable. They indicate that Japan, like most European nations,
had a high rate in the past but that this is now on the decline.
This fact is of much significance, indicating the same general
pattern of decline in Japan as in most Western countries. The
birth rate of Japan in 1938-41 (28.0) was about what that of
England and Wales was in 1900 (28.8) and but little above
that of the United States for 1910 (27.4). From these data
it appears rather probable that the decline in Japan may possibly
be a little more rapid than in most Western countries. For the
rest of Asia about all that can be said about the birth rate with
reasonable certainty is that it is very high, probably above 40
in most countries and possibly as much as 50 in some areas.

This brief review of birth rates may be summed up by saying that rates of 40-50 per 1,000 of the population have by no
means been unusual in the past and are still found in many
agricultural populations, perhaps in 60 percent of the world's
population today. Rates of 30-40 were quite common even in
the West several decades ago, and are not uncommon now in

Southern and Eastern Europe and in many parts of South and Central America. Rates of 25, and often under 20, are now common in Western Europe and North America although in some years during the war and since the United States and Netherlands have had rates above 25. But let us not forget that 60 to 70 years ago, even England, Germany, the United States, and most of the other countries with present rates under or but slightly above 20, had birth rates of between 30 and 40 and had apparently had rates as high or higher in the past. Adjustments in crude birth rates to allow for the differences in proportions of women married, and in age and sex would not impair the general validity of the preceding comparisons.

Birth Rates and Differential Population Growth.—The full significance of the changes which have taken place in the birth rates of the several countries during the last 50 to 70 years cannot be fully appreciated until after we have investigated their death rates; but it should be pointed out here that these changes in birth rates have increased the possibility of widely different rates of population growth in different parts of the world. Thus when practically all peoples had birth rates of 40 or more, all of them could have a large natural increase at any time they could control their death rates even in moderate degree. But when the birth rate falls below 20 only a small increase is to be looked for, because death rates of less than 15 can only be maintained as long as the population remains relatively young (see Chapter 4). A death rate of 15 means an average expectation of life at time of birth of 66.6 years.

The differentials between the birth rates of nations which have just been noted will be discussed more fully in Chapter 6 and some of their political and economic implications will be discussed in Chapter 7.

The Recent Rise in the Birth Rate

Since 1941 much publicity has been given to the fact that the number of births in the United States (also in certain European countries) has increased very substantially. In the United States the birth rate rose from about 18.9 per 1,000 in 1941 to about 23.3 in 1946 and at the time of writing (April 1948) is provisionally given as 25.9 in 1947. Many people consider this an indication that the long-time downward trend in the birth rate noted above has not only been stopped but has been reversed.

As has been shown above, the crude birth rate is not a very reliable measure of reproduction. Moreover, in a period when the crude birth rate is fluctuating considerably even the net reproduction rate now so widely used to measure the trend of reproduction in the future is not a satisfactory measure.[2] Both these rates may reflect to a significant degree changes in the marriage rate and/or changes in the intervals following marriage during which first and second births are taking place. They may merely indicate a change in the age at which women are having their children. Hence these higher rates do not prove that families are actually growing larger. Thus if a considerable number of women rather suddenly (under war conditions) decide to marry younger and to have a child or two sooner than they would have had them under prewar conditions, a rather large increase in the crude birth rate and in the net rate of reproduction may not mean a larger average number of children per woman.

---

[2] The net reproduction rate is based on the births per 1,000 women of each age, 15-19, 20-24, etc. which occur in a given period of time and, making allowance for the deaths which will occur among these women before they have completed their reproduction, it shows how many daughters they will bear. Thus a net reproduction rate of 100 means that each woman will bear one daughter and thus population will just be maintained. A rate above 100 indicates the proportional gain in population in a generation if birth rates and death rates remain at the given level and a rate below 100 indicates the rate of loss in a generation under existing birth rates and death rates.

Are Families Getting Larger?—Since the women born in 1901 are the youngest for whom complete reproduction data are available it is impossible to say what the complete reproductive performance of women born since then will be. However, tables prepared by P. K. Whelpton of the Scripps Foundation showing the number of children borne by women of the same age at different dates throw some light on this point. These data show that each 1,000 of the women born in 1900-1904 had had 2,150 children by the time they reached 35 years of age, while those born in 1905-1909 had 1,963 children by the time they reached 35, and those born in 1910 and 1911, the last groups to reach 35 by January 1, 1946, had borne only 1,934 and 1,914 children, respectively. Since the depression of the 1930's affected the birth rates of women of different ages differently, we cannot be positive that 1,000 women born in 1910 and 1911 will not have more children between their 35th and 40th years than the women born in 1900-1904 (240 children per 1,000 women 35-39). However, since all the evidence now available shows a steady decline in birth rates to women over 35, it seems highly unlikely that this will happen.

But it should be noted that women born in the years 1910-14 had had only 1,470 children per 1,000 by the time they were 30, while those born in 1915 and 1916 had had 1,494, and 1,533, respectively. This is a significant increase particularly for the 1916 women, but still is far below the 1,729 children born to the women of 1900-04 by the time they were 30 years of age. These data do not prove that the recent rise in the crude birth rate will not lead to a somewhat larger number of children per 1,000 women within the next few years than in the recent past, but since this increase is largely in first and second children it appears quite improbable. It seems more reasonable to believe the increase in number of children born to fairly young women represents merely a slightly different distribution of births by age among women whose early years of childbearing came during the fairly prosperous times (1940-47) as compared with those whose early childbearing years lay in the depression period. It appears that the recent rise in the birth rate is, in part, the result of the consummation of marriages which had been postponed during the depression and of the advancing of marriages which would not have occurred so soon except for prosperity and the war, aided by a tendency to have the first child as soon after marriage as possible and perhaps to reduce the interval between the first and second child.

Another indication that families are not increasing in size and are not likely to do so in the near future is found in other calculations from this same study. Of the women who were 35 years old in 1920, 57.7 percent had 0, 1, or 2 children. When these same women were 45 in 1930 there were still 50.7 percent who had 0, 1, or 2 children. Thus only 7.0 percent of all women who survived from 35 to 45 passed into the group having 3 or more children during the decade of the 1920's, a generally prosperous period. By 1930 the proportion of all women 35, who had 0, 1, or 2 children had risen to 61.4 percent and when these same women were 45 years of age in 1940 the proportion with 0, 1, or 2 children had decreased only to 55.3 percent, or 6.1 percent.

This comparison can be carried 5 years farther. The 62.8 percent of women 35 in 1935 who had 0, 1, or 2 children fell only to 58.7 percent when they were 45 in 1945, a decline of only 4.1 percent. Since 1935 the proportion of women 35 who have had only 0, 1, or 2 children has increased very rapidly, to 68.5 percent in 1940 and to 70.6 percent in 1945. If the proportion of these who pass into the group with 3 or more children by the time they are 45 continues to decline, as it has in the past, we are forced to conclude that the size of the average family must continue to decline, at least until the young women who are now contributing so largely to the increased birth rate have completed their families. Until then we shall not know positively whether the size of the family has been affected materially by the 1941-47 baby boom, but the data now available certainly do not justify the very common belief that the average size of the family is increasing.

GROUP DIFFERENCES IN BIRTH RATES

By Size of Community.—It should not be assumed that differences in birth rates are confined to national groups. There are differences in birth rates within a nation which are also of much interest. In the United States we have known for 50 years or longer that there was a considerable difference between the birth rates of urban and rural people. The ratios of children 0-4 to women of childbearing age based on census data show that this has been true at least since 1800. A few facts will show how important these differentials have been and still are. In 1820 our one city of over 100,000, New York, had 827 children under five per 1,000 white women 20-44 and all the cities of 25,000-100,000 at that time had 786 children, while in the rural population there were 1,286 children per 1,000 white women. In 1920, 1,000 native white women in cities of over 100,000 had only 350 children under five while 1,000 rural native white women had 745. In 1940 these ratios were 332 in the urban population and 584 in rural communities.

If rural communities are further divided into farm and non-farm the 1940 ratios are 658 for the farm women and 522 for the nonfarm women. If cities are divided into the three groups (1) over 100,000, (2) 10,000-100,000, (3) 2,500-10,000, the ratios are 302, 349, and 402, respectively (see Figure 4). Since these differences in ratios approximate differences in birth rates we can safely say that not only is the rural birth rate higher than the urban, but also that within the urban population the birth rate decreases as the size of the city increases and that the portion of the rural population which is most like an urban population—the rural nonfarm—has a lower birth rate than the rural farm population.

By Social and Economic Status.—Differences in birth rates by size of community are not the only differences within the nation. Within the urban population in particular there are large differences between economic, occupational, and educational groups. In general it may be said that the lower the economic status of the family, the larger the number of children; also, that the less the skill and preparation involved in the occupation of the father, the larger the family; and the less the schooling of the wife, the larger the family. In the 1935 Health Survey, Kiser[3] found that among native whites the birth rate in the unskilled laborer group in the cities was one

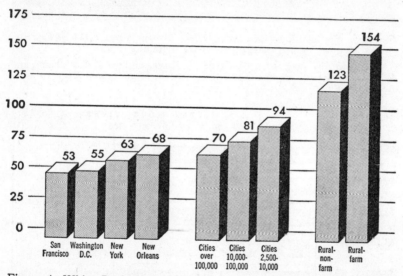

Figure 4. White Replacement Indexes for Selected Communities in the United States, 1940

In the above indexes a ratio of 429 children aged 0-4 to 1,000 women aged 20-44=100, which is exact replacement when age composition and death rates are those in the 1939-41 life tables for the United States. Indexes so calculated give an indication of the way populations are likely to increase (over 100) or decrease (below 100) in a generation, but are not to be regarded as exact predictions.

[3] Clyde V. Kiser, *Group Differences in Urban Fertility; A Study Derived from the National Health Survey,* Baltimore: The Williams and Wilkins Co., 1942.

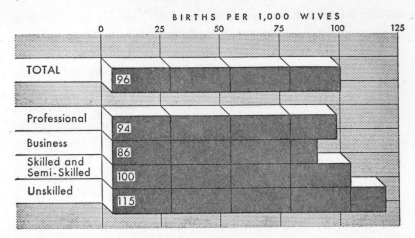

Figure 5. Fertility Rates of Native White Urban Wives 15-44 by Occupational Class of the Head of Family, 1935

Redrawn, by permission of Clyde V. Kiser, author, and Williams and Wilkins, publishers, from the illustration on p. 57 of *Group Differences in Urban Fertility*.

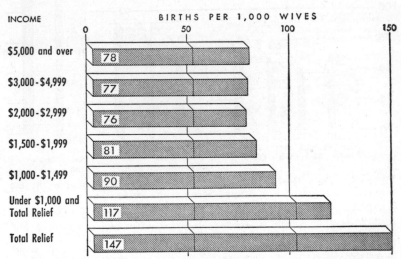

Figure 6. Fertility Rates of Native White Urban Wives 15-44 by Size of Family Income, 1935

Redrawn, by permission of Clyde V. Kiser, author, and Williams and Wilkins, publishers, from the illustration on p. 125 of *Group Differences in Urban Fertility*.

third greater than in the business group (see Figure 5); that it was over one half larger in the group with an income of less than $1,000 a year than in the group with $2,000-$3,000 a year (see Figure 6); and over one third greater among women who had less than a seventh grade education than among women with college education.

Birth Rates According to Economic Status in the Rural Population.—In the rural population the situation is much the same as in the urban population, as regards differentials in births between upper and lower economic groups. When the rural-farm and rural-nonfarm populations of the United States are divided into 10 groups on the basis of the level-of-living indexes calculated by the United States Department of Agriculture for each county, very substantial differences in ratios of children to women are found (see Table 3).

The facts which stand out most clearly in Table 3 are: (1) in the farm population there is a steady decline in the ratio of white children to white women from 885 in Group 1, which has the lowest level-of-living index, to Group 8 and then a very small rise to Group 9, with the lowest ratio of all (465) in Group 10, which has the highest level of living; (2) in the non-farm population the downward trend persists from Group 1 to Group 10 without exception; (3) among rural nonwhites in the South, both farm and nonfarm, there is the same decline from Group 1 to the higher groups, although the downward progression is not as regular as among whites, probably because there are so few nonwhites in Group 4 and above that the ratios for them are of little value; (4) for both whites and nonwhites the ratio of children to women is very substantially higher at comparable levels of living in the rural-farm population than in the rural-nonfarm population.

Exceptions and the Rule.—There are, of course, many individual exceptions to the general statements regarding the relation between social and economic status and the birth rate given above. There are many well-to-do people and many well-educated people with large families and many poor people with little education who have small families. There is also some evidence that urban people with good incomes, let us say with incomes above $5,000, have more children than those with incomes of $3,000-$5,000 although both groups have smaller families than do the poor. But such exceptions are not suffi-

TABLE 3

STANDARDIZED RATIOS OF CHILDREN TO WOMEN AND REPLACEMENT INDEXES FOR WHITES AND NONWHITES IN THE RURAL-FARM AND RURAL-NONFARM POPULATIONS OF THE UNITED STATES, BY ECONOMIC GROUPS, 1940

| | United States—White | | South—Nonwhite | |
	Standard-ized ratio	Replacement index	Standard-ized ratio	Replacement index
	Rural—farm			
United States	564	157	746	197
Group 1*	885	246	770	204
2	785	218	721	191
3	672	187	710	188
4	620	172	763	202
5	583	162		
6	546	152	772	204
7	515	143		
8	493	137		
9	499	139		
10	465	129		
	Rural—nonfarm			
United States	417	116	449	119
Group 1*	619	172	477	126
2	559	155	424	112
3	526	146	396	105
4	478	133	386	102
5	453	126	} 399	} 106
6	430	119		
7	417	116		
8	401	111		
9	373	104		
10	330	92		

* Group 1 is the lowest in the economic scale.

ciently common to invalidate the general statement that the people with better incomes and better social status have smaller families than those of lower economic and social status and it makes no difference whether they live in cities or in rural areas, or are white or colored. Finally, it should be noted that these group differences in birth rates are not peculiar to the United States. They prevail throughout the Western World and probably in Japan also. The small amount of evidence known to the writer leads him to doubt their existence in China and India at the present time. In these countries, as has already been indicated, there is little control over births (or deaths) in any class but it is not improbable that the upper economic classes have somewhat lower death rates, for reasons which will be discussed in Chapter 4.

The Significance of Birth Differentials

There are two consequences of these group differences in birth rates to which attention should be called in passing, although the discussion of their significance must be postponed to later chapters. In the first place, it is at once clear that if the city people have only about 75 percent enough children to maintain their numbers, without in-migration, while the rural people not only have enough children to replace themselves but to add about 40 percent to their numbers in each generation, an increasing proportion of the population of the future will come from the rural areas. But with a declining proportion of rural population (see Figure 7) which also has a declining birth rate, its excess will not be sufficient to make up the deficit of the urban population for more than a few years.

In the second place, as long as present differentials continue our future population will come more and more from the less fortunate, less privileged portion of the community. Since the children of these less fortunate groups are certainly less able to get an education, to obtain good medical care, and are otherwise handicapped in getting a start in life, this differential birth rate will raise many problems increasing in importance as time goes on. There is reason to believe, however, that class differentials in birth rates are decreasing and, although it is by no means

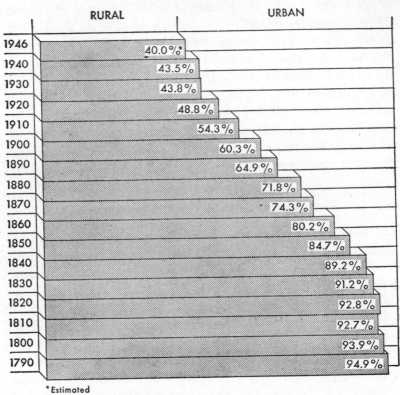

RURAL	URBAN
1946	40.0%*
1940	43.5%
1930	43.8%
1920	48.8%
1910	54.3%
1900	60.3%
1890	64.9%
1880	71.8%
1870	74.3%
1860	80.2%
1850	84.7%
1840	89.2%
1830	91.2%
1820	92.8%
1810	92.7%
1800	93.9%
1790	94.9%

*Estimated

Figure 7. Percentage Rural of the Total United States Population, 1790-1946

certain that they will ever disappear, they may not be as important in the future as they are now.

To help the children of the poor overcome their social and economic handicaps is, perhaps, the chief challenge of the differential birth rate within the nation. We have already done a little to meet it, but not much. We do have more public education now than in the past, we do recognize some small measure of community responsibility to see that children have a decent neighborhood in which to live, we have made some slight adaptation of the school system to the needs of those who have little means of their own, and we have expanded our public health services. But we have not done nearly enough along any of these lines to insure equal opportunity to the economically handicapped and we may very well suffer from this neglect if the comfortable classes continue to fail to reproduce.

CHAPTER 3

THE BIRTH RATE—FACTORS IN ITS DECLINE IN THE WEST

The great decline in the birth rate in the Western World noted in the preceding chapter raises two very important questions regarding the future growth of population among different peoples and in different regions of the earth. The first is whether this decline can be stopped, or reversed where necessary, in time to prevent a decline in numbers if this is desired, or to produce an increase if this is wanted. The second is whether a similar decline in the birth rate is likely to take place in those lands where there is as yet little evidence of any decline. Although we shall not be able to answer the questions just proposed as definitely as we should like, we shall certainly be in a better position to take an intelligent look ahead if we examine as best as we can the factors which seem to be associated with the decline of the birth rate in the West and in the light of this information try to foresee the future course of the birth rate among the different peoples (see Chapter 6) of the world and in different groups within a nation.

URBANIZATION AND THE BIRTH RATE

In the first place, there is a close connection between the development of modern industry and commerce and the decline of the birth rate. The great urbanization of the population which has accompanied the development of manufacturing and commerce since about 1800, has produced new modes of living for a great proportion of the population in most Western lands. Even the peasants of Europe, the share croppers in our South,

48

and the mountain folk in our Appalachian and Ozark regions, have been influenced significantly by these new ways of living. There can be little doubt that it is the changes in modes of living accompanying the development of modern industry and commerce which lie at the basis of the recent decline of the birth rate in the West. It will not be possible to go into much detail regarding just how these changes in modes of living have affected the birth rate, partly because we do not know a great deal about this matter, and partly because of space limitations. But certain of these changes do merit brief attention.

Economic Value of Children.—One of the most important changes accompanying the urbanization of population is the lessening of the economic value of children over 8 or 10 years of age. Among an agricultural people where there is little formal education, children begin to share in their own "keep" at a tender age. There are many ways in which even a five- or six-year-old can help on the farm, or in the kitchen, while in the simpler types of farming where handwork predominates a boy of ten to twelve can frequently do nearly as much as his father, and a daughter of like age can almost keep pace with her mother. As a matter of fact, until quite recently even in industrialized countries child labor has been a very important economic factor in the life of the people and it still is in a large part of the world.

In contrast with the economic assistance which parents receive from their children while still very young in an agricultural civilization, or even in an agricultural community in the United States or Canada today, a modern industrial community offers comparatively little opportunity for children to become of real economic value before they are 15 years of age and often older. The trend in nonagricultural communities for a hundred years or more has been towards a longer period of complete unproductiveness for children. More years in school are being required, many kinds of labor are forbidden to children under 16 to 18 years of age, and more and more elaborate preparation is necessary for the many special and technical tasks of urban life. A large family is a much heavier handicap in nonagricultural communities than on the farm, even when school attendance laws are enforced with equal vigor in both types of communities.

Mobility vs. Children.—A second factor of importance and also quite closely associated with modern urban life is that children, particularly if there are several of them, tie a family closely to the home for many years. Since most types of farming require the constant presence of the family at home to care for livestock and crops, children do not limit the freedom of the farm family to travel and to move about to the same extent as they do that of the nonfarm family. Hence, the desire to be foot-loose is not as strong a motive for restricting the size of the family among farm folk as among nonfarm folk.

Vocational Training of Children at Home.—The differences between urban and rural living already mentioned all contribute to another difference that is of importance, viz., the greater ability of the farmer and his wife to train their own children for a similar type of life. The farmer can still supervise much of the preparation of his boys for farming, in spite of the increasing need for expert guidance in many aspects of farm work. He is regularly working at the tasks his sons need to learn, he can be with them while they work and can show them what to do and how to do it. Most city fathers cannot be directly in touch with their sons when they are at work; nor could they, if they were, provide them the training they need to follow the same occupation, to say nothing of a different one. The community has definitely decreed that no physician is equipped to make a physician of his son. Most other professional men are in like case. Even in most types of skilled work and technical training the father is no longer in position to keep his son with him while being trained, nor to instruct him in his job. The same is true in the field of merchandising. As regards daughters, they can still learn housekeeping at home to a considerable extent but if they are going to work for a few years between school and marriage they need training which they must secure outside the home.

One important result of this greater loosening of economic ties within the city family, in comparison with the family in the country, has been to make it seem less important to raise children to carry on the family affairs and thus to make the raising of children more and more a matter of personal concern and convenience. In addition to these differences in urban and rural attitudes affecting desire for children we also find more widespread knowledge of effective contraceptive practices in urban communities.

It is not claimed that these differences in rural and urban attitudes are adequate to explain fully the present differences between urban and rural birth rates. The writer does, however, believe they are important factors in producing these differentials, and thus in accounting for the rapid decline in the birth rate in most Western nations in recent decades as these nations have become more industrial and commercial.

FACTORS IN BIRTH DIFFERENTIALS BETWEEN CLASSES

Ambition.—The differences in birth rates within the urban group to which attention was called above also need explaining. The close relation of low birth rates to good economic and social status suggests the likelihood that ambition to achieve good status in these respects is an important element in this situation. City people who want to get ahead in their profession, or to achieve a better than average economic and social position, find children a heavy handicap. Each child not only adds to the cost of running the home but takes time and effort from the achievement of the more conventional types of success. This point need not be argued. It is obvious that if one's position depends on the amount of time that can be given to his work, on the means available for entertaining or making social contacts, on the opportunities to travel, or on the undisturbed concentration on the problems of business or profession, children limit the economic resources available for these purposes in at least nine out of ten families. They also absorb much energy which might otherwise be used for personal advancement.

In business, where the accumulation of capital, even of relatively small amounts, is of great importance, the spending of money on several children rather than on none, or one, or two, may seriously interfere with getting ahead. It is easier to save and at the same time to live well, with one child than with three or four. On the other hand the less ambitious people, economically and socially, may find a satisfaction in children which is greater than any they could hope for by devoting their energies and income to "getting ahead."

Finally, it appears that as people become more and more preoccupied with position, with economic success, and with "making good," the family ideal fades out. Children become an incidental factor in life, not a prime factor; personal desires tend to crowd out the family values which might make it worth while to trouble with children. In other words, our modern industrial civilization has set up economic and social ideals and values which make it very difficult, if not impossible, for most (not all) ambitious people to raise fair-sized families. Quite naturally, any civilization which values only, or chiefly, the economic contributions which an individual can make, taking no account of the family, exerts most influence on the people who are most deeply involved in it, viz., the urban population at economic levels appreciably above the average.

There is little chance that there will be any significant change in this attitude of the well-to-do classes towards children until our whole social order comes to place a different value on reproduction than it now does. Furthermore, as the poorer part of our population increasingly imitates the family pattern of the upper groups we shall be faced squarely with the problem of a rapidly declining national population. This may or may not be a misfortune, but it is certainly a new situation which we must meet with forethought and planning if it is not to result in a high degree of community disorganization.

Desire for Ease and Luxury.—The desire for ease and luxury also has a depressive effect on the birth rate. There can be no serious doubt that in a world where one's social position is judged largely by the ease and luxury of one's living many people come to prefer the evidences of "high" living to children. No woman who has raised a fair-sized family (three to four children) would for a moment doubt that she could have had an easier life if she had had a smaller family. Only a few of the very well-to-do can raise fair-sized families and not be deprived of many of the "nice" things, the luxuries, they would have liked to have in their homes. Very few people can afford both children and ease and luxury. In the competition between them, ease and luxury frequently, perhaps generally, win out.

Desire to Maintain a Customary Standard.—The desire to maintain a decent though modest level of living is much more effective in reducing the birth rate than the less laudable desire for ease and luxury, because it affects so many more people. Most people can do little to increase their incomes as the number of their children increases. They can, however, see to it that they do not have more children than they can care for at a given level of living. Hence it is not surprising that the small family, i.e., the family with only one or two children, is rapidly becoming the standard pattern in the urban population. (In addition somewhere between 10 and 15 percent of all married couples have no children.)

Although the factors mentioned above have been more effective up to the present in reducing the birth rate among urban people than among rural people it should not be inferred that they have not operated to reduce the size of families among the latter. There is a very marked decrease in fertility in the rural population as economic status rises as was shown in the preceding chapter. Up to the present, however, rural birth rates remain much higher than urban rates and there is much reason to believe that the basic differences between urban and rural living will continue to maintain such differences in birth rates for some time to come. However, as it becomes increasingly difficult for farm boys to get a start as farmers it is quite possible that the lengthened period of education and the expensive training they need will have an increasingly depressing effect on the rural birth rate.

Involuntary Factors in the Decline of the Birth Rate.—In what precedes it is assumed that conscious personal choice rather than any physiological change in fecundity or any change in marriage rate, lies at the basis of the reduction in the size of the family. This is justified because we now have definite proof that contraception is the chief means used to reduce the birth rate. Though there can be little doubt that there has been some increase in sterility in modern urban populations and that impairments of fecundity are on the increase, they will nevertheless account for only a minor part of the decline in the birth rate. On the other hand, there is no proof for the frequent assertion that age at marriage has increased to a point where it is a significant factor in reducing the birth rate. It may be that certain small groups, e.g., the professional classes, marry later but for the population as a whole there has been a decrease rather than an increase in age at marriage. Finally, the proportion of women marrying has been increasing almost steadily during the last few decades. This, by itself, should lead to a higher rather than a lower birth rate. The only reasonable conclusion therefore, is that the desire for smaller families is the most important cause of the decline of the birth rate. Contraception is merely a means of accomplishing this desire. Some of the conditions which are likely to make people want

smaller families have been suggested above, but these sugges-
tions are far from supplying a satisfactory answer to the question, Why do so many of our people want small families,
families too small to maintain the population? Much research
must yet be undertaken before this question can be answered
with confidence.

THE BIRTH RATE AND ECONOMIC CONDITIONS

Good and Bad Harvests.—It has long been known that there
was a rather close connection between annual or short term
fluctuations in the birth rate and economic conditions. It was
noticed in the latter part of the eighteenth century that the
Swedish birth rate varied more or less directly with good and
bad harvests in the preceding year. A good harvest was followed by a rise in the birth rate while a bad harvest was
followed by a decline. Since Sweden, like practically all other
lands, was then primarily an agricultural country the size of
the harvest was a fairly reliable measure of general economic
conditions. If the harvest was good times were good, if the
harvest was poor times were hard, the degree of suffering depending on how much it fell below a normal yield. This variation in harvests resulted almost immediately in a considerable
variation in the number of marriages which in turn resulted in
a corresponding increase or decrease in first births in the following year or two as well as in some variation in births among
those already married. At the same time, as might be expected,
the death rate moved in just the opposite direction. Thus an
unusually small number of marriages in 1772, a year of very
poor harvests, was followed in 1773 by a very low birth rate
(25.52 while the average for the five years preceding was
32.16) and a very high death rate (52.45). Dorothy Thomas
quotes Sundbärg on these relations as follows:

> "Not only marriage rates but crude birth rates and
> married and unmarried fertility rates rose following
> adequate harvests and declined in years following har-

vest failures; whereas death rates showed an equally
strong tendency to rise after a failure and decline in
periods of abundance." [1]

In more recent times the direct relation between a good
harvest and a high marriage rate in one year followed by a high
birth rate and a low death rate in the ensuing year is not so
obvious, because there is no longer the same high degree of
dependence on local harvests and the size of the current crop
that there was in the days before steam transportation and
more passable roads. Besides, with the improvements in agriculture and in the processing of foods in the last century the
degree of variation in agricultural production has been somewhat reduced, while the total amount of food in storage
(canned and dried fruits, vegetables, etc.) has been increased.
In any event, the relation in the West, between good (or bad)
harvests and marriages, births, and deaths is less direct than
formerly. The relation between the general level of economic
activity and marriages and births is taking its place. To show
the relation between the level of economic activity and the marriage rate, and, in due course, with the birth rate, there is no
need to go farther back than the great depression of the 1930's.
But it should be clearly understood that we are now concerned
only with annual or short-term fluctuations, not with the long-
term secular decline in the birth rate.

**The Marriage Rate and the Birth Rate in the United States
Since 1930.**—In the United States the number of marriages and,
of course, the marriage rate began to fall off in the first depression year. In the four years ending in 1933 the total number
of marriages reported was about 800,000 under what would
have been expected if the 1925-29 rate had been maintained.
This deficit was equivalent to almost two thirds of the annual
number of marriages that were to be expected in 1933, that is

---

[1] Dorothy Swaine Thomas, *Social and Economic Aspects of Swedish
Population Movements, 1750-1933,* New York: The Macmillan Co., 1941, pp.
83-84.

to say, the number of marriages in these four years was only equal to the "expected" number for three and one third years. This decline in marriages was followed by an unusual decline in birth rate, from an average of 20.2 in the years 1925-29 to 18.9 in 1930 and to 16.6 in 1933. That there was a causal

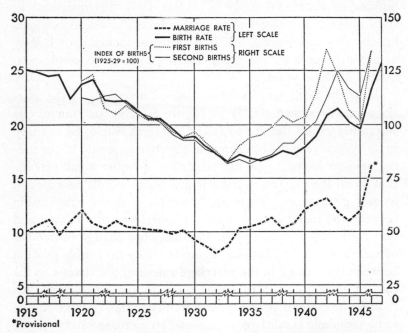

Figure 8. Marriage Rates and Birth Rates per 1,000 Population, United States, 1915-47

connection between the depression, the decline in marriages, and the decline in birth rate is shown by the fact that the decline in the birth rate was largest in first and second births and in the births to younger women. Likewise, the subsequent rise in the birth rate, which has received so much favorable comment, must be attributed largely to the same cause, viz., to the great increase in marriages which has taken place since 1933. In 1934 the number of marriages was the largest ever celebrated in the United States up to that time and was slightly larger than the "expected" number.[2] From 1934 to the present the marriage rate has been continuously higher than the 1925-29 rate. In 1942 the number of marriages rose to 1,772,000, or about 300,000 above the expected number, and then fell off during 1943 and 1944 only to rise again to the unprecedented number of 2,286,000 in 1946. After 1941 the variations in the number of marriages were much affected by war conditions, but the very rapid increase 1939-41 must be looked upon largely as a consequence of the rapid improvement in economic conditions in those years.

How the birth rate in due course of time follows the marriage rate is shown clearly in Figure 8. But, of course, one would not expect the rise or fall of the birth rate to be as sharp in any given year as the change in the marriage rate in the preceding year because new marriages are a rather small proportion of all the marriages from which births might be expected in any given year. There is, however, a closer relationship between the increase or decrease of marriages in one year and first births the following year than between change in number of marriages and all births. There is also a noticeable relation between the change in the marriage rate and the change in the rate of second and third births three to six years later. Although the lapse of several years attenuates this connection, the same economic conditions which lead to increase in marriages, or to their postponement, in a given year also lead many of those already married to decide upon the time of arrival of their next child and quite possibly whether or not there will be a next child.

Our interest in divorce here is confined to its demographic aspects, that is, its effects on population growth. The social aspects of the problem, which are of wider significance, lie outside our discussion. During the five years 1930-34 the average annual number of divorces was about 180,000. During the

---

[2] This was calculated by assuming the continuance of the marriage rate of 1925-29.

years 1941-45 this average more than doubled (375,000) and passed the half million mark in 1945 with the number still rising. Obviously, such an increase in the number of broken marriages might have a very considerable effect on the birth rate if divorced women have fewer children during their lives than women whose marriages are not broken. Many people believe that divorce does tend to reduce the average number of children a woman will bear, but we have no definite evidence on this point. We can be reasonably certain, however, that as divorce grows the proportion of all marriages which are re-marriages will grow and that an increasing number of remar-riages of divorcees will introduce a new element into the demography of divorce. At first thought it may appear reason-able to assume that anything which adds to the disorganization of the family, as divorce certainly does, will tend to reduce the average size of the family. However, it may be that many new couples—even where it is not a first marriage for one or both of the partners—will want children of their own with the result that many remarried women will have as large or even larger families than if they had married but once. Until we have defi-nite evidence on how divorce affects childbearing we can only speculate on its demographic consequences.

This discussion of the factors in the decline of the birth rate has no doubt been quite unsatisfactory to the reader. If it is any comfort, he can be assured that it is also unsatisfactory to the writer. But the discussion has not been useless, even if we cannot state definitely and precisely the reasons why an increas-ing proportion of all couples have no children or only one or two. The opinion so frequently expressed above that the birth rate will continue to decline, but more slowly than in the past, is based on the belief that the factors discussed above are signifi-cant even though we cannot measure their effects precisely. Further, they will not only continue to operate about as in the past on that portion of the population where they are now effective but will also extend their influence into that portion where as yet they have had little influence. This does not mean that the community can do nothing to change its birth rate if it so desires but it does mean that in the absence of deliberate community action to change the birth rate the present trend is likely to continue, although more slowly.

It is easy to understand *why* small families, or even no children at all, are of advantage economically to most urban couples. It is less easy, but still not too difficult, to understand the broader social and psychological factors which must be at work alongside the economic motives, and which contribute to the conviction of people that small families, or even no children, are to their advantage. But this is not sufficient if we would control population growth for the benefit of the community. Until we know more concretely how the community "climate of opinion" acts on the A's and the B's in deciding to have only one or two children, or none, the community can do little to adjust its numbers to its economic and social needs, as contrasted with the adjustment which individuals are making for their personal advantage. Some progress is being made in the understanding of motives to reproduction as influenced by community attitudes, but it is slow. As yet the community has manifested little interest in the problem of the desirable size of its population, in its quality, or in its distribution. These problems will be discussed in later chapters.

CHAPTER 4

THE DEATH RATE

The crude death rate, like the birth rate, is expressed as the number of deaths per 1,000 of population. Thus a community with 10,000 persons in which there were 140 deaths a year would have a death rate of 14. This is merely an example of the way in which a crude death rate is calculated; it is not implied that 14 is a usual or normal death rate. In fact, there is no such thing as a *normal* death rate for all communities or populations. However, if the death rate of any community is well known and has remained near a given level for some time it comes to be accepted there as normal. Any appreciable departure from it or from the trend which has prevailed is likely to attract attention and lead to investigation of the reasons for the departure from the normal for that community.

DIFFERENCES IN AGE COMPOSITION

As with crude birth rates, the comparison of crude death rates for different peoples and at different periods may be quite misleading, chiefly because of large differences in age composition between populations. But when differences in age composition are small, differences in crude death rates are a reasonably good measure of differences in health conditions which are in large measure due to differences in levels of living.

Reasons for Age Changes.—Several demographic factors are generally at work in producing any significant age changes, but at any given time a particular one may be predominant. Thus, any considerable migration of young adults from rural areas to cities will change the age composition of both com-

61

munities. A more rapid improvement in the death rate of one age group, e.g., babies, than in that of another group, e.g., young adults, will raise the proportion of children in the population while this change is in process. A rapid decline in the birth rate would work in the opposite direction to lower the proportion of children but would not greatly change the proportion of adults for some time because its effects are spread over a longer period. All such changes are important in thinking about the death rate because at any given time each age group, 0-1, 1-4, 20-24, etc., has a characteristic death rate which may be quite different (higher or lower) from that of other age groups. Thus, children in their first year of life often have a death rate thirty to fifty times as great as in their tenth year of life and people in their fortieth year have a death rate only about one tenth as great as people in their seventy-fifth year. A crude death rate must, therefore, be used with caution. When adjustments are made to allow for significant differences in age composition the rates are known as *adjusted* rates, and measure with fair accuracy differences in health conditions in the populations compared.

COMMUNITY DIFFERENCES IN DEATH RATES

The United States' death rate for the years 1942-46 averaged 10.5 per 1,000 and has been hovering in this vicinity for several years. In most parts of the country a death rate that was as much as 1.0 or 1.5 points in excess of what the rate had been in that area for the past several years would lead the vital statistician and public health official to look for some mild epidemic, while a rate 2.5-4.0 points above the usual would immediately arouse great concern because it would clearly indicate the operation of new and unusual destructive forces.

On the other hand, a death rate of 35-40 in most Chinese communities would probably be regarded as normal and a variation of 4 or 5 points in either direction would occasion little surprise, even if it were known. In the small Chinese community of 20,000 (Hsiao Chi), referred to in Chapter 2, where a determined effort was made to record births and deaths during four years, the average death rate during this period was 38 and the variation within this short time was from 52 in a year of poor crops and severe epidemics to 24 in the favorable year following this bad year. The reasons for such high death rates are not far to seek. There is no public health work whatsoever in most of China, there is almost no understanding of the sources of such diseases as typhoid fever, cholera, dysentery, and malaria, and even where a disease like smallpox is known to be contagious almost no effort is made to prevent its spread. In addition, diarrhea and enteritis and other diseases bearing most heavily on babies undoubtedly kill off one fifth to one fourth of them in their first year of life. In much of Asia and Africa the usual death rate is about the same as in China and in the more backward regions of South America it is but little lower.

DISEASE AND THE DEATH RATE

Prior to the Industrial Revolution, man had comparatively little control over his death rate. He took it for granted that a large part of the babies born would die within a few weeks or months. (In Sweden in 1751-60 over 20 percent of the babies died before the end of their first year.) He also expected that the children who survived infancy would succumb in large numbers to such ailments as diphtheria, smallpox, scarlet fever, measles, etc., as well as to all the other contagious and infectious diseases which regularly visited the community. Those who survived these children's diseases were almost constantly exposed to typhoid, dysentery, cholera, and smallpox, and in many regions to malaria, as well as to the frequently recurring epidemics of typhus, bubonic plague, pneumonic plague, black death, etc., and to all the continuing ills following in the train of such diseases. In addition, the people of those days must have been even more afflicted than we are by all those organic ailments which naturally develop as age advances.

While there is no generally accepted proof of what the usual death rates were among any people prior to about 1750 (Sweden's death rate in 1751-60 was 27.2 and in 1781-90 it was 27.9) and almost none for a considerable part of the world even now, it is quite safe to assume that until about 1800 death rates had always and everywhere been extremely high according to present standards, and that they varied greatly from year to year. It could not have been otherwise as long as people were almost completely ignorant of the connection between the terrible sanitary conditions of their daily life and the diseases which ravaged the community. As the connection be-

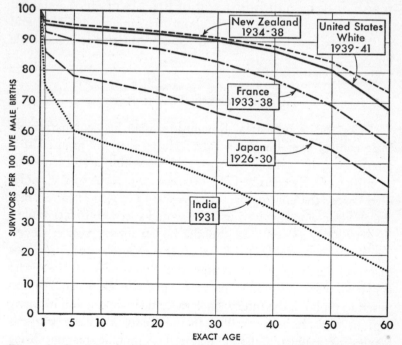

Figure 9. Survivors at Given Ages Out of 100 Live Male Births (selected countries, latest life tables)

tween these diseases and living conditions became known, e.g., between open sewers in London, which were also the sources of the water supply, and typhoid, dysentery, cholera, and enteritis, it slowly became apparent that most disease was of community origin rather than retribution for personal sins, and that only community action could prevent the worst of its ravages. For the way in which differences in the incidence of disease in different countries affected the number of survivors see Figure 9.

The Individual and His Health.—The individual had to use the common well. Even if he had known it was a source of infection he could not have obtained water elsewhere. He could not avoid contact with his neighbors who may have had diphtheria, scarlet fever, smallpox, etc., because there was no quarantine. Nor could he refuse to buy dangerously contaminated foods, even if he had known they would make him ill. There were no other foods available for most of the year! Moreover, the very term sanitation in its modern meaning was unknown until perhaps a century ago. The aquaducts of the Romans and other ancient peoples were installed not as health measures to insure a *good* water supply but to insure an *adequate* water supply, although such aquaducts undoubtedly reduced the death rate in most communities because they did furnish better water.

If this picture of the helplessness of the individual in the matter of health protection seems an exaggeration, it must be remembered that the germ theory of disease was not proved, even to the satisfaction of the scientists, until 1878 and did not become common knowledge in the West for at least another generation. But by 1800, or a little later, a few communities, by installing improved water supplies and better sewage disposal and by enforcing a few simple health regulations, had begun to control their death rates and great progress had been made in this direction even before Pasteur's discovery of the relation of bacteria to disease. The Swedish death rate, which averaged about 27.5 from 1751 to 1810, averaged only 18.3 in the decade of 1871-80 and fell to 11.7 in the decade 1931-40. Thus the absolute decline was greater in the 60 to 70 years preceding Pasteur's great discoveries than in the years since that time, although the proportional decline was greater in the later period.

TABLE 4

CRUDE DEATH RATES (DEATHS PER 1,000 POPULATION) IN SELECTED COUNTRIES 1838-1946. FIVE-YEAR AVERAGES, EXCEPT 1943-46

Date	United States	Germany	France	Sweden	Rumania	Italy	Japan
1943-46..	10.6		16.6	10.6	18.9	14.2	20.2
1938-42..	10.6	12.5	16.7	11.1	19.1	13.8	16.4
1928-32..	11.5	11.5	16.4	12.0	20.7	15.2	18.8
1918-22..	13.5	16.7	20.0	14.2	23.9	21.1	24.0
1908-12..	15.6	16.9	18.5	14.1	25.6	20.8	20.8
1898-02..	17.3	20.8	20.7	16.2	26.4	22.6	20.6
1888-92..	19.8	23.9	22.2	16.8	30.2	26.3	20.4
1878-82..	19.2	25.8	22.4	17.6	30.6	29.0	18.1
1868-72..	19.5	28.0	26.6	19.3		29.8	
1858-62..		25.1	23.4	19.9			
1848-52..		27.0	23.5	20.6			
1838-42..			23.6	21.7			

The data for Sweden are used here because they are believed to be the most accurate from 1750 to date, and also because they are believed to show the general pattern of the decline in the death rates of Western nations since about 1800 (see Table 4). They prove beyond question that a very modest public control of the sanitary conditions of the community, coupled with a rising level of living, paid large dividends in the saving of life even before there was a strong and well-supported public health movement such as we have today.

FAMINE AND THE DEATH RATE

We Westerners are apt to think of famine as something that occasionally afflicts China and India but we find it hard to believe that until about a century ago famine was an ever-present scourge in most of the world. We can, perhaps, better appreciate its effects if we try to think of what would have happened to the people in our "dust bowl" if there had been no means of getting food into that area except by wheelbarrow or pack-a-back, and no way for the people to get out except by walking. If, in addition, the "Okies" had not been allowed to enter other states or even other counties in their own state because of the fear that they would become an intolerable economic burden (California did try to keep them out), or a dangerous group of brigands, or would carry deadly epidemics, there can be no doubt that many would have died of starvation and the epidemic diseases which always accompany famine. This is essentially the situation which actually existed in most of the world until a little over a century ago. A crop failure almost always meant famine and epidemics in the area of dearth, and the epidemics were frequently spread quickly over whole nations.

The dearth in the "dust bowl" is also a good illustration of the local character of most famines. While the "dust bowl" people would have starved if compelled to look after themselves and if forbidden to move, there was abundant food in most other parts of the United States. Seldom, if ever, is the whole of China, or India, or any other large country, afflicted with serious crop shortage. But in the days when crops could not be moved more than a few miles because of the cost of transport, the surplus in one area could not be made available to the people in an area of dearth.

Famine and Transport.—In 1930-31 the writer spent some months in Nanking, China. At that time rice was so cheap in Nanking that many farmers were going bankrupt. They could not get enough for their bounteous crop to repay the production loans they had contracted. At the same time people were starving by the hundreds of thousands (some say by the millions) in northwest China. Money could have been found to buy considerable amounts of rice in the Yangtze Valley and to transport it by river, railroad, and truck to the end of passable roads, but once there, the coolie pushing a wheelbarrow of rice would have had to eat the load he started with and a little more while making a round-trip to the stricken area. Clearly, no relief is possible in such cases.

This situation has been so common in the past that we must list famine as one of the important causes of a high death rate all over the world until quite recently, and in perhaps half of the world even today. Moreover, such prosperous and well-organized countries as England, France, and Sweden had severe local famines from time to time, even during the first half of the nineteenth century. Their death rates often varied by 8 or 10 points within a given five-year period, e.g., the death rate in Sweden in 1857 was 27.6 and in 1860 dropped to 17.6. Only recently and in a comparatively small part of the world has a "famine factor" been eliminated from the death rate.

THE INDUSTRIAL REVOLUTION AND THE DEATH RATE

It was not until about 1800, and then only in Western Europe, that man began to gain any significant degree of control over his death rate. For some time this control was haphazard and precarious because there was little knowledge of the cause of disease and because the productivity of the economic system was so low there was very little surplus which could be used to improve the general level of living and to provide better sanitation, even when its importance came to be realized. Moreover, medical science was only in its infancy. That control of the death rate remained quite precarious until the middle of the nineteenth century is shown clearly in the Swedish data. In that country in the second half of the eighteenth century the death rate varied from a high of 52.4 in 1773 to a low of 21.7 in 1780, and although averaging lower in the first half of the nineteenth century, its variation even then was from 40.0 in 1809 to 18.5 in 1835. There is no good reason to believe that the variations in the death rate in the remainder of Western Europe were substantially different from those in Sweden at this time. If anything, Sweden's death rate may have been somewhat lower than that of most other countries of Western Europe and its fluctuations somewhat narrower. Why did Western Europe show this new trend in the death rate beginning about 1800? What happened then to change so radically an age-old pattern of the death rate, to produce such a great, such a steady, and such a prolonged decline?

Increased Productivity.—Undoubtedly the chief factor in lowering the death rate in Western Europe at this time was the increase in the productivity of labor which took place as machine industry replaced hand industry, as agriculture was improved, and as opportunity for emigration to new lands expanded. Together, these factors resulted in increased per capita productivity, which provided the means to make possible the public control of sanitation referred to above, to raise the general level of living, and to advance medical knowledge and train its practitioners. For the first time in human history, man had the economic means which made it possible to exercise an appreciable and fairly secure control over his death rate.

Higher Level of Living.—Particular attention should be given here to the improvement in the general level of living as a factor in the decline of the death rate. Terrible as were the living conditions of the workers in the early days of the Industrial Revolution according to present-day standards, they were an immense improvement on those of the workers in the cities and villages of the preindustrial period. The filth and squalor of eighteenth century Europe are incredible today. The open sewers of the cities, the shack housing of London or Paris, or any other city of that period, the complete lack of control over food sold, the absence of quarantine and of segregation hospitals, and, above all, the mere subsistence level at which all but a tiny fraction of the people lived, made a high death rate inevitable. There

simply were no means of securing a reasonably healthy existence to any significant proportion of the population. The conditions which we deplore today in visiting China, or India, or
any other backward agriculture country, are almost exact sur-
vivals of those which existed in eighteenth century (and earlier)
Europe. Such deadly conditions of daily life are inevitable as
long as human labor produces only enough for a bare existence
for only a part of the people who are born. Increased productivity is and always has been the absolute prerequisite for any
substantial lowering of the death rate. It was not until the
Industrial Revolution was well started that a higher level of
living became possible and until this happened the death rate
remained high. Note the relationship between wages and death
rates shown in Table 5. This is an important point to remember because it seems quite likely that during the next several
decades the change from hand industry to machine industry and
the improvement in sanitation will begin to affect the death

TABLE 5

INDEX OF WAGES AND DEATH RATES, ENGLAND AND WALES, 1780-1941

Date	Index of wages (1890-99 = 100)	Date	Death rates
1780-90	40		
1790-00	45-50		
1800-10	55-65		
1810-20	65-70		
1820-30	65		
1830-40	60	1838-42	22.1
1840-50	60	1848-52	22.6
1850-60	65	1858-62	21.9
1860-70	75	1868-72	22.2
1870-80	95	1878-82	20.3
1880-90	90	1888-92	19.0
1890-99	100	1898-02	17.4
1900-09	110	1908-12	14.2
1910-14	116	1918-22	13.7
1924-30	231	1928-32	12.2
1931-33	221		
1934-36	227	1938-41	12.7

rates in nations not yet much industrialized in the same way it affected those of the nations of Northern and Western Europe during the nineteenth century, and will thus make possible an unprecedented growth in the world's population since the total is now about two and one half times as great as in 1800.

The Agricultural Revolution and the Death Rate

The very brilliance of the achievements of industry since 1750 has tended to blind us to the fact that an equally significant revolution has taken place simultaneously in agriculture. From about 1750 up to the present time the efficiency of agricultural labor has been improved almost as much as has that of labor in industry. More productive crops were continually being discovered, better livestock was being bred, more effective methods of conserving and improving soil fertility came into use, machinery was being vastly improved and its use greatly extended. The net result has been that one worker in agriculture today produces several times as much food and fiber as an agricultural worker did before 1800.

This increase in the productivity of human labor, both in the factory and on the farm, may very properly be called the essential condition for the decline in the death rate which has taken place in almost all parts of the Western World during the last century and has more recently got under way in other regions. The revolution in transportation, although an essential part of the Industrial Revolution, was a very important part and should not pass without special mention. At the same time that man found out he could make things more cheaply and grow more food with less labor, he developed new ways of moving things about which were so much more economical than those he had employed previously that he revolutionized the entire structure and location of both industry and agriculture. (This will be discussed more fully in Chapter 8.) Because of its effect in removing the danger of famine from a large part of the world in the last century better transport should be counted as an important factor in reducing the death rate.

BENEFITS OF THE ACCUMULATION OF HEALTH KNOWLEDGE

During the last century man has learned more about how to maintain health than in all his previous history. We now know how the community can organize to prevent the worst ravages of the epidemic diseases, of tuberculosis and of the deadly ailments of infancy and early childhood. Barring some great catastrophe, e.g., war, we know how to keep our death rate at a low level and we know about what it will cost to do so. It would seem reasonable, therefore, to expect that declines in the death rates of those countries still having high death rates would be even more rapid in the future than those of Europe in the past if it were not for the fact that the open spaces of the world have largely been filled during the last century. The decline in the death rate in Japan in the last 30 to 40 years and in the Soviet Union in the last 15 to 20 years may be considered typical of what will happen in other high death rate lands when they, too, tackle their health problems in earnest and begin to reap the benefits of a more productive economy.

Benefits to the Soviet Union and Japan.—The Soviet Union and Japan did not have to wait to establish their public health service until they could, by their own efforts, accumulate the knowledge of sanitation and medicine needed to make such service effective. As soon as their governments had the means and the will to employ trained health workers, they could undertake the control of the death rate. Even before their economic means permitted any considerable improvement in the level of living they could establish fairly effective control over the death rate from epidemic disease because they could draw upon the accumulated experience and knowledge of the West. The extent to which they did profit by the experience of West-

ern Europe in reducing their death rates is seen in the fact that
the Soviet Union was able to lower its death rate in two decades
about as much as England did in a century or more preceding
1900 and that Japan was able to reduce its death rate since 1900
about as much as the United States did during the nineteenth
century.

**Benefits to India, the Philippines, and Other Oriental
Lands.**—If further proof of the great importance of the accumulation of health knowledge is needed it can be found in the
experience of countries like India, the Philippines, the Netherlands Indies, and Malaya where, according to our standards,
only very modest amounts are spent on public health work. In
all of these lands considerable progress has been made in the
control of epidemic disease in spite of the fact that not a great
deal of progress has been made in raising the general economic
level. However, in these lands the control of the death rate is
still as precarious as it was in Europe in 1800-50, and seems
likely to remain so for some time to come. Nevertheless, with
our present accumulation of health knowledge, we may rather
confidently look forward to a time not far distant when "high"
death rates will be a thing of the past, if only we have the good
sense to avoid war and to make a rational adjustment of our
birth rates to our means of livelihood.

THE DEATH RATE AND FUTURE POPULATION GROWTH

In Low Death-Rate Countries.—Although the decline of
the death rate has been the chief factor in determining the
growth of population in the world in the past century and a
half, and will be the chief factor in the less industrialized regions for some time to come, it is no longer the chief factor in
the more industrialized countries. In most of the lands now
inhabited by people of Northern and Western European stock
the death rate has been reduced to a level which cannot be low-

ered sufficiently to have any great effect on future population growth. This can be illustrated by some estimates of the future population of the United States. One estimate was based on the lowest death rate it seemed reasonable to expect after a long and careful study of what has happened to death rates throughout the world. Another was based on a "medium" death rate. In both, the same birth rates ("medium") were used. The difference in population between the two in 1975 is only 2.5 percent in favor of the population with the ex-

TABLE 6

FUTURE POPULATION OF THE UNITED STATES, CALCULATED ON ASSUMED FERTILITY AND MORTALITY TRENDS, 1945-75

| Date | Without immigration | | | With 500,000 immigration each-5-year period |
	Low fertility High mortality	High fertility Low mortality	Medium fertility Medium mortality	Medium fertility Medium mortality
1945.........	139,621	139,621	139,621	139,621
1950.........	144,922	146,987	145,460	145,959
1955.........	147,990	152,970	149,840	150,911
1960.........	149,827	158,559	153,375	155,075
1965.........	151,047	164,434	156,692	159,055
1970.........	151,627	170,845	159,847	162,888
1975.........	151,090	177,304	162,337	166,069

tremely low death rate. On the other hand, when "medium" and "low" birth rates were used with "medium" death rates the difference was 6.3 percent in favor of the population with "medium" birth rates. Since the future growth of population in the countries now having low death rates like the United States will be affected in much the same way by similar "expected" changes in birth rates and death rates it is reasonable to assume that their growth, like that of the United States, will also depend primarily (migration apart) on the changes in the birth rates. If birth rates continue as they were before World

War II, most of them will soon begin to lose population; if they stay on the level of the last five years they will continue to grow slowly for some years. Table 6 shows how the population of the United States may be expected to grow if certain combinations of "high" (the highest reasonable estimate), "medium," and "low" (the lowest reasonable estimate) fertility and mortality rates prevail over the next 25 to 30 years and how a given amount of immigration will add to these numbers. The demographic situation in which changes in the death rate that are within the bounds of reason will have comparatively little effect on population growth is something quite new in human experience.

In High Death-Rate Countries.—On the other hand, in China and India, in most of the rest of Asia and the adjacent islands, in most of Africa and South America, in lands containing perhaps 60 percent of the population of the world, death rates are still so high that the future growth of population, for several decades at least, will be determined chiefly by changes in the death rates since changes in their birth rates are certain to be relatively small. This is as it always has been.

In Medium Death-Rate Countries.—But, of course, not all countries belong to these two extreme groups—the one with high death rates and birth rates and the other with low death rates and birth rates. Perhaps, one fourth of the world's population lives in regions having medium death rates, and medium to high birth rates. In these lands, as in those with high death rates, the death rate is the more controllable factor at the present time and, hence, largely determines population growth from year to year. Judging from what has happened elsewhere during the past century the death rate will continue to be the decisive factor in such countries until it reaches a moderately low level. But once having reached such a level (perhaps 14-17) experience would lead us to expect that further decline in the death rate will be slower than the decline in the birth rate and,

TABLE 7

AVERAGE FUTURE LIFETIME FOR MALES AT SPECIFIED AGES AND AT
DIFFERENT PERIODS IN SELECTED COUNTRIES

	United States—white			England & Wales		
	1900-02	1919-20	1939-41	1881-91	1920-22	1937
0	48.2	54.0	62.8	43.7	55.6	60.2
20	42.2	44.3	47.8	40.3	45.8	47.1
40	27.7	28.8	30.0	25.4	29.2	29.6
60	14.4	14.6	15.0	12.9	14.4	14.3
	Japan			New Zealand		
	1921-25	1926-30	1935-36	1901-05	1921-22	1934-38
0	42.1	44.8	46.9	58.1	62.8	65.5
20	39.1	40.2	40.4	46.7	48.7	49.9
40	25.1	25.7	26.2	30.3	31.6	32.0
60	11.9	12.2	12.6	15.4	16.0	16.1

hence, that the rate of natural increase will decline. Furthermore, from that time forward, fluctuations in the birth rate will probably be as great as those in the death rate and will gradually become more important in determining population growth.

FUTURE DECLINE IN THE DEATH RATE

In the long run, of course, no country with a birth rate below 18 can have much increase in numbers, simply because it cannot have a death rate which will long remain below 14 or 15. Such a death rate is the lowest to be expected, once the age composition of a slowly growing population is achieved, unless the actual span of life is prolonged, and there is no evidence that this has happened or is likely to happen. We have made it possible for more people to live out the normal span of life, i.e., to live to extreme old age, but there is no evidence that extreme old age is higher than in the past. Figure 9 (page 64) shows the changes in the expectation of life for males (years yet to be lived) at different ages for several countries, at periods shortly before World War II. The significant point to notice is that in recent decades there has been comparatively little increase in years yet to be lived after people reach 40 years of age and almost none after they reach 60. On the other hand, the increase in the expectation of life at birth is very large and is, except in Japan, greatest where it was very low 30 or more years ago. The highest expectation of life at time of birth shown here is 67 for New Zealand in 1934 and there is every reason to suppose that pushing this up to 70-71 will be a slow, hard job. The crude death rate in a stationary population in which the average baby born alive could expect to live 70 years would be 14.3. As the low death rate and low birth rate countries approach the age composition of a stationary population —and they are moving rapidly in this direction—they cannot maintain death rates of 10-12. Their rates will move to 14-15 because they will have so many more old people. This is one important reason for saying that in the present low death-rate countries very little increase in population is to be expected from any future lowering of the death rate.

This does not mean that we will cease to make conquest of disease or to improve health. It does mean, however, that we encounter increasing difficulty in reducing the death rates of people at any age, once they have fallen to a relatively low level. Hence, future saving of life in populations with low death rates becomes slower and more costly. What is most reasonable to expect is that people can be shown how to live out a life span in better health rather than how to prolong the span; e.g., people of 65 or 70 may be kept more vigorous and healthy but it is more doubtful whether a larger proportion of those who live to be 70 can expect to live to be 80 or 85. The human organism seems to be wound up for only about a given span of years and while it can be made to function more efficiently during this span and a larger proportion of people can be helped to fulfill the span there is as yet no conclusive evidence of a lengthening of this span.

CHAPTER 5

WAR AND POPULATION GROWTH

Because of our experience in two World Wars and because of the chaotic social and economic conditions following these wars we are all much interested in the ways in which war affects the growth and composition of the population. These effects will be discussed under four main headings, put in the form of questions with chief emphasis on the first: (1) What are the effects of war on numbers? (2) What are the effects of war on the make-up or composition of the population? (3) What are the effects of war on the hereditary quality of the population? (4) What are the effects of war on the distribution of people?

THE EFFECTS OF WAR ON NUMBERS

There is a widespread belief that war is one of the great destroyers of mankind and is to be classed with hunger and disease as one of the three most important factors preventing the more rapid growth of mankind throughout much of his history.

The Nature of War Losses.—Until quite recently deaths of soldiers from wounds and disease were, as a rule, far greater in number than the deaths occurring immediately in battle. Sanitation both in camp and along the line of march was generally unspeakably bad and a large proportion of those who were wounded in battle died from the uninhibited infection of their wounds. Furthermore, an army not only generated its own illnesses but also it could not fail to contract diseases from the communities where it was stationed or through which it marched. It is little wonder that armies were generally more disease-ridden than the local populations among whom they lived, and that disease was more to be feared than bullets or spears.

In the past armies have, of necessity, lived largely "off the country" since transport of food was practically impossible. As a consequence, even after depleting the food supplies of the natives the soldiers themselves were often, if not generally, badly nourished and thus fell easier prey to all manner of disease, while the natives often starved because the soldiers destroyed what they could not eat or carry away. Besides the direct confiscation or destruction of food, "scorched earth" policies have been very common both as a means of defense and retaliation against an aggressor. This great destruction of property often reduced the productive power of a population for many years and thus contributed to a high death rate long after the fighting ceased.

It is quite clear that under these circumstances the only fairly accurate knowledge of losses was that of total military losses, where armies were well organized and disciplined. This condition was by no means common. And no one could make even a fair guess at civilian losses in most wars. About all that can be said concerning the losses in most past wars is that if the duration of the war was short, and if the war was confined to a limited area, the number of deaths was correspondingly small. If, on the other hand, the war involved a vast invasion, sweeping for hundreds of miles over a well-peopled area, many tens of thousands or even hundreds of thousands of deaths might occur of which no one had any definite knowledge. Moreover, a great many of these uncounted deaths would be among the soldiers, because of the inefficient organization of the army itself. This is especially likely to be the case in civil wars because of the guerilla character of much of the fighting. In such wars the whole economic structure of the community not infrequently breaks down. Famine and disease then sweep over great areas, almost denuding the countryside of population.

Examples of War Losses.—In China the Taiping Rebellion (1848-65) is often said to have cost 50 million lives. Starting in South China and spreading to areas north of the Yangtze River, it probably affected half or more of the population of China. The estimate that 50 million lives were lost is only a wild guess and is probably much too high, but even so the loss exceeds one's power of imagination. The writer has seen areas devastated at that time which have not yet recovered from the effects of this war. To come closer home it is well known that The Thirty Years War (1618-1648) left considerable areas in Central Europe almost unpeopled. In such cases how can one speak with any assurance of military and civil losses in war? When the great mass of a population lives close to the subsistence level anything which seriously interferes with the production or harvest of crops or any widespread destruction of shelter raises the death rate and thus reduces population growth or even thins out the population. There can be no doubt that war has frequently been an important destroyer of men. In his day Malthus was justified in looking upon war as one of the important causes of man's high death rate and, hence, a "positive" check on his increase in numbers. Are we justified in doing so today? In trying to answer this question we shall review briefly the losses of population associated with the two World Wars, about which we have fairly reliable information.

Military Deaths in the Two World Wars.—It is impossible to state precisely the number of military deaths which took place in the whole of Europe in World War I largely because of the uncertainty regarding such losses in Russia. However, the following estimates are probably not far wrong. Europe, west of Russia, had about 6.5-7.0 million direct military deaths. Russia's military losses were probably in the neighborhood of 2 million, but may have been more. In World War II military losses were probably of about the same size as in World War I but were distributed between countries quite differently.

France suffered comparatively few direct military deaths and those of England and Italy were far below their losses in World War I. The Soviet Union, on the other hand, had losses which may have amounted to 5 million or more and Germany's losses were probably somewhere between 2.5 and 3.0 million. Although the margin of error in these estimates is still rather large, it appears doubtful whether military losses in the whole of Europe were quite as large proportionally in World War II as in World War I. On the basis of the above estimates the military losses in the first World War in Europe amounted to almost 2 percent of the total population and in the second to perhaps 1.7 percent.

This may not seem a large proportion and may seem to indicate that in modern times war does but little to retard population growth. But even if for Europe as a whole military losses were relatively small this is not true for every country. In World War I France's military losses were slightly over 3.3 percent of her population, in Serbia nearly 10 percent and in Italy about the average—2 percent. Certainly these are not negligible losses and, as we shall see below (age composition), are more significant than the numbers and proportions might lead one to suppose.[1]

Excess of Civilian Deaths.—As was noted above, war often brings a large excess of deaths to the civilian population. The size of this excess of civilian deaths depends on the circumstances prevailing in each country or area and on the definition of civilian war losses. If all the excess of civilian deaths in Europe, west of Russia, in the years 1915-19 is attributed to the war, then there were perhaps 5 million civilian war deaths in this region or about three fourths as many as the military losses. But attention may be called to the fact that the excess

---

[1] For a discussion of war losses in more detail, but still in summary form, see: F. W. Notestein et al., *The Future Population of Europe and the Soviet Union: Population Projections, 1940-1970*, Geneva, League of Nations, 1944; and Dudley Kirk, *Europe's Population in the Interwar Years*, Geneva, League of Nations, 1946.

of deaths in 1918 over those in 1917 was extremely high in practically all countries for which statistics are available. Since 1918 was the year of the great influenza epidemic it seems reasonable to conclude that perhaps one third of all this war excess of civilian deaths in Western Europe was due to this disease. Even in the United States, where the civilian population was not directly affected by the war, the number of deaths in 1918 was almost one third higher than in 1917, nearly all of which excess is to be attributed to influenza.

But if direct civilian war losses were not large in most of the countries of Western Europe, they were huge in many other parts of Europe. In Serbia and Montenegro it is estimated that excess civilian deaths amounted to about 450,000 or to about one seventh of their 1914 population. In several other countries the excess civilian deaths amounted to 2 or 3 percent of their 1914 populations. In any event, in all of Europe, west of the Soviet Union, the excess of civilian deaths by the end of 1919 over those which would have been expected if there had been no war was great enough to people at least two cities the size of Chicago.

It seems quite reasonable to call all these excess deaths, both of military personnel and of civilians, war deaths. Taking this view, the excess of deaths in Europe, west of the Soviet Union, which are attributable to World War I up to the end of 1919 amounted to 11-12 million or somewhat over 3 percent of the prewar population of this area.

The effect of World War I on the civilian population of the Soviet Union cannot be calculated apart from the effects of the revolution and the great famine of 1920-22. Several years ago the writer estimated roughly that between 1914 and the middle of 1922 (about eight and one-half years) the Soviet Union probably lost from all causes all of the natural increase which might have been expected if there had been no war and no revolution—probably about 20 million persons. This figure now appears too low in view of Dr. Lorimer's more detailed calculations.[2] His estimate for total losses up to 1926, about four years later, is 26 million, of which about 14 million were civilian losses.

Reduced Birth Rate During War.—In the preceding paragraph reference was made to over-all or total losses of population by war. Clearly, if war leads to a reduced birth rate the deficit from this source is just as much a war loss as the deaths already noted. In World War I the reduction of the birth rate was very marked during the years 1915-19 in practically all countries engaged in the war, and even in some of the neutrals. A part of this reduction was due to the continuance of the long-time downward trend of the birth rate, but even when this is taken into account the deficit in births in Europe, west of the Soviet Union, probably amounted to 12-13 million and in the Soviet Union to about 10 million up to the time of the 1926 census. Thus it is probable that in Europe about 22-23 million children were not born as a consequence of World War I, the revolution and the famine in Russia, and general disorganization of life which followed it in many areas. Adding these figures, the total losses of World War I may be estimated at about 48 million. Since practically all the losses in Europe, west of Russia, occurred by the beginning of 1920 but some of the Soviet Union's heaviest losses occurred during 1920, 1921, and 1922 the writer has tried to arrive at an estimate for the whole of Europe for the beginning of 1920 in order to get a bird's-eye view at that date. His conclusion is that if Europe's population had continued to grow as might reasonably have been expected by a demographer studying the question in 1913, it would have amounted to about 500 million by the beginning of 1920 but that it actually numbered about 470 million or a little less, depending on just how the population of the Soviet Union is divided between Europe and Asia. This is

[2] Frank Lorimer, *The Population of the Soviet Union: History and Prospects,* New York: Columbia University Press, 1946.

about the same population Europe had in 1913. If it is assumed, as seems reasonable to the writer, that the losses in the Soviet Union in the three years from 1920 to 22, which were very heavy, about balanced the growth in the rest of Europe, it would appear that there was comparatively little change in Europe's population for the period of about nine years, 1914 to 1922 inclusive. Thus while Europe did not actually decrease in numbers as the direct consequence of the war it probably remained about stationary for nine years.

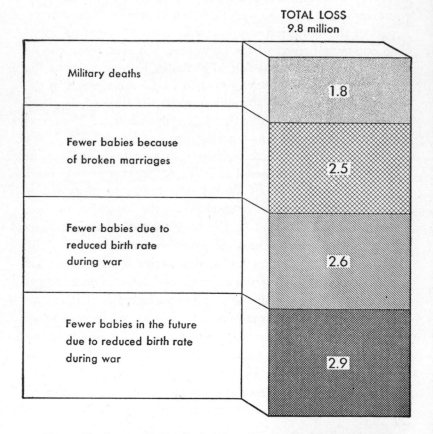

TOTAL LOSS
9.8 million

Military deaths — 1.8

Fewer babies because of broken marriages — 2.5

Fewer babies due to reduced birth rate during war — 2.6

Fewer babies in the future due to reduced birth rate during war — 2.9

Figure 10. Germany's Population Loss Due to World War I (total population loss 9.8 million)

Deficit in Future Births.—But the deficit of births during the war years and in the Soviet Union in the years immediately following, while quite obvious, is by no means the only effect of war on the birth rate. This may be illustrated by some calculations for Germany the results of which are shown in Figure 10. Germany's military losses in World War I were 1.8-2.0 million. Of these somewhat over 70 percent were under 30 years of age and about 85 percent were under 35 years of age. Clearly, these deaths reduced the number of children born to hundreds of thousands of couples, not only in cases where the husband was killed before the family was completed, but also because soldier deaths prevented the establishment of other hundreds of thousands of families. The probable deficit in births from this source during the 25 years following 1918 may be estimated at about 2.5 million. Finally, the babies who were not born during the war and the 25 years following it could reasonably be expected to have had about 2.9 million children by about 1965, when most of them would have passed their reproductive period. Adding all these losses together it appears that by 1965 World War I would have reduced Germany's population by a total of 9-10 million below what could have been expected at that time, had it not been for the war. As an estimate, little importance should be attached to this figure, since many other factors, both political and economic, which could not be taken into account might well come into play during this period and would be far more decisive in determining Germany's future growth. World War II would in itself form one such factor. But a calculation such as we have made does show how persistent may be the influence of war on population growth, even in modern times when the *direct* effects on the civilian population are probably far less than in earlier times.

In the Soviet Union conditions were more favorable than in Germany for continued population growth at a rapid rate after World War I. As noted above, once the revolution was accomplished, it appears that up to 1926 the consequences of World

War I reduced the population by about 26 million below what could otherwise have been expected. Practically all of this loss occurred before 1923. Looking ahead to 1970 on the basis of what could reasonably have been expected in 1913, the Soviet Union's population may very well be 40-50 million smaller by that time because of the losses in World War I and the revolution. This leaves out of account entirely the effects of World War II.

World War II, of course, gave another great setback to the growth of population in the Soviet Union. Lorimer's estimate of the actual population in the Soviet Union in 1945, "adjusted for hypothetical war losses," is 169 million whereas there would have been about 189 million if World War II had not intervened. This is a retardation of 20 million although an actual decline of only 3 or 4 million from the 1940 population. If there had been no retardation of population growth in the Soviet Union because of World War II its 1970 population could reasonably have been expected to be about 251 million. The present "expected" population is only about 222 million, a difference of 29 million; the 9 million increase in deficit after 1945 being due to the accumulation of unborn children discussed above in calculating an overall deficit for Germany.

Clearly, war can have a very marked effect on population growth. But the effect of these losses on future growth will vary greatly from country to country, depending upon the size of the losses and the changes in birth rates and death rates which may be attributed to the war. In Europe west of Germany, where losses in World War II were comparatively small, they could be made up in a few years by a rise of a few points in the birth rate which in 1939 was already below the replacement level in many countries and was being kept low largely by voluntary control. On the other hand, the further reduction of the death rates cannot be expected to contribute much to the replacement of war losses in these countries since their rates are already very low. Future growth in the next decade or two depends therefore, chiefly upon the will of the people. They can increase the average size of their families if they desire to do so.

In the Soviet Union and in the Balkans the situation is somewhat different. There the voluntary control of births is much less common than in Western Europe and the birth rates are still relatively high. Moreover, there is reason to expect important future declines in their death rates because of a fairly rapid improvement in the level of living. Under these conditions there is reason to expect that the prewar rate of population growth will be maintained or even increased somewhat in the next few years. The continuation of past trends would lead to the replacement of actual war losses, i.e., to bringing the population back to the 1940 level by 1946 or 1947 in the Soviet Union and within a few years even in Yugoslavia, which suffered very heavy losses. But the total population will increasingly fall below prewar expectations until a new generation unaffected by war losses comes to reproductive age.

As a general proposition one can say that the existence of low and voluntarily controlled birth rates means that the birth rate can be voluntarily increased by several points, if the people really want to do so. A population with a low birth rate which has suffered comparatively small war losses could, therefore, not only replace these war losses in a few years but could also bring its total numbers to the level that would have been expected if there had been no war losses if any considerable proportion of the people were willing to raise larger families. On the other hand, where the birth rate is already quite high and the death rate is only partially under control any significant increase in the rate of population growth over that of prewar years could not be as readily achieved by the will of the people to raise larger families. Actually it appears that war losses are seldom made up, in the sense that the population of a country 5 or 10, or 25 years after the war is as large as it would have been without the war. But it should also be noted that war

losses, even when as great as those of the Soviet Union in World
War II (let us say 20 million), are small when compared with
the effect of a slightly larger decline in the birth rate than in
the death rate over a period of a generation or two. Thus in
a population of 170 million with a birth rate of 35 and a death
rate of 20 the annual rate of increase would be 15 per 1,000.
If this rate were sustained for 25 years, the 170 million would
grow to about 247 million. But if the birth rate and death rate
were to decline in such proportions that the rate of increase
averaged only 10 per 1,000 per year for this period the population would only grow to 218 million, a difference of about 29
million and the decline in the birth rate could be said to have
had almost half again as great an influence in one generation
as the war. In other words, over a period of time as long as a
generation (about 25 years) the retardation in population
growth arising from moderate decline in the birth rate may
easily exceed the loss of even a very destructive war. Furthermore, Western experience to date is to the effect that once a
downward trend in the birth rate is established it continues for
some decades, at least. At present it is not certain that we
know how to raise it, even if we desire to do so.

War and Birth Rates.—The preceding discussion might
leave the impression that war always depresses the birth rate
during war years. This was certainly the effect of World War
I in most countries and many demographers, among them the
writer, believed that we could quite reasonably expect the same
sort of decline in World War II. However, the pattern of
births in World War II turned out to be quite different in some
countries from that followed in World War I (see Table 8).

In the United Kingdom the crude birth rate rose from 15.3
in 1939 to 15.6 in 1940, the first year in which births were
somewhat affected by the war and to 15.7 in 1941 the first full
year in which births would be expected to show the effects of
large-scale mobilization. It continued to rise and was 19.9 in

1944 but fell to 18.3 in 1945. It rose again in 1946 to 20.2 and is estimated at 22.3 for 1947. This is quite a different pattern from that followed from 1913 to 1919. Considering the fact that the birth rate of the United Kingdom had been declining fairly steadily from 1922 to 1938 the recovery during World War II is rather remarkable.

TABLE 8

BIRTH RATES, 1939-47, DURING AND FOLLOWING WORLD WAR II

Year	United States *	United Kingdom	Germany	Italy *	France *
1939	17.3	15.3	20.5†	23.5	14.9
1940	17.9	15.6	20.4†	23.4	14.0
1941	18.9	15.7	18.9*	20.8	13.3
1942	20.9	17.5	15.2*	20.4	14.8
1943	21.5	18.5	16.2*	19.9	15.9
1944	20.2	19.9	15.4‖	19.2	16.4
1945	19.6	18.3	12.3‖	18.3	16.2
1946	23.3	20.2	14.6‖	22.4	20.6
1947	25.9	22.3‡		22.6§	21.9§

* "Monthly Bulletin of Statistics," Statistical Office of the United Nations, December, 1947, Number 12.
† *Statistical Year Book of the League of Nations, 1942-44.*
‡ Estimated from data for 9 months.
§ First 6 months.
‖ Estimate, *Population,* July-September, 1947, Vol. 2, Number 3.

For France and Germany the data given are affected by territorial changes and invasion, but their general trend is clear. In Germany the 1913 rate was 27.5. This fell to a low point of 13.9 in 1917, rose to 14.3 in 1918 and then to 20.0 in 1919. Just before World War II (1939) the birth rate of Germany reached the highest point (20.5) it had attained in recent years and then fell to 15.2 in 1942. It recovered a little to 16.2 in 1943, but according to the latest estimates available fell again in 1944 (15.4) and 1945 (12.3). Thus we see that in Germany during both World Wars the birth rate remained well below what it was in the years immediately preceding.

In the whole of France the 1913 birth rate was 18.8. It declined rapidly in 1915 and 1916 to 9.5 in the latter year (uninvaded territory) and only recovered to 12.6 in 1919. In 1939 the birth rate in France was 14.9. It declined to a low point of 13.3 in 1941 and then recovered to 16.4 in 1944 and remained about at that level in 1945 (16.2). Thus France's birth rate never fell in World War II as it did in World War I and from 1941 onward was as high or higher than it had been prior to the war in spite of the deportation of hundreds of thousands of slave laborers. Since 1945 it has risen still more to 20.6 in 1946 and 21.9 in 1947.

There is no need to go into more detail, as Table 8 tells its own story. In Western Europe and the United States World War II did not depress the birth rates as did World War I.

Why, in World War II, the birth rate in several countries should have followed a course different from that it followed in World War I is by no means clear, but one difference is worth noting. In general the period preceding World War I was a time of prosperity. In such a period marriages and, in due course, births, are generally more numerous both absolutely and relatively than in a period of depression such as preceded World War II. (Due to the preparations for war Germany had an earlier recovery from the depression than took place in most other countries in Europe and in the United States.) When World War II broke out there was in many countries an accumulation of postponed marriages and births which was being rapidly reduced as economic conditions improved. For many countries, both belligerent and neutral, unemployment vanished shortly after war began and people were generally better off than during the depression. As has been noted in Chapter 3, prosperity generally leads to increased marriages and births. This explanation is not offered as completely covering the case but there seems to be little doubt that this change from depression to boom was a factor of much importance in the United States and probably in some of the European countries also. It seems likely, however, that there were also other factors of a less tangible sort (psychological) which operated to raise the birth rate chiefly through increasing the number of marriages and reducing the interval between marriage and a first birth. We can only guess at the nature of these factors now and may never know a great deal about them since they may be more or less temporary and may vanish before they can be studied.

Summary of Effects of War on Numbers.—By way of a brief summary it may be said that the effects of war on population growth are of many degrees and vary considerably from country to country. Any judgment regarding how long it takes to make up war losses depends upon what we mean by "making up war losses." If war losses are considered made up when the military losses and excess civilian deaths are equalled by the excess of births over deaths, then it will seldom take most countries more than a few years to make up their war losses and quite frequently there may be an increase in total population even during the war. If, on the other hand, by making up war losses we mean that the population will be as large at a given time, say 20 years after the close of the war, as it would have been without the war then only those countries which have had comparatively small losses are likely to make them up. If a country has reached the stage of demographic development, like France, where at most there is a very small excess of births over deaths and in some years an excess of deaths, and where there appears to be great reluctance to increase the size of the family, then it may not again reach its prewar population within any foreseeable period, except through immigration from abroad.

In contrast with France, whose birth rate was very low before the war and whose military and civilian deaths were about 820,000 (an equivalent number for the Uuited States would have been about 2.5 million), or with the Soviet Union, whose total loss of population is estimated at about 20 million, the United States had military losses and losses of merchant seamen of a little over 400,000. Moreover, our birth rate instead of declining below the 1939 level rose above it and remained well above it all during the war. Even in 1945—the low year —it was 2.3 points, or a little over 13 percent, higher than in 1939, and the actual number of births in 1945 was 444,000 larger than in 1939. Thus the excess of births in 1945 alone more than equalled our war losses. In our case, therefore, it may seriously be asked whether our total population was not increased rather than diminished by the changes in social and economic conditions which accompanied the war, i.e., whether it was not larger at the end of the war than it would have been had there been no war.

While no one can answer such a question with assurance, we do know that in prosperous times marriage rates and later birth rates rise and there is no question that on the whole economic conditions were very favorable for most of our people during the war. How far these favorable economic conditions were responsible for the psychological atmosphere favoring a high marriage and birth rate cannot be told; the fact remains that this set of conditions, coupled with the making up of marriages and births postponed during the depression, led to such an increase in births that in 1950 our population will be larger by perhaps 4 or 5 million than one could reasonably have estimated it on the data available at the time we entered the war. Whether it will be larger by that number 25 years hence is an altogether different question, one which will depend on how far this increase in births represents a drawing on future births during the war (and in the years immediately following) and on how far it represents a genuine halt in or possibly even a reversal of the long-time downward trend in the birth rate. As pointed out in Chapter 2, there is as yet no evidence of an increase in the average size of the family.

Effects of War on the Composition of the Population

Effects on Sex and Age.—How war affects the composition of the population depends on the extent and the nature of the losses suffered. If military losses are very large, as they were in Germany and in the Soviet Union in both World Wars, and are heavily concentrated in the 15-34 age groups then the most noticeable effects on the make-up of the population will be the decline in the sex ratio (males per 100 females), at the ages where the military losses were greatest. This will also be noticeable in the excess of females in the total population. Thus

TABLE 9

SEX RATIO BY AGE GROUPS OF THE POPULATION OF THE SOVIET UNION, 1926 AND 1939, AND OF GERMANY, 1939

	U.S.S.R. 1926 *			Germany 1939 *			U.S.S.R. 1939 †
	Males	Females	Sex ratio	Males	Females	Sex ratio	Sex ratio
	(In thousands)			(In thousands)			
Under 5..	11,238	11,085	101.4	3,949	3,788	104.3	102.3
5-9	7,650	7,620	100.4	2,242	2,166	103.5	99.7
10-14	8,643	8,448	102.3	2,478	2,406	103.0	99.4
15-19	8,133	8,844	92.0	4,168	4,031	103.4	97.5
20-24	6,712	7,101	94.5	2,245	2,176	103.2	99.4
25-29	5,490	6,547	83.9	3,561	3,506	101.6	93.2
30-34	4,297	4,768	90.1	3,597	3,562	101.0	90.9
35-39	3,994	4,458	89.6	3,336	3,362	99.2	83.0
40-44	3,393	3,562	95.3	2,569	3,076	83.5	78.5
45-49	2,893	3,015	96.0	2,161	2,712	79.7	78.1
50-54	2,343	2,698	86.8	2,040	2,424	84.2	81.9
55-59	1,887	2,318	81.4	1,838	2,098	87.6	82.2
60-64	1,709	2,126	80.4	1,704	1,898	89.8	77.5
65-over ..	2,610	3,357	77.7	2,876	3,407	84.4	69.8
Unknown	50	38					
Total ..	71,043	75,985	93.5	38,762	40,614	95.4	92.0

* Population figures from *Statistical Year Book of the League of Nations, 1942-44.*
† Based on estimated distribution of population of 1939. From Frank Lorimer, *The Population of the Soviet Union: History and Prospects,* New York: Columbia University Press, 1946, p. 143.

the 1926 census of the Soviet Union showed a total of 71 million males and 76 million females, with especially large sex differentials in the young adult age groups most depleted by war and revolution.

If, in addition to heavy military losses there has been a large decline in the birth rate during the war years, as there was in most countries in World War I, there will be a contraction in the size of the group born during war years as compared with the groups born immediately before and after the war. This contraction will be clearly apparent throughout the lifetime of the group.

Since actual military losses have generally affected only young males there will commonly be relatively large proportions of young women in these same groups who are unmarried and widowed. As already noted, this, in turn, will have an affect upon the birth rate of the group during the reproductive life of this war-decimated generation. The effect of the disparity of the sexes on the birth rate depends upon there being no significant change in the proportion of children born outside of wedlock or in the importance of monogamous marriage. These provisos are mentioned because there were some indications that in Germany both of these limitations on births as a consequence of war losses might be weakened intentionally.

Effects on the Labor Force.—Perhaps the most important economic effect of the heavy loss of young men is to reduce the labor force of the nation since men of military age are also the most productive workers. It is highly probable, therefore, that the productive capacity of a country suffers more economic loss proportionately than the loss in numbers would lead one to expect. The effects of this economic loss will last until the men of the war generation have passed into the less productive ages; nor can it be fully compensated for by the larger proportion of the unmarried and widowed women who will enter the labor force.

War and the Sex Ratio of Births.—It is frequently said that nature takes measures to redress the imbalance of the sexes due to war by producing a larger proportion of male babies during and after a war. The following table shows there is no clear evidence that this was the case in World War I. Normally there are 104-107 male births per 100 female births with 105.5 being about an average, but there is considerable variation about this norm from time to time so that a temporary rise or a fall of 1.0 to 1.5 points in the ratio cannot be regarded as unusual.

TABLE 10

RATIO OF MALE LIVE BIRTHS TO FEMALE LIVE BIRTHS, SELECTED COUNTRIES, 1911-42

Country	1911-13	1915-17	1920-22	1930-32	1940-42
Japan	104.2	104.2	104.3	104.9	105.1 (1936-38)
Australia	104.7	105.5	105.9	105.7	105.2
New Zealand	105.3	105.4	105.4	106.1	105.4
Germany	105.6	106.3	107.2	106.2	
Austria	105.8	105.4	106.6	106.2	
Belgium	103.9	104.8	105.5	104.5	
England & Wales	103.9	104.4	105.1	104.8	105.7
France	104.3	104.7	105.3	104.2	104.5
Hungary	105.4	106.4	107.1	106.1	107.6 (1939-41)
Italy	105.3	105.5	105.6	104.9	106.1
Finland	106.8	105.9	106.0	105.7	106.1
United States		105.7	105.7	105.4	105.6
Chile	104.9	105.3	104.6	106.4	104.5 (1939-41)
Sweden	105.9	105.6	105.5	105.2	105.6
Netherlands	105.0	105.6	105.9	106.5	

It should be noted, also, that the changes in the sex ratio of births shown in Table 10 do not coincide very closely either with the war period or with the immediate postwar period. Nor are the variations much more evident in countries engaged in war than in countries not at war. Finally, the changes in the sex ratio of births are not equally large or continuous in countries almost equally involved in the war. In Germany the sex ratio rose from 105.6 in 1911-13 to 106.3 in 1915-17 and to 107.2 in 1920-22 and then fell to 106.2 in 1930-32. In

France, on the other hand, there was a rise of 1.0 up to 1920-22 and then a decline to slightly below the level of 1911-13. In Japan there was no appreciable change until 1930-32 and then the change was small. In Italy there was no significant rise at any time during this period but a definite falling off between 1920-22 and 1930-32. In fact the only countries in which a fair case might be made for some effect of war on the sex ratio of births are Germany, Austria, and Hungary and the rises in these countries would by no means compensate for the war losses they suffered. If the sex birth ratio of 107.2, the highest attained by Germany just after the war, prevailed for a generation, 25 years, in place of the ratio of 105.6 of 1911-13, it would only make up about one fourteenth of Germany's direct military losses. But as we have seen, the ratio fell to 106.2 by 1930-32 and with this ratio only about one thirty-sixth of the war losses would be made up in a generation.

It is too soon after World War II to find much information on sex ratios at birth, but in the United States the sex ratio at birth, 1936-40, was 105.3 and for the years 1941-45 it was 105.6. In Sweden the ratios were 105.6 in the years 1936-40 and 105.9 in 1941-44. Both of these differences are small and are well within the limit of variations the demographer has learned to expect from year to year. With what is known on this matter at present the most reasonable conclusion is that nature does not automatically provide compensation for the excess losses of males in war. This may be a good thing in the atomic age when losses of life in war will probably fall far more heavily on the civilian population than on the armed forces.

Effects of War on the Quality of the Population

The effects of war on the quality of the population have long attracted the attention of biologists. Their conclusions have generally been to the effect that a disproportionately large number of men of good physical constitution became soldiers and because they suffered heavy mortality they left disproportionately few children. Thus because the weaklings and the less competent were left at home to become the parents of the next generation the population suffered biological deterioration. Needless to say, there is no definite proof that such a deterioration in the quality of any people has taken place. There was perhaps more reason to argue to this effect when armies were made up largely of volunteers, but even then there is serious question whether the qualities which lead men to volunteer for military service are more beneficial to society than those of the people who do not volunteer. In these days of mass wars and universal service there is certainly no good reason to assume that the men most exposed to death are "fitter" citizens than those less exposed. Besides, as has been shown above, the excess of civilian deaths in the two World Wars may be almost as great as that of soldiers and it may very reasonably be argued that these deaths, aside from those due to aerial bombing, fall especially heavily on the poor and the weak and thus offset to a considerable extent any evil effects of direct military losses among the "fittest." In modern armies there is also a selection of the better trained men from the more favored economic classes for special technical work and for desk jobs which are certainly less dangerous, on the whole, than actual combat service.

With regard to the often-made statements that the decline of the power of Rome, of the British Empire, or of France, is proof of biological deterioration among these peoples it must be said that we know almost nothing about biological changes in national populations, either in the past or in the present, which can be considered relevant to the problem of quality. What little we do know of changes in national populations relates chiefly to changes in social and economic characteristics as shown in national institutions. History tells us nothing regarding *biological* changes in populations.

Even the tremendous losses sustained by Russia in 1914-22 did not prevent the Soviet Union from staging the most impressive industrial revolution the world has ever known from 1929 to 1941, nor from being able to put in the field against the German army a fairly well-equipped and well-trained army and one whose morale was far superior to that of any Russian army in the past. As regards the effects of war on Germany's ability to organize for war and for production there is certainly no evidence in the fighting ability of her army, in the effectiveness of her economic organization, nor in the quality of her military equipment that her great losses in World War I or her smaller losses in previous wars, had undermined the quality of her population. The deterioration in humanely decent conduct among the Germans is certainly to be attributed to the Nazi ideology rather than to any biological change. (For a discussion of other aspects of the problem of the quality of population see Chapter 12.)

It should be made clear in this connection that biological deterioration of a population is not the same as its physical deterioration. Quite clearly, war may weaken a generation because of malnutrition and the prevalence of disease, but this is not proof of any deterioration of the hereditary quality of the people. The most reasonable conclusion regarding the effects of war on the hereditary quality of people is that this quality is little affected by war, so far as can be judged by information now available. But it should be noted that if war losses amount to as much as 15 or 20 percent of the total population, as they occasionally do, and if there is reason to believe that certain classes or groups have been especially selected for destruction, then this conclusion might need to be modified as regards that particular country or people. Even this is by no means certain! In addition, if new types of weapons, e.g., A-bombs, emit rays which damage the germ cells as well as the body cells it may well be that the hereditary qualities of vast numbers of people will be so changed by future wars or so weakened by these rays that their offspring will be inferior. Such a type of weapon might very well weaken the biological quality of vast populations.

EFFECTS OF WAR ON THE DISTRIBUTION OF POPULATION

There can be no doubt that the great invasions of history have had long-lasting effects on the distribution of population in certain areas and regions. At times very considerable areas have been almost depopulated and the surviving people have been forced to live in peculiar forms of distribution. However, we are not concerned here with the historical consequences of war on the distribution of population but, rather, with the probable effects of current military practice on the distribution of people over the land.

Although there was but little bombing of cities from the air in World War I there remained little doubt that another war would bring a vast amount of destruction from the air to the great centers of population and industry. The development of the airplane in speed, in radius of action, and in carrying capacity rendered it more and more certain that it would be the most formidable weapon in another war. Finally, the boasts of the Germans after about 1935 left no doubt that they intended to use the threat of aerial bombing to frighten their enemies into submission and, if threats did not avail, that they would actually bomb civilian populations. If there had been any lingering doubt about the potential destructiveness of aerial bombing in anyone's mind what happened at Warsaw in 1939, at Rotterdam in 1940, and in the blitz against England in 1940, certainly laid these doubts to rest. Nevertheless, it took the use of the atomic bomb at Hiroshima and Nagasaki to make us realize fully the helplessness of man to protect himself from destruction by air-borne weapons.

Aerial Bombing and the Large City.—It is now obvious to everyone that the modern large city, with its highly concentrated business center, with a large proportion of its population living within a radius of three to five miles from this center and with a heavy concentration of large factories either within the city itself or close to its outer border, makes an ideal target for an enemy bent on destroying a nation's fighting power. The question we are interested in here is: Will this new type of warfare have any significant effect on the distribution of population in the foreseeable future? Strange as it may seem, in view of the facts regarding the vulnerability of the modern city with the weapons we already have, and the practical certainty that far more destructive weapons will be developed in the near future, there is practically no evidence of any effort either to break up the large city or even to disperse large industrial and commercial enterprises. The increased building of branch plants and warehouses by many large corporations can scarcely be expected to contribute very much to the reduction of the vulnerability of cities, or even of particular industries, when these new branches are located on the outskirts of cities as large as Cincinnati, Atlanta, Houston, Dallas, Los Angeles, or San Francisco. These branches generally represent additional capacity for the firm involved and not a dispersion of production and workers to smaller cities and plants. In addition, it appears that many of the 103 largest electric power plants, furnishing over half of our total electric power, are among those being increased most in capacity.

On top of all this, as far as the writer can find, most if not all city plans now being overhauled are concerned almost exclusively with the problem of how to get more and more cars and people into and out of the downtown areas and the factory districts of the city in a given length of time. In this they recognize the importance of the suburban movement of population and industry. But there is not the slightest glimmer of recognition that the basic structure of the modern city is an anachronism in the atomic age as long as the atom remains politically untamed as an agent of destruction. Finally, it should be added that many people who know what is going on in the field of biological warfare consider the large city fully as vulnerable to attack by this as yet unused weapon as by the atomic bomb.

The amazing fact, in view of the terrible potency of these new weapons, is not that we are failing actively to undertake the dispersion of population and industry but that we are not even seriously discussing the ways and means of bringing it about. The practical difficulties in the way of dispersion are colossal; but so was our war effort, to the tune of about 300 billion. This amount, about equal to our national income (at the present rate of production) for a year and a half, would do wonders in reducing our vulnerability to atomic and biological warfare. Nevertheless, we are not even discussing the need of adapting the distribution of population to these new weapons. Perhaps this is not surprising in view of the fact that not even the Europeans who have had direct experience of the destructiveness of aerial warfare are giving the redistribution of population any more serious consideration than we are. This indifference on both sides of the Atlantic surely cannot be attributed to a belief that the United Nations will be able to exercise effective control over these new forms of warfare. It must be attributed largely to the fact that we have not been able to imagine vividly enough the devastating effects of atomic and biological warfare on the physical plant of our cities, and on human life. Perhaps it is grimly true that "whom the gods would destroy they first make mad."

In contrast to the Western nations, the Soviet Union began to give effect to strategic considerations in the building of cities under its first 5-year plan (1929). The fact that much of its new industry was built beyond bombing range from Germany paid off in a big way in the last war. But no city in the world will long be beyond the range of airplanes from some possible or probable enemy. Whether the Soviet Union is now actually dispersing its industries no one knows but the fact that its rulers have given weight to strategic considerations in the past is reason to believe that they will do so in the future, once the most urgent projects of postwar reconstruction have been accomplished.

We would do well not to ignore the dangers from the atomic bomb and from biological agents in planning our future cities. (For some facts showing our present vulnerability to aerial attack see Chapter 9.)

CHAPTER 6

THE FUTURE POPULATION OF NATIONS

It has been shown in preceding chapters that there have been significant differences in the rates of growth of different peoples within the period during which we have dependable knowledge of this growth. It has also been shown that in times past these differences in population growth arose out of differences in death rates more than out of differences in birth rates. Until the Industrial Revolution, which increased per capita production of goods and made possible better sanitation and higher living standards, death rates had always been high and rapid sustained population growth was a rare occurrence anywhere. In the past it was also usual for death rates to vary greatly from season to season, depending on the quality of the harvest, the incidence of epidemics, and other conditions affecting the volume of the food supply. The situation in India was dwelt upon as an illustration of the way in which the fluctuations in the death rate affect population growth in a preindustrial agricultural civilization. This was done not because conditions are worse in India than in many other lands, but because there are more reliable data for India than for most other regions where birth rates and death rates are under but little control.

THE IMPORTANCE OF POPULATION FORECASTS

One of the chief reasons for the brief survey of the factors affecting population growth among different peoples made in the preceding chapters is that it enables us to look ahead and to make reasonable guesses regarding where, and under what conditions, population is likely to grow in the future. The guesses for any particular area must, of course, be within very broad limits and they must rest on certain assumptions which appear reasonable in the light of the known facts. These estimates can never be precise because we can never know exactly what will happen either to the birth rate or the death rate. However, as knowledge accumulates regarding the factors affecting these rates, we are justified in using it to make forecasts if we do not endeavor to make them too precise and do not forget their shortcomings when we use them. Calculations of population growth in the more industrialized nations over the next few decades should not be very far wrong, barring new wars. An evaluation of the factors likely to affect the death rates in the nonindustrialized areas should also enable us to estimate their probabilities of growth within limits of usefulness, although less exactly than in the industrialized countries. For a number of reasons it is important to get as accurate a picture of future population growth as is possible, for changes in population growth are certain to be influential in determining the future course of history just as they have been in the past. But such changes in growth are probably of more importance today than in the past because we live in a world in which there is a growing likeness in the processes of industrial production. Today, more than ever before, changes in population growth are accompanied by changes in industrial potential. By changing the balance of power in the world such changes are more than ever likely to exert a decisive influence on the course of world events. A Japan in a feudal state of development (before 1878) was not a dangerous competitor of Western nations, either economically or militarily. But a Japan industrialized after the modern pattern became a threat to the economic dominance of Europe in Asia and the Pacific, and by 1930 felt strong enough to undertake a vast expansion of her empire.

The way in which the influence of Europe spread during the nineteenth century, both in the new areas opened to settlement and in the nonindustrialized parts of the world which could not defend themselves, is sufficient proof of the importance of the differential growth of population in determining the course of history although, as frequently noted above, the expansion of industrial capacity has been a prime factor in the growth of population in the West and also in the increase of military power and is steadily becoming of increasing importance in many other parts of the world. The way in which differential population growth will affect several important countries in the next 25 years is shown in Figure 11.

THE EXPANSION OF EUROPEANS

It may be well to point out briefly the political position which Western Europe had attained in the world after the somewhat more than a century of rapid population growth which ensued upon the application of steam to industry and transportation.

European Colonies.—By 1914, in addition to the vast areas actually settled by Europeans, they dominated most of Africa, India, the Philippines, and the islands of the Pacific and Indian Oceans. Even China, nominally independent, was in effect a European colony until 1931. In Asia, Japan alone was truly independent and she only cut European leading strings about 1900, after she had developed enough industrial power to make her exploitation as a semi-colonial area dangerous, and after her population had begun to grow at a rapid rate. Because we must assume an improvement in the industrial efficiency of all backward peoples in the not-distant future, probably even more rapid than that of Western lands (since they can profit by our experience), population growth is likely to become an even more highly significant factor in determining the strength of nations in the near future than it has been in the past. It is of the greatest importance, therefore, to search out to the best of our ability what changes in the growth of nations are likely to

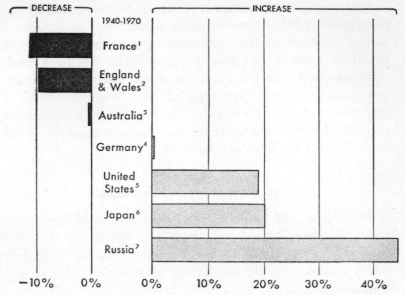

Figure 11. Estimated Population Increase or Decrease in Selected
Countries, 1940-70

[1] Fertility and mortality rates remain the same as in 1935; no immigration. Alfred Sauvy, "Perspectives statistiques sur la population, l'enseignement et la chomage," *Jour. de la société de statistique de Paris,* No. 6 (June, 1937), pp. 16-17.

[2] Estimates assume fertility and mortality rates same as in 1933; no immigration. Enid Charles, "The Effect of Present Trends in Fertility and Mortality upon the Future Population of England and Wales and upon Its Age Composition," Executive Committee of London and Cambridge, Economic Service, London, August, 1935.

[3] From 1938 to 1963 fertility rates decline at a rate equal to one half of the decline experienced during 1925 to 1930, then stabilize; mortality rates as 1932 to 1934; no immigration. S. H. Wolstenholme, "The Future of Australian Population," *Econ. Record,* Vol. 12, No. 23 (December, 1936), p. 205.

[4] Same number of births (1,162,000) as in 1927; same mortality rates as 1924 to 1926; no immigration. Friedrich Burgdörfer, "Volk ohne Jugend," Vowinckel, Berlin, 1935, p. 135.

[5] Medium birth rates and medium death rates; no immigration. See "Estimates of Future Population of the United States, 1940-2000," National Resources Planning Board, Washington, 1943.

[6] Average of the 1970 estimates of the Institute for the Research of Population Problems in Japan and of Dr. Teijiro Uyeda. See Inouye Masaji, "Population of Japan," Tokyo Bureau of Social Affairs, Kojimachi-Ku, 1937.

[7] Frank W. Notestein, "Some Implications of Population Change for Postwar Europe," *Proceedings of the American Philosophical Society,* Vol. 87, No. 2, 1943. Because of her losses in World War II the population estimate for Russia of 251,000,000 people by 1970, is probably too high by 28-30 million.

occur in the next few decades. That significant demographic changes, i.e., changes in birth rates and death rates, and, therefore, in growth, are taking place has been shown in preceding chapters. It will be in order, therefore, to sketch briefly the world population picture of tomorrow as it appears from the facts we now have.

World Differentials in Population Growth

For our purposes, the different regions of the world may be divided into three classes from the standpoint of their present and probable future growth. The basis on which the different countries are assigned to these growth classes is simply the degree of control exercised over their death rates and birth rates. The proof of control is found in the decline in either birth rates or death rates, or both, or in low rates which, if not still declining have been maintained long enough to justify a belief that they can be maintained in the future.

Class I.—Without attempting to name every small political area belonging in this group the following countries may be placed in this class: United States, United Kingdom, France, Denmark, Norway, Sweden, Netherlands, Germany, Austria, Czechoslovakia, Hungary, the Baltic countries Estonia, Latvia, Lithuania (now part of the Soviet Union), Belgium, Finland, Switzerland, Italy, Canada (although French-Canadian Quebec still has a large increase), Australia, and New Zealand.

In these countries there is now a large measure of control over both death rates and birth rates. In general, they have low death rates so that as a class not a great deal of increase in numbers can be expected from further improvement in health (see Chapter 4) although in those that have but recently entered this class (e.g., Italy) there is still considerable room for improvement. These countries also have low and, in most cases, declining birth rates which are largely under voluntary control. The net result is that there is little or no natural increase in them when due allowance is made for the fact that most of them still have young populations in which the number of births is high and the number of deaths low compared with what it will be within two or three decades (see Chapter 2). In those countries in which there is still a fair natural increase, e.g., Italy, Netherlands, and United States, the birth rate appears to be declining as fast as, or even faster than, the death rate so that the natural increase is declining and bids fair to disappear altogether within a relatively short time. It appears, therefore, that unless some change takes place in the attitudes of these peoples, causing them to want more children, there is not much likelihood they will have any considerable population increase in the foreseeable future although most of them will continue to grow slowly for the next decade or two and some for a little longer. In this group at present, crude death rates vary from about 10 to 14 or 15 and crude birth rates from about 15 or 16 to 22 or 23. The aging of their populations, however, will soon bring these rates closer together, as had already happened in France before World War II. This will take place even if there is no further decline in the number of births per 1,000 women of each age, which is an improbable assumption. France has had a low birth rate long enough to become an "old" nation. Although her crude birth rate is higher than that of some other Western European countries, her death rate is now more like that of a stationary population, so that even in these postwar years of higher crude birth rates there is but a very small excess of birth over deaths.

One can say with certainty that unless the average number of births per woman actually increases and remains well above the level of recent years, most of these Class I countries will have fewer people three to five decades hence than they now have, regardless of the effects of the last war. In some of them, e.g., United Kingdom, France, and Sweden, the decline in population may begin within a decade or two, while in others it may be four or five decades off. But as a group these countries cannot be expected to grow much in the future. In the United States, where conditions are more favorable for growth than in most of the others, it appears probable that we may add about another 20 percent to our population in the next 30 or 40 years, bringing our total to perhaps 165-170 million before we begin to decline. This is a smaller proportional increase than we had in any single decade up to 1910-20.

It is especially noteworthy that these Class I countries which are now growing slowly and will probably soon cease to grow are, with few exceptions, the countries which grew most rapidly during the last century and a half. In 1800 they had a population estimated at approximately 115 million or about 12.6 percent of the world's population and by 1914 they had grown to 358 million, or by 200 percent, and then constituted about 20.8 percent of the world's population. Between 1914 and 1940 their populations increased by only 77 million, of which almost one half was in the United States and Canada, which were still increasing rapidly up to 1920. In 1940 they still contained about 20.9 percent of the world's population but there can be no doubt that this proportion is now declining.[1] Can these countries continue to play the part they have in world history as they become a smaller and smaller part of the world's population?

Class II.—The following countries may be placed in Class II: Spain, Portugal, Greece, Yugoslavia, Bulgaria, Rumania, Poland, South Africa (white), Japan, and the Soviet Union; possibly also French North Africa (Algeria, Tunis, and Morocco), Brazil, Argentina, and Uruguay. The term possibly is used with regard to these latter areas because their vital statistics are so inadequate that one cannot feel at all certain just what their population growth is but it seems reasonably

---

[1] These figures are only approximate because the many changes in boundaries between 1800 and 1940 make it impossible to ascertain their population with precision at any given time.

certain that their death rates have fallen sufficiently faster than their birth rates to create a fairly wide gap between them.

These are countries in which both birth rates and death rates have been declining in recent decades but in which the death rate has declined more rapidly than the birth rate. Their vital rates may still be called *medium* to *high*. Birth rates are generally from 25-35, and sometimes even higher, probably averaging 30 or more, while death rates are 15-25 and may average 17-20. At present the natural increase of population is greater in these countries than in most other parts of the world. They can be counted on to have a fair to high natural increase year after year for some time to come, again assuming no war losses. In due course of time they may be expected to pass into Class I and gradually cease to have any natural increase. They are now in much the same stage of evolution as regards their vital rates as most Class I countries were during the 30-50 years before World War I.

If all the countries named above are included in Class II it contained in 1940 about 432 million people, or 20.7 percent of the world's population. In 1914 it had a population of about 333 million or 19.3 percent of the world's population, and in 1900 it had about 238 million or only 15.6 percent of the world's population. So little is known about 1850 populations in most of these countries that no estimate is attempted, but they certainly contained a much smaller proportion of the world's population then than in 1900. Class II has not only gained more in absolute numbers since 1914 than Class I but also has, of course, gained at a much faster rate. Since the death rate is under somewhat less secure control in Class II than in Class I countries, its fluctuations are likely to affect population growth in some of them from time to time. To be specific, it is more probable that the death rates of Japan and the Soviet Union will fluctuate significantly than will those of the United States or of England. This does not mean that a significant rise in the death rate is not possible in the United

States but that such a rise is less likely because of our better established health service and the larger means we have available to use in any health crisis which may arise. Despite the possibility of wider fluctuations in population growth in some of these Class II countries there is no doubt in the mind of anyone familiar with their demographic trends that they will continue to grow fairly rapidly for 3-5 decades. The Office of Population Research at Princeton has recently made some calculations of the future growth of population in different parts of Europe which may be cited as illustrative of the differences in the rates of growth to be expected in Class I and Class II lands in the future. Taking no account of the effects of war, the Soviet Union could have been expected to grow from about 174 million in 1940 to 251 million in 1970, while Northwestern and Central Europe would reach a maximum of 237 million in 1950 and then decline to 225 million by 1970. In these comparisons the Soviet Union may be regarded as representing about the maximum rate of growth in our Class II, and Northwest and Central Europe as the minimum in our Class I. But even when this *maximum* spread in natural increase is reduced to a *medium* it is abundantly clear that Class II nations will rapidly outstrip Class I in numbers during the next few decades.

Class III.—The remainder of the world may be placed in Class III. In these countries neither the birth rate nor the death rate has come under reasonably secure control. As will be explained later, even when the death rate appears to be under a certain measure of control, general economic and social conditions are such that it may get out of control at any time. In most lands in this Class a poor harvest is likely to result in serious malnutrition or, if much below the average, in severe famine. This shortage of food will almost certainly be accompanied by more or less devastating epidemics. Furthermore, local epidemics of typhoid, dysentery, cholera, smallpox, and other deadly diseases, and particularly of enteritis among children, are always present and take a terrific annual toll, while in the tropics and subtropics malaria is all but universal. The growth of population in these lands is, therefore, likely to be quite erratic. If, as in the case of India, the Philippines, and the Netherlands Indies, the government is quite efficient, and by improved health service does manage to reduce the ravages of epidemic disease for a time, and by the extension of irrigation makes possible a fairly rapid increase in food supply, and by the suppression of internal quarrels, eliminates the effects of war, the growth of population is rapid because the birth rate still approaches the physiological maximum.

There is no assurance, however, that the controls over the death rate just described can be permanently maintained. They may fail at any time for a number of reasons. In passing from colonial status to independence, civil disturbance may become, widespread as appears to be happening in India, the Netherlands Indies, and Indo-China. This, in turn, may lead to the disorganization of the meager public health service built up during the last two or three decades. In addition, the expansion of agriculture through irrigation may be stopped and the agencies concerned with the improvement of crops and livestock may have their support withdrawn. Under these conditions, industrial expansion will also be slow. Consequently, in these Class III lands the abundance or the scarcity of the means of subsistence and a highly precarious control of epidemic diseases, or the complete lack of epidemic control as in China, now determine their growth in numbers. To use Malthus' phrase, the "positive checks," i.e., those which tend to make the death rate high, are at present the chief determinants of population growth in these Class III lands.

There is no reason to doubt that in the course of some decades many of the Class III lands will achieve more and more secure control over death rates and will make a beginning

in controlling birth rates, but the control of the latter is certain
to lag by several decades behind that of death rates. For the
present we cannot make any very assured prediction as to how
rapidly population will grow in any Class III country. In some
of them, e.g., in India, population has already grown to the
point that any future increase can only be regarded with much
misgiving by all who would like to see a higher level of living
in that country. Population growth is creating problems of
population pressure which are causing much anxiety to those
in responsible positions because they believe India is now on
the horns of the Malthusian dilemma: her population is increasing faster than the means of subsistence and the adjustment will be effected through an increase in the death rate
resulting from increasing poverty and hardship.

Much the same situation is arising in the Philippines, Java,
and Indo-China. Their populations have been growing quite
rapidly during the last few decades and, because the cheapest
means of reducing death rates have already been put into operation, the outlook is gloomy and the future highly uncertain.

That these Class III countries may grow very fast is clearly
proved by what has happened in several of them since 1900.
That their growth may fluctuate greatly is also proved by the
same experience. That they will slowly increase the security
of their control over their death rates seems a reasonable
assumption but the speed with which this is accomplished will
depend largely upon the speed with which birth control spreads.
Because most of these peoples, except in parts of Africa and
South America, do not have new lands into which to spread,
as was the case with Europeans of 1800, and because many of
these countries already have dense populations, they will encounter far more severe "positive" checks to their growth
during the next several decades than Europeans have known
since the middle of the eighteenth century. No matter how
great their efforts to use the experience and knowledge of the
West to hasten their industrial development and the improve-

ment of their agriculture they will not soon acquire a secure control over their death rates. They have a long, hard pull ahead.

From what has been said above regarding the growth of Class I and Class II countries in recent decades it appears that Class III countries have not held their own in the recent past, decreasing from about two thirds of the world's population in 1900 to perhaps three fifths in 1940.[2] It also appears that this is due to their extremely high death rates, for they undoubtedly have the highest birth rates in the world.

But while there is great uncertainty regarding the future growth of population in any Class III country and of this Class as a whole, it should be said that there are vast potentialities of growth in it. Once these peoples develop a control over their death rates similar to that of Class II countries we may witness a growth in numbers far greater than that of Europeans during the nineteenth century.

In closing this statement on the probable future growth of nations the writer will hazard the general predictions, (a) that during the next four or five decades the proportion of the world's population living in the Class III nations as named above will probably change but little or even decline slowly, (b) that the proportion in Class I countries will continue to decline, and, (c) that a large relative increase in population will take place in Class II countries. If internal strife remains severe in India and China the absolute increase in Class II countries may even be greater than that in Class III countries. But almost certainly before a half century has passed some Class II countries will have passed into Class I and some of the minor Class III countries will have passed into Class II. This latter movement appears less certain within five decades.

---

[2] These proportions are arrived at by taking the population of Class I and II countries from the estimated population of the world, and are not very exact. They are sufficiently accurate, however, to leave little doubt that in the last four decades this Class, as a whole, has not maintained its relative position in the world's population, although certain portions of it have grown in relative size.

CHAPTER 7

POLITICAL AND ECONOMIC IMPLICATIONS OF DIFFERENTIAL NATIONAL GROWTH

Assuming that the outlook for the future growth of different countries is about as pictured above, why is this change in the source of population growth from West to East, from the more industrialized to the less industrialized countries, of economic and political importance? The answer is that, assuming also a diminishing differential between West and East in the efficiency of their economic systems, the center of economic strength, and with it the center of political and military power, is certain to shift in the direction of the more rapidly expanding populations.

During the century and a half ending about 1910 the economic and political power of Western lands had grown much faster than that of Eastern lands, including the Soviet Union, largely because a new dynamic factor had entered in the life of the West while that of the East remained relatively static. This relative increase in the power of the West was closely associated with those changes which are called, collectively, the Industrial Revolution. One important consequence of this Revolution was the rapid growth of Western populations. Changes in population growth may be regarded as a symptom of important changes taking place in the economic and social organization of peoples and since growth is one of the first visible symptoms of these underlying changes which can be measured and evaluated it is very important to study it carefully. It is the harbinger of other changes yet to come which are quite likely to determine the future structure and organization of world economy and world politics.

The growing economic efficiency of the West, together with its increase in numbers, gave it a vast advantage in production, in trade, and in military power over the more static regions of the earth. It was, therefore, able to extend its political power over a large part of the East which was still agricultural and whose small industry still depended almost entirely on hand labor. Looking back, we can see that the growth of population was both cause and effect of the political and economic expansion of the West into the less industrialized areas of the earth. Without this population growth it is very doubtful whether the Industrial Revolution alone could have furnished the drive to make Western Europe the dominant economic and political power in the world during the past century or century and a half.

PROBABLE CHANGES IN THE LOCUS OF ECONOMIC AND POLITICAL POWER

As was shown in the preceding chapter, the expansion of the Western European people is about over. The future expansion of population within the foreseeable future will be chiefly in Eastern and Southern Europe, in Asia and in other so-called *backward* lands, because these backward lands (lands in which hand industry and hand agriculture still prevail to a considerable extent), are not going to remain economically static much longer. Some of them already know how to control their death rates to a significant degree and are also rapidly increasing their productivity thus already providing an economic base for a growth of population similar to that in the West during the nineteenth century. In general these are the Class II countries. The Class III countries have scarcely begun to industrialize or to develop effective public health services. But there is good reason to believe that even in these latter the process of industrialization once started will go forward steadily and in some cases quite rapidly. We have only recently been forced to realize just how effective Japan's industrial revolution has been.[1] Since 1929 the Soviet Union has startled the world by the rate at which it has industrialized and the control it has gained over its death rate. The quantity and quality of its industrial products are best attested by the way it stood up against the military might of Germany. Its increase in population during the next few decades will probably exceed that of any other nation.

Industrialization in India and China.—The Chinese and the Indians alike are laying plans for the extensive industrialization of their countries. The younger leaders are convinced that only through the wider and more efficient use of their natural resources can they make a place for themselves in the world today and maintain that place in the future. India, under British guidance, made significant headway in industrialization and, if internal troubles can be avoided, should go forward quite rapidly. But widespread civil strife may not only stop progress but may even destroy much that has already been achieved. How quickly China can make a real beginning in industrialization and how fast she can proceed will depend in the first instance on how quickly she can establish internal order. Until stable political conditions are attained there will be little chance for her to secure loans, or machinery, or personnel from abroad, and without these progress will be very slow even in those areas where civil order is maintained. But it is a fact that everywhere in the backward lands the ferment of industrialization is at work. Their people are convinced that machine industry is the one way to assure themselves a better living and to develop the strength by which they can defend themselves against aggression by the peoples already industrialized. There can be no doubt that the wide differential in economic achievement which has in the past characterized

[1] For a somewhat more comprehensive discussion of Japan's economic development in the past years see the author's *Population and Peace in the Pacific*, Chicago: University of Chicago Press, 1946, Chs. 7-10.

the West and the East has already begun to diminish and will most certainly disappear at a more rapid rate in the future as capital and skill accumulate. This does not mean that these agricultural lands in the East or in South America can quickly attain the industrial status of Western Europe or of the United States, because many of them never may attain such a status, due to their lack of basic mineral resources. It does mean, however, that even those which have as yet scarcely begun to industrialize are going to make increased efforts to develop efficient machine industry, and it seems only reasonable to believe that they will achieve a substantial amount of success, although less than many of their more sanguine prophets are predicting. As a consequence, we in the West will soon cease to have sole possession of the economic and political advantages of an efficient machine industry and a rapidly growing population to which we have become accustomed.

Economic Needs and National Expansion

The growth of population in lands which heretofore have had but a small and uncertain increase will help to stimulate the development of their industry as it did in the West. As a consequence, their need for more secure access to larger resources will grow just as it did in the West. Once industry begins to expand and the mass of the people begins to secure a few of its products, the need for materials grows by multiplication rather than by addition. What is likely to happen in China and India and in other backward lands in this respect can be foretold to a certain extent by studying what has taken place in Japan in the last three or four decades.

The Growth of Japan's Needs.—The agricultural and mineral resources of Japan were ample at a stage of development when the Japanese people lived on a very simple home-grown diet and used only a small variety and quantity of nonagricultural goods made by hand and made out of their small native mineral resources. These resources became inadequate as a more productive industry made a higher level of living possible and led to a reduction in the death rate, thus stimulating population increase. Once the nation's industry was well started it became more and more voracious because of the growing demands of a growing population. It needed ever larger and larger amounts of more and more kinds of raw materials.

Whether the increasing industrialization of a country and the accompanying effort to keep raising the level of living will result in the attempt to get larger resources by force, as in the case of Japan, depends upon a variety of factors. If a nation can find its raw materials and its markets at home to the extent that has been the case in the United States and the Soviet Union, there is little economic need to seek colonies abroad. There is, therefore, only a comparatively mild public urge to bring new areas under the nation's political and economic control, except as they may have definite strategic value or may enhance the power of the ruling class or clique. If, on the other hand, the domestic raw materials are limited both in amount and variety, as they were in Japan, then they must either be secured by trade through the regular channels of foreign commerce, or they must be brought under the political control of the nation in colonies, if the level of living is to keep on rising.

All this may seem so evident that it need not be mentioned, but we seem to forget it when we think about the rise of new powers which do not have the same secure access to resources and markets as the powers having great rich territories in a solid block like the United States and the Soviet Union, or those having large colonial possessions like Great Britain, France, and the Netherlands. The increase in the industrial strength of Eastern Europe and of the Far East and the accom-

panying growth in population portend a shift in political and
economic power from West to East. Japan has already shown
how a determination to secure a larger share of the world's
resources which will enable her to live better at home and to
play a larger part in the political and economic life of the
world, may lead to a war of conquest. If we fail to appreciate
this aspect of Japan's militarism and merely assume that her
aggression was entirely the work of a few evil men, we shall
almost certainly make serious blunders in our efforts to establish a peaceful Japan.

Population Growth and the Need for Political and Economic Adjustments

Population growth in new lands today may, in the beginning, be largely the consequence of the establishment of public
health work and/or of the improvement in living conditions
associated with the growth of a more efficient economic system
and better government. But once the growth of population
begins it becomes a dynamic factor in forming the structure
and organization of the nation's industry and trade and in
developing the world outlook of its people. The underlying
economic changes which made it possible for Japan to grow
from a nation of 32-33 million to one of 73 million in a comparatively short time (70 years) inevitably led to a quite
different outlook on Japan's position in the world and her
economic needs by the 73 million from that held by the 32
million. This very growth in numbers, which was not planned
and which, under the existing conditions, could not have been
avoided, made it seem reasonable to many Japanese, who were
not militarists, to demand larger resources and the political
control of the areas possessing these resources. Experience
had shown that this was the most certain way to secure them

in an intensely nationalistic world, and one growing steadily more autarchic.[2]

Population growth alone does not necessarily change the balance of power and make inevitable a new allocation of the world's resources. But, as was stated above, changes in the source of population growth are proof that basic social and economic changes are taking place in the areas where growth occurs. These changes may foretell the need for a different distribution of the world's resources which cannot be ignored by the peoples in power except at great peril not only to themselves but to all the world. These changes in population growth were a dynamic factor of the greatest significance in expanding the economic and political life of Europe before 1914. More recently, the increase in Japan's population and economic strength played an increasing role in world politics and it can truly be said that they were important factors in bringing about World War II. The basic changes in Japan's position in the world which were the inevitable consequence of the growth of her population and industry were largely ignored by the peoples in power. They were ignored, in part, because they were not realized, but even when realized the governments of the great powers were almost helpless because they had no organization through which any basic political and economic adjustments could be effected.

Can anyone doubt that the very rapid growth of the population of the Soviet Union, coupled with its great industrial expansion, will pose even greater political problems in the near future than it does now (1948)? This may seem impossible but it is highly probable.

---

[2] Space cannot be taken here to show how Japan's efforts during the interwar years to expand her trade and thus to secure the needed resources abroad were frustrated at almost every turn by the great powers. This, however, was the case and it unquestionably made easier the task of the militarists in selling their solution of Japan's industrial dilemma (aggression) to the public. See Ch. 10 of the author's *Population and Peace in the Pacific*.

Furthermore, we must not overlook the fact that India did grow in numbers from about 305 million in 1921 to 389 million in 1941 and that further growth at about the same rate only awaits the expansion of her productive capacity in about the same way as in the recent past. The possible growth of China from 350-400 million to 500-600 million in the next few decades also awaits only increased productive capacity. Such increases in population and productivity will inevitably raise new economic and political problems, problems of raw materials, of markets, of colonial government, etc., which cannot be solved within our present political structure any more than we are able now to solve those created by the rise of the Soviet Union as a great power. Either we must organize the world economically and politically so that the inevitable changes in the needs of peoples for economic improvement can be met, i.e., those changes which follow naturally upon changes in industrial structure and the growth of peoples, or we must look forward to periodical and devastating explosions. These are the alternatives. It may be that we are not wise enough to know how to organize for the peaceable adjustment of the problems that will arise as the balances in population growth and industrial power shift from nation to nation and region to region, but it would seem worth trying to anticipate these inevitable changes, instead of resigning ourselves to future cataclysms even greater than that which we have just gone through.

POPULATION PRESSURE AND WAR

At the risk of some repetition it should be made clear that population growth is not necessarily an initiating cause of disturbance in the relations between nations, nor does intense population pressure, such as now exists in India, China, and some other parts of the Orient, directly endanger the peace of the world. These pressures in the nonindustrialized countries do not at present endanger peace because only very few of their people are aware that they might live better if they had access to new lands and larger resources and that the use of organized force on a large scale might make this possible. Furthermore, there is no integrated group of political and military leaders in these more backward industrial countries which can organize and direct the efforts of the whole people towards acquiring new lands for colonization, larger resources for their industries, and wider markets for their manufactures. In a measure this also was true of Japan before about 1890-1900.

Absolute population pressure such as we commonly associate with great poverty is not, then, a cause of war on a large scale. Extremely poor peoples are too feeble to wage war with any hope of success against the great powers already entrenched in the desirable areas. Moreover, the hardships of life due to population pressure have become a part of the "cake of custom" in the more backward regions of the world, and are accepted as inevitable. Once industrial development is started, however, and the people come to believe that improvement in living conditions depends largely on political expansion, they can apparently be led into great military gambles to obtain these better living conditions. The greatest degree of *felt* population pressure is generally found among peoples who have tasted some of the good things of life, and who believe that they are being deprived of their desserts by those who have arrived ahead of them. This confusion of *felt* and *absolute* population pressure as a motive for aggression has led many people to believe that population pressure has no influence in leading people to war.

Birth Control—the Ultimate Solution of Population Pressure

This brief discussion of the political implications of changing areas of population growth and industrial power cannot be closed without pointing out that there can be no hope of ever stabilizing the relations between nations and peoples for more than very short periods if population growth is to remain uncontrolled in any considerable part of the world while it is controlled in other parts. Even the fulfillment of the most sanguine hopes of science and industry for increasing the means of living will be inadequate to supply more than a meager existence to our increasing numbers for more than a few years unless birth control becomes the rule in all the world. There can be no rational hope of a decent life for all mankind if birth rates remain at more than about one third of the physiological maximum in any considerable part of the world's population. Sooner or later, and in the writer's judgment relatively soon, the death rate must rise to approximate equality with a high birth rate, or the birth rate must fall to approximate equality with a low death rate. We can choose between these alternatives but we cannot long support the population arising from a high and uncontrolled birth rate and a low and controlled death rate.

For the most part, the Western World has already made its choice; the Eastern World and the industrially backward peoples still have to make it. There seems little doubt that in time they, too, will choose low death rates and low birth rates. It must be recognized, however, that this choice cannot be made in a moment. The facts show that it was a century or more between the time the death rate began to fall in Great Britain and the time the birth rate began to decline. Apparently there was also much the same lag in Sweden and Finland. The lag need not be as long as that today in countries like the Soviet Union, Japan, India, and China because effective techniques of contraception are now fairly well developed and the means of communication are better. But he would indeed be a hardy optimist who would expect a rapid spread of birth control in China, or India, or most of the other lands in Class III, within the next three or four decades. There is, however, a possibility that simpler, cheaper, and more effective methods for the control of conception will be developed which will make its spread even more rapid than now seems possible. It is to be hoped that this will happen. But the economic condition of these peoples, their habits of living, their sex mores and their social values are all organized to support the present system of uncontrolled birth rates. It will take some time, even under the most favorable conditions, for most of the people in these backward industrial lands to appreciate the fact that when the death rate is halved the birth rate can be halved and survival will remain just as sure as now, perhaps surer because of less violent fluctuations in the death rate. Such changes cannot be produced by wishing for them. They will come only after the masses are made to realize that improved living conditions mean increased chance for survival.

Temporary Palliatives.—Since it is not reasonable to expect that birth control can become an effective means of securing population control in the Class III countries for several decades, and as we must assume that it will be only partially effective in Class II countries for the next two or three decades, it behooves us to search for other means of adjustment to the probable changes in the sources of population growth which will occur within this period. It will do no good to blame dictators and militarists and demagogues for rapid population growth, which is the inevitable consequence of changing social and economic conditions. We need to recognize the probable trends in population growth which the facts foretell, and to try to work out adjustments which will take account of them.

DIFFERENTIAL POPULATION GROWTH AND POLITICAL FRICTION

As long as there actually are great differentials between nations in the economic opportunities available to their people because of differences in the adequacy of their basic resources, it will almost certainly be easier for Hitlers and Mussolinis among the less fortunate peoples to stir up hostility against the more fortunate peoples than if such differentials were small or did not exist. This relative poverty actually does exist today in a number of lands and the argument here is that we should recognize it and honestly attempt to remove the disadvantages under which these backward peoples labor, as far as is in our power.

Since the history of population growth in the last century or more shows that we cannot expect such countries as India, China, etc, to adopt birth control on any significant scale for some decades, and since even in Japan, in the Balkans and in other Class II lands, population will also continue to increase for some time yet, the practical question we face is: Is there any way to avoid the use of force in resolving the conflicts of interest which are almost certain to arise out of these changing differentials in growth in the face of the existing differentials in resources? Certainly the question cannot be answered with an unqualified "Yes!," but attention should be called to the fact that there are still rather large areas of the earth which are inefficiently used, and considerable areas of good land which are scarcely used at all. Why cannot these areas be used as shock-absorbing areas during the period of inevitable population growth which will ensue in the backward countries as they proceed to industrialize and to improve living conditions? This matter cannot be discussed here in any detail but it may be pointed out that not more than one fifth of the area of the Netherlands Indies is effectively used at present, although the used area is probably the most productive area. The British portions of Borneo and New Guinea are almost untouched. The greater part of tropical Africa has a very thin population and tropical Australia, though not of great value, is almost uninhabited. South and Central America, with a few exceptions, still have abundant room for the expansion of their own peoples and probably could accommodate a considerable immigration. If it is said that most of the little-used areas just mentioned are tropical and as such are not suitable for colonization, it should be pointed out that most of the Indians and perhaps one third to one half of the Chinese are tropical peoples and that still another third of the Chinese and about that proportion of the Japanese are accustomed to a semi-tropical climate. These peoples have shown that they can use new tropical lands for genuine settlement, not merely for colonial exploitation. Settlement of these tropical areas by these industrially backward peoples will, of course, be slow but it should not be impossible. Furthermore, merely to have the right to settle in these areas, even if it were not used to any great extent, would do much to lessen the bitterness of these Eastern peoples towards the Western peoples, who now hold such a large part of the tropics and whose attitude towards them is that of the "dog in the manger."

Temperate Australia is also far from well settled. It can undoubtedly support three to four times its present population at a high level of living. Canada, too, is far from its limit in the support of population. In addition, the Pacific islands not included in the above enumeration can support many additional millions at better levels of living than those now prevailing there. If plans are made to use these thinly settled lands, as well as to provide for much freer trade between the nations of the world at all times, the inevitable increase in the world's population during the next few decades can be better cared for. Thus the danger of armed conflict can be lessened and possibly avoided. This means, of course, that the Western Europeans and the United States must relinquish much of the diminishing control they still exercise over the unused portions of the world. Since, in any event, their present type of control by force is doomed, it would seem that a liberalization of access to unused world resources would be well worth considering. It would probably involve much less hardship in the long run than that involved in attempting to maintain the present status.

Objections of Colonial Powers to Asiatic Settlement.—The European objections to such a suggestion by an American quite frequently take a form similar to that of Sir Norman Angell in the following statement:

> For we know that this country (the United States) could never be persuaded to hand over California to Japan or Pennsylvania to Germany; and what Americans are not prepared to face themselves they could hardly urge upon Australians, or Canadians or the British.[3]

If Sir Norman or any other good Britisher is prepared to argue that the less than 7,000 Europeans, chiefly Australians and British, "possess" one half of New Guinea (about 180,000 sq. mi.) in the same sense that we possessed California in 1936 with about 6.0 million whites on 157,000 sq. mi., no serious reply need be given. Either he does not recognize the realities of the situation, or is deliberately trying to throw dust in the eyes of those who are anxious to find some way of avoiding the necessity of defending the colonial system by a war every few years.

TABLE 11

POPULATION DENSITY OF SELECTED COUNTRIES, 1939

Country	Persons per sq. mi.
Australia	2
Canada	3
Brazil	13
Argentina	13
Columbia	21
Mexico	26
United States	44
India	241
Germany	352
Italy	365
Japan	492
Great Britain	505

[3] Sir Norman Angell, *Raw Materials, Population Pressure and War,* Boston: World Peace Foundation, 1936, p. 10.

Furthermore, in the course of my rather extensive reading I have found no serious student of these problems, certainly not among Americans and none that I can recall among the Indians and Chinese, who has proposed that Australia allow Asiatics to settle in areas where the Australians actually do "possess" the land. Whether Australia can properly be urged to take measures which will result in a white population of 20-25 million (Griffith Taylor's estimates of its capacity to support a population with good standards of living) rather than be content to become stationary at about 8 million, as now seems likely, is a question of very great concern to those nations Australia will ask to guarantee her against future attacks by Asiatic peoples. If Australia would prefer her present immigration policies, which practically restrict immigration to English-speaking peoples and which contemplate a maximum of about 70,000 immigrants annually, that is her business. But she should realize that it is highly improbable she can secure 70,000 English-speaking immigrants annually and that even if she does her population will only grow from about 7 million to 9.5 million in 25 years unless the birth rate also rises well above what now seems probable. If she continues to follow her present policies she must be prepared to take the consequences and not look to outside aid from Britain and North America to secure her in her favored position.[4]

The Australians and New Zealanders have a hard choice to make. They must either embark very energetically upon a program of immigration which will steadily dilute the Britishness of their people or they must face the expansion of the Asiatic peoples with a population so small and so weak militarily that they will have no chance in the struggle that will ensue. Unfortunately this decision is largely in the hands of people who will not be here to suffer from their shortsightedness.

---

[4] For a more detailed discussion of Australia's population questions see the author's *Population and Peace in the Pacific*, Ch. 4.

INDUSTRIALIZATION AS RELIEF FROM POPULATION PRESSURE

As regards relief from population pressure the outlook is not bright among most of the peoples who will grow most rapidly in numbers during the next half century. Industrialization, the remedy usually proposed, has very grave limitations. It was possible for Western Europe and the United States to absorb a great increase in numbers by industrialization but it should not be forgotten that at the same time the settlement of America, South Africa, and Australia offered an enormous outlet for emigrants from Europe. It is more than doubtful that European standards of living would have risen nearly as fast as they did had this new and fertile land not been available. The Soviet Union still has opportunities to expand agriculture within its own boundaries, and it has large unused mineral resources, but several of the Class II countries and most of the politically organized Class III countries are already rather thickly settled. Besides, many of them are not as richly endowed with natural resources as was America. While the importance of industrialization in providing a better living for a larger population in the backward regions of the world should not be underestimated neither should it be regarded as a sure cure-all for the poverty of these peoples. There is need for the more effective use of the tropics, for a freer trade throughout the world, and for a world political organization to see that all peoples have fair access to the world's resources. The role of migration in caring for the increase of these growing peoples is discussed briefly in Chapter 9. But all of these together probably will not be sufficient to raise the level of living among these backward peoples to that enjoyed by Western Europe before 1939.

CHAPTER 8

THE DISTRIBUTION OF POPULATION

There are two aspects of the distribution of population to which the writer wishes to devote most of the discussion directly concerned with this topic because he believes they are the most important for an understanding of how the present distribution of population in different lands has been effected and what the trends in distribution are. In this chapter the discussion will be confined largely to a description of the conditions determining the distribution of population between rural and urban communities. Most of the illustrative material, though not all, will be drawn from the experience of the United States. The conclusions would not be different, except in detail, if the illustrations came from other countries.

In the following chapter some of the more important types of migration affecting the distribution of population will be discussed, with emphasis on regional distribution rather than rural-urban distribution although this latter cannot be ruled out in discussing many aspects of regional population distribution.

Without attempting, for the moment, to give a precise definition of "rural" and "urban" as applied to population it may be said that until quite recently the vast majority of people in all lands were rural. Moreover, practically all rural people lived in small villages from which the farmers, who constituted perhaps 90 percent or more of all villagers, went out to till their lands. Even a large part of the nonagricultural workers lived in these villages, where they carried on the simple service operations needed by the tillers of the soil. Such cities as there were usually contained only a few thousands of people and had comparatively little direct influence on the lives of the peasants who constituted 80-85 percent of the total population.

Conditions Determining Urban and Rural Distribution

Under a simple hand agriculture the agricultural laborer produces so little that there is only a tiny surplus beyond his own needs. Besides, if the agricultural population becomes dense the peasant is likely to have too little land to keep him employed even half of the year. This is the situation in China today. She probably cannot support a nonrural population much, if any, in excess of one fifth of the whole. In India, which is only a little better off, it appears that about one fourth of the population is nonagricultural. In Czarist Russia the rural population was 85 percent, or more, of the total and it was still over 82 percent in 1926. In spite of the very rapid industrialization and urbanization after 1929 the census of 1939 showed that two thirds of the population was still rural. Because the size and distribution of the nonagricultural population prior to the use of steam was determined largely by the productivity of local agriculture the distribution of population for ages past in most civilized lands was about as follows: A large part of the population, 80 percent or more, lived in small agricultural villages, many of them very small (100-200 people), only a few having as many as 500-1,000 persons. Another 10-15 percent of the people lived in larger market towns or small cities, very few of which contained as many as 10,000 inhabitants.

The remaining population, perhaps 5 percent or less, lived in larger cities with only an occasional large city of 50,000 or over. These large cities were usually the seats of government or important trade centers with good water transportation. The number of cities and their proportion of the total population has always depended more on the efficiency of agricultural production than any other factor. The size of the individual city depended on the area it serviced and this in turn depended largely upon its transportation facilities. Thus a great empire like Rome, or China, or Russia could support a few fairly large cities even before the days of steam because of the tribute collected either by the government or the landlord class from vast agricultural areas. Some of these large cities, e.g., Rome and Peiping, which did not have good natural water transport were provided with it at great cost (Peiping) or were close enough to the coast that the land haul was not prohibitive (Rome).

THE INDUSTRIAL REVOLUTION

The effects of the Industrial Revolution and the accompanying agricultural revolution on the growth of population have already been discussed. Their effects on the distribution of population in a considerable part of the world have been no less revolutionary as Figure 12 shows. There seems little doubt that they will accomplish a similar revolution in population distribution (in the remainder of the world) in the course of the next century, in that part of the world not yet industrialized. The effects of the revolutions in industry and agriculture are treated together because they were and are so inextricably interwoven that neither alone could have brought about the redistribution of population which has taken place in the West during the last century. If there had been no appreciable improvement in the productivity of agricultural labor the Industrial Revolution could have changed the distribution of the nonagricultural population by concentrating it somewhat more in a few large cities, but it could have done little to change the proportions of urban and rural people. This could take place only as a farm worker was able to produce an increasing surplus beyond his own needs. When one agricultural worker had so increased his productivity that he was able to supply food and fiber for himself and his family and one other worker and his family instead of for himself and one fourth of another worker, then the proportion of the rural population could fall from 80 percent to 50 percent, but not before. On the other hand, without the revolution in transportation growing out of the application of steam, both the area the city served and its size would have remained small, although the number of small cities would probably have increased as the growing efficiency of agriculture released more and more farm workers from the local farms.

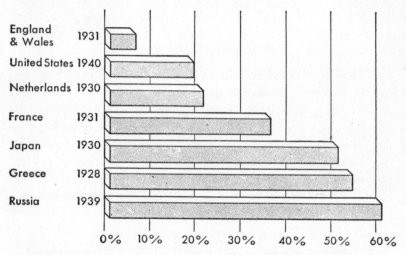

Figure 12. Percentage of Population Engaged in Agriculture in Selected Countries

How this improvement in agriculture has made possible a new rural-urban distribution of population is clearly seen in the United States. Here the farm population in 1940 was only 23 percent of the total population, and the persons engaged in agriculture amounted to only 18.5 percent of all persons gainfully employed. The proportion is even smaller today—perhaps 14 or 15 percent. But in spite of this small percentage of workers in agriculture we still produce enough farm products to care for ourselves. In England and Wales the proportion employed in agriculture had fallen to about 6 percent by

1931 because cheap transport enabled them to trade factory products with newer countries for food and other raw materials, and not because 6 percent of the workers could produce enough agricultural products for the nonagricultural 94 percent.

Apparently man has always developed his towns and cities —his nonagricultural communities—to the extent that his agricultural productivity permitted. But only within the last century or a little over could any national political unit support a nonagricultural population significantly in excess of 20 or 25 percent of the total even if, like Rome, it had large colonies nearby from which grain could be brought most of the way by water, and only within the same period could the size of more than a very few city units exceed 20 or 30 thousand.

The Modern Urban Movement

The period when movement of population from country to city began to be of significance varied considerably from nation to nation because the agricultural and industrial revolutions did not come simultaneously to all lands. In regions with much new land, like Canada and the United States, the attraction of free or cheap land was so great that industrial development was, for a time, retarded by the inability to get adequate labor in spite of high wages and large immigration from abroad, and by the lack of capital. In some countries this cityward movement is still largely in the future but there is no reason to believe that it will be essentially different in the long run from that in Western Europe and the United States, although in community structure and in location within a country a different distribution of people may take place because of the development of different forms of economic organization and because of weapons peculiarly destructive to the modern type of city. (See Chapter 5.) For this reason a description of the urbanization of the United States will serve to illustrate what has happened in the West and what is likely to happen in most of the regions which are still largely agricultural, if the location and organization of industry develop freely as they did in the West.

The Urban Movement in the United States.—In 1790 only a little over 5 percent of our population was urban according to the definition used by our Bureau of the Census, viz., persons living in places of 2,500 or more. Since even in 1790 a significant part of the rural population lived in villages and was not engaged in agriculture directly, such a division of the population exaggerates the proportion of the people dependent on agriculture. It may well be that even in these early days 20 percent of our population was nonagricultural, for Whelpton found that in 1820 only 71.9 percent of the gainful workers of the nation were engaged in agriculture[1] while 28.1 percent were in other pursuits. The proportion of the gainfully employed in nonagricultural occupations in 1820 was about four times as large as the proportion of the population that was then urban (7.2 percent).

But the proportion of the population that was urban was by no means uniform throughout the nation even at the end of the eighteenth century. In New England and the Middle Atlantic States about 8 percent[2] of the population was urban in 1790 while in the South only 2.3 percent was urban and it was not until 1810, after the acquisition of Louisiana, that any state or territory west of the Alleghenies had any urban population and even then less than one percent of the population in this western territory was urban. It is also of interest that although urban population has grown faster than rural population throughout our national life, except 1810 to 1820, the urban proportion did not begin to grow rapidly until about

---

[1] P. K. Whelpton, "Occupational Groups in the United States, 1820-1920," *Journal of the American Statistical Association,* Vol. 21 (September 1926), p. 340.

[2] United States Bureau of the Census, "Urban Population in the United States from the First Census (1790) to the Fifteenth Census (1930)." Census release dated October 31, 1939.

1840, at which time almost 90 percent of the total was still rural. After 1840, however, the proportions of rural and urban population changed rapidly and the shift still continues, although the rate varies somewhat from decade to decade depending upon general economic conditions.

Reasons for Slow Urban Growth Before 1840.—The chief reasons for the relatively slow growth of our urban population between 1790 and 1840 probably were: (1) American agriculture had not yet felt the full effects of the improvements in agriculture which had taken place in Western Europe, particularly in England. Hence, there was not as rapidly increasing a surplus of agricultural products which could be spared from the farms as there was at a later period, when certain new implements came into more general use (by 1840 the McCormick harvester was coming into use and steel plows were becoming common). Our agriculture was, therefore, still largely a subsistence agriculture. (2) Besides, even if there had been a more rapidly increasing surplus, it would have been practically impossible to move much of it from the farms because of the lack of transportation. Not until the Erie Canal was completed in 1824 was it possible for the eastern seaboard to take advantage of the increased agricultural productivity arising from the use of the new and fertile lands of western New York and of those of the Middle West lying relatively close to the Great Lakes; nor could manufactured goods be sent to the West at a price to compete with local village industry until transport had been cheapened. (3) In addition, this was a period when cheap or free land was more attractive to farmbred people than city jobs. This was almost as true of our foreign immigrants as of our native rural youth.

Extent of Urbanization.—The proportion of the population that is urban is now about a dozen times as great as in 1790, while the proportion of workers engaged in agriculture is less than one fourth as large. The percentage engaged in manufacturing is about three times as great as in 1790, and that engaged in trade and transportation is over 14 times as great.

From these data several conclusions can be drawn: (1) that there were comparatively few workers who devoted their major efforts to manufacturing; (2) that whereas it took about three or more agricultural workers to support one nonagricultural worker in 1790 it now takes only one to support five or six such workers; (3) most of our population was either self-sufficing economically in 1790 or it secured the few articles it needed from others by local barter; (4) there has been a very large movement of people from rural areas to towns and cities from the time of the first census, since the rural population has always had the higher rate of natural increase.

TABLE 12

PROPORTION OF POPULATION, RURAL AND URBAN, AND ENGAGED IN
PRINCIPAL OCCUPATIONS, UNITED STATES, 1790-1940

Year	Rural	Urban	Agri-culture	Manufac-turing	Trade and trans-portation
1790*........	94.9	5.1	75.2	9.7	2.0
1820.........	92.8	7.2	71.9	12.2	2.5
1850.........	84.7	15.3	64.5	16.4	5.4
1880.........	71.8	28.2	48.9	24.1	12.2
1910.........	54.3	45.7	31.2	28.4	21.3
1940.........	43.5	56.5	18.5	28.0	28.7

* The occupational percentages for 1790 are estimates on the basis of trends 1820-40 and are only approximate at best.

More detailed data for recent years and for other lands would only confirm the general trends shown by the changes in these broad classes of workers in the United States. As fast as the improvements in agriculture and the mechanization of its tasks have released men from producing subsistence they have been drawn into manufacturing, transportation, trade, the professions, and clerical work until in the more highly industrialized countries only a small minority of the people now work at agriculture. That nearly all these new kinds of work are carried on in cities rather than in small communities is due to the improvements in transportation as well as to the greater efficiency of larger-scale machine operations.

THE GROWTH OF CITIES IN THE UNITED STATES

The vast improvement in transportation which, like manufacturing, was based on the use of steam, made possible the really large cities of modern times, cities many times larger than any ancient large city. The use of steam for transport not only made it possible to assemble cheaply great quantities of raw materials for manufacturing and to distribute the products quickly and cheaply over long distances, but also to supply great and concentrated aggregations of people with food, fuel, building materials, and other goods and services needed to maintain health and comfort. But it should be remembered that almost none of this concentration of population in cities would have been possible had it not been for the vast improvement in agricultural production, a considerable part of which is due to improvements in agricultural practices which cannot be attributed to the increased efficiency of agricultural machinery. In this class must be placed the breeding of better livestock, the development of better practices to maintain soil fertility, and the improvements in plant breeding and selection which have produced better varieties of corn, wheat, cotton, etc.

For about 100 years now the forces making for a great and rapid movement of population into the cities, and particularly into larger and larger cities, seem to have operated without let or hindrance throughout the Western World. They have concentrated an incredibly large proportion of our total population in huge cities. Over 12 percent of the people of the United States now (1940 census) live in cities of over 1,000,000 and another 5 percent in cities of 500,000-1,000,000, i.e., 17 percent

in cities of over 500,000.[3] An additional 12 percent live in
cities of 100,000-500,000. Thus 29 percent of us live in cities
of over 100,000 while only 23 percent live on farms. But this

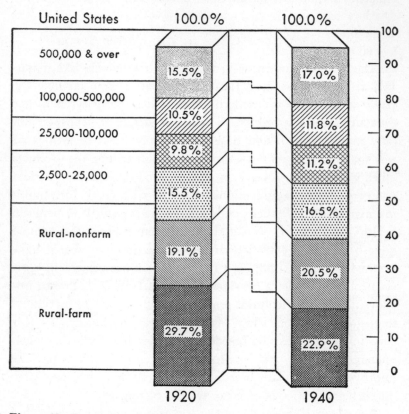

Figure 13. Percentage Distribution of Population by Size of Community,
United States, 1920 and 1940

is not all; in 1940 the 140 metropolitan districts—large cities
and their satellite, urbanized areas—contained almost 63 million people or 47.8 percent of the total population of the United

[3] In agricultural civilizations only an occasional great city had over
500,000 inhabitants; great capitals like Rome and Peiping were probably between 500,000 and 1,000,000 in their heydays.

States and these districts grew by 8.1 percent between 1930 and 1940, while the population in the rest of the country grew but 6.5 percent. It is true that the larger part of the growth of metropolitan districts, in absolute numbers as well as in proportion, was outside the central cities—these cities growing by 2,070,000 or 5.1 percent, while the territory immediately surrounding them grew by 2,645,000, or 15.1 percent. But this is all a genuine urban increase, despite the fact that of the 2,645,-000 increase in satellite areas 1,785,000, or 67 percent, took place in rural areas and that their rate of increase was 30.0 percent. These 140 districts drew a total of 4,715,000 while all the rest of the country increased by only 4,179,000. Thus 53 percent of our total increase during the decade went to these few large communities.

Since 1920 the parts of the metropolitan districts outside the central cities have grown faster than the cities themselves. This is a new trend which has been greatly accelerated since the use of the automobile has become general. Up to the present it has led only to retarding the growth of the large city and not to any real dispersion of population and industry to smaller communities. The slower growth of metropolitan districts during the decade 1930-40 as compared with the decade 1920-30 seems to have been reversed during the war, and the rather scanty evidence available since the war indicates that the metropolitan districts have increased even more rapidly, with the return of the men from military service. It seems highly probable, therefore, that much the major portion of our total increase in population during this decade will be found in our metropolitan districts in 1950 (see the following chapter).

STEAM AND THE LARGE CITY

While it is not difficult to understand why the urban population should have become an increasingly large part of the total population as agriculture was able to release workers, it is not as easy to understand why people crowded into the larger cities in such steadily increasing proportions, instead of locating in a larger number of small cities. It will be of some interest to look into this matter a little because it is a phenomenon of very great importance in modern life from a number of standpoints.

Steam and the Concentration of Manufacturing.—When machines driven by other than man power first began to come into use they had to be located at a water-power site. However, soon after the Industrial Revolution got under way the steam plant became the important focus for the location of industry. Until about 1900-10 the accepted means of transmitting power from waterwheel or steam engine to machines was by shaft, pulley, and belt. This was true until the internal combustion engine and the electric motor had been perfected and their advantages for many purposes came to be realized, i.e., until 25 or 30 years ago.

Since the very nature of water power and steam power, when used directly to operate machines, necessitated the concentration of the machines within a very short distance of the point of power generation it was to be expected that many, perhaps most, successful enterprises would increase in size at or near the sources of their power by enlarging the existing plant. In addition, there were decided advantages in locating a new plant near other plants of the same character. In such a locality trained workers could more readily be found, raw materials could be assembled with less difficulty, machine maintenance and repair were easier and marketing problems were better understood. Thus the very nature of steam power made it advantageous to concentrate more and more workers in a small area and the services they needed to live according to accepted standards, of course, developed around them. The use of steam for transport, like its use for manufacturing had a concentrative effect when applied directly to machines used to move people and goods. Steam was less well adapted to local transport, with its many starts and stops, than to longer hauls and the movement of large quantities of goods and large numbers of persons. It was not until electricity and the internal combustion engine were used for local transportation that the concentrating effects of steam transportation were somewhat nullified.

Steam and Communication.—In addition, the function of steam as an agent of communication was confined entirely to its conveyance of persons and of written or printed material. In the actual management of business, steam did, of course, make it easier for concerns owning factories in several places to keep in touch with them, both by personal visit and by letter; it did not, of course, provide the instant and continuous communication which appears so essential today. Only the telephone could do this and it can scarcely be said to have come into common use in the United States, even for business purposes, until about the time of World War I. In much of the world it is not yet in common use. Until the telephone did come into common use for long-distance communication there was a decided advantage in concentrating production in a factory where the manager could be in personal touch with his technical staff, and generally, also, with his sales staff, although this was less necessary. Personal communication was confined within much the same bounds in pretelephone days as the transmission of power was in the days before the internal combustion engine and the electric motor had become effective.

Therefore, when account is taken of the development of the techniques of power transmission, of transport, and of communication, it is not surprising to find that until the last two or three decades there was a strong tendency for industry to concentrate in larger and larger units, which also gathered together in larger and larger cities.

OTHER FACTORS IN THE GROWTH OF LARGE CITIES

In addition to the technical and economic factors favoring large cities which have already been mentioned, there were financial factors favoring larger and larger business units. Financiers found great profit in consolidating railroads, steel plants, oil refining, and a hundred other industries. Not infrequently, consolidations and reorganizations led to the closing down of many small local plants and the enlargement of those already large. They also frequently resulted in the concentration of a significant proportion of the whitecollar staffs of the several combined corporations in a single center, often the center where financial control lay rather than a center of production. The increasing importance of sales organization has also worked in this direction. The fact that insurance, too, gravitated to large financial centers where it employed great staffs has aided the growth of great cities. The stopping of large numbers of immigrants in the ports of debarkation added further to the growth of our large cities on the eastern seaboard, while the heavy industries of the Great Lakes also attracted great numbers of unskilled workers from abroad.

In Europe all these factors, except foreign immigration, were also at work drawing people from the smaller cities and towns and the rural areas into the large cities. In addition, the more strongly centralized administration in many countries increased the drawing power of the capital city which was also the financial center, the center of most of the advanced education and the center of the more expensive cultural activities as well as the locus of much industry. Greater London has for some time contained about one fifth of the population of England and Wales. Before the war the Department of the Seine (Paris) had about one tenth of all France's population. Greater Berlin had about one twelfth of Germany's population and Greater New York had about one eleventh of all ours. The movement of population into large cities has been a world-wide movement and there is no evidence of its slackening, except possibly in the Soviet Union where much of the new industry is located in cities built with strategic considerations in mind.

ELECTRICITY AND THE DECENTRALIZATION OF CITIES

The growth of modern large cities was, then, greatly encouraged, if not made inevitable, up to the end of World War I by the direct use of steam for machine operation, for transport, and for communication. It is not surprising that the momentum thus developed did not slacken, once new techniques were developed. It is obvious, however, that when electric power can be generated cheaply in great centralized plants and can be distributed cheaply and instantaneously to places several hundred miles distant, there is no longer the same technical advantage in concentrating many types of production in huge factories as there was when steam was used directly to furnish power. Today, in locating new industries and in building additional capacity, it is possible to give more weight to the efficient size of a productive unit in the industry concerned and to the advantages of location with reference to raw materials and markets than it was in the days of the direct use of steam.

In addition, with efficient and cheap telephonic communication and with airplane travel becoming general, there is not the least reason why a general manager cannot keep in close touch with plant managers in a dozen different places at a very small cost. In other words, efficient manufacturing operation is no longer dependent on the concentration of plant or personnel to anything like the extent it formerly was.

The same is true of most types of commercial operations. Modern techniques of communication have largely wiped out distance as a factor in business organization. As yet, we have only begun to use these new techniques so we do not know just what they can accomplish in the way of dispersing the operations of large business. It should be made clear that although it is now possible to disperse the operations of much of our business this does not mean that modern techniques make big business organizations unnecessary. Huge operating units both in manufacturing and commerce and huge business organizations are two different things. Modern techniques of power transmission and of communication do make possible an organization of industry and commerce on an even larger scale than in the past, where such organization is needed for efficiency. But these improved techniques do this without making it necessary to concentrate such huge populations in small areas as has been customary in the past. Moreover, they also make possible the reestablishment of many small local businesses which could not compete with larger units as long as steam was used directly as power and also was the chief agent of rapid communication.

DIFFICULTIES OF DECENTRALIZATION

That comparatively little use has been made of these new techniques to break up business enterprises into relatively small units and to scatter them in small communities is due to many factors, most of which cannot even be mentioned here, but attention may be called to a few of the more important. Once a factory is established and its personnel settled, it is not an easy matter to break it into smaller units or to move it to a smaller community. The immediate loss involved in abandoning buildings and in the disruption of moving is generally considerable and cannot be shouldered by the great majority of concerns. Besides, many workers object to moving from a community in which they have a home. The best chance for the rapid dispersion of an industry comes when a concern is expanding and is relatively free to locate new plants wherever the economies of production and marketing may dictate.

Prestige.—There is also a prestige value which attaches to New York, or Chicago, in general, and to Detroit, or Akron, for particular industries which does not attach to Kenosha, or Hagerstown, or South Bend, or Conshohocken. The same product will often command a better market, or a better price, or both when coming from large centers or from centers specializing in particular products than when it comes from a smaller place. A somewhat similar prestige often attaches to the product of a big plant as compared with that of a small plant, even though the latter product may be better.

This matter of the prestige of bigness is also closely bound up with the ability to sell over a wide market under brand names which only a large concern can do. If the public can be made to believe that a shirt made in Troy is better than one made in Muncie or Baton Rouge, or that a product of General Electric is preferable to one of local manufacture, then there is apt to be a concentration of shirtmaking in Troy and of the manufacture of electrical goods in large concerns. The lack of standards for goods which could easily be standardized without loss of style or the curtailment of personal choice often makes it possible for the producer or distributor with a long purse, or a clever and unscrupulous advertising agent, to dominate a market where the merit of the product would not justify such domination. This in turn tends to keep large factories and large sales forces in large centers long after there is any economic justification for such concentration.

Finally, the present state of employer-employee relations often makes the former reluctant to become dependent on the labor supply of a small community and the latter unwilling to live where he cannot have some choice of jobs and employers.

LARGE CITIES AND REPRODUCTION

To most people this great concentration of population in a few large centers will not cause any concern. It is commonly believed that if economic considerations or even the convenience of business leaders demands the further concentration of industry and commerce, and hence of population, nothing should be done to counteract this movement. This seems a very short-sighted view because there is one desideratum which outweighs all others and which seems altogether impossible of attainment in a population crowded into the great cities of today, viz., the need to reproduce. Any population which does not value its position in the civilization of its day sufficiently to take the trouble to reproduce itself is following values which are funda-mentally antagonistic to its long-time welfare. The failure to reproduce, where this is biologically possible, means that people find other values which absorb their time, their interest, and their means so exclusively that they are not willing to raise children. Obviously a civilization which thus sterilizes, or nearly sterilizes, a considerable part of the population cannot long endure. In a country like the United States where there can be no serious question of the availability of the resources needed to support our present numbers, and our probable future increase, not only in decency but in abundance, we cannot plead the excuse of poverty as might well be done in England, the Netherlands, or Germany. Besides, as we have seen, it is the more comfortable who raise the fewest children.

At the risk of boring the reader, some of the material on the differential birth rate will be repeated in order to make this point clear. Twenty-nine percent of our population lived in cities of 100,000 or more in 1940. According to the 1940 census the number of children under age five in this population was only 72 percent of the number needed to maintain the existing population if the birth rates of 1935-39 and the death rates of 1939-41 had continued. Even in the cities of 10,000-100,000 the birth rate was sufficient to replace only 83 percent of the population and in the very small cities, 2,500-10,000 it was only 96 percent sufficient. Only in the rural areas was the birth rate sufficient to produce an increase (41 percent). But there, too, it is now declining rapidly.

It may not be that rural life is the only manner of life which will induce people to raise enough children to maintain their numbers, but in the Western World as now organized practically all populations in cities are failing to do so by a large margin—the larger the city the greater the margin of failure. This failure is not due to biological deterioration but, rather, to the impact of social and psychological factors on the willingness of the city dweller to raise children. It seems that since man has found relatively easy and effective means to control his birth rate the city dweller is not willing to forego the social and economic advantages of relative childlessness. Survival as understood by the biologist means less to him than the economic and social gains resulting from having very few or no children (21.2 percent of the native white women aged 45 in 1940 were childless, 15.6 percent had borne only one child and 18.6 percent had borne only two children.) Although it is impossible to give similar figures for urban and rural women separately, the data given in Chapter 3 leave no doubt that women who are childless or have only one child are relatively much more numerous in the urban population.

The failure of city people to replace themselves with children is in itself of sufficient importance to demand that we give serious consideration to the redistribution of population. We should be asking ourselves how we can redistribute our urban population into environments where the replacement of its numbers can be reconciled with the values of its daily life, where raising children does not appear so arduous a task that a considerable proportion of all city people will remain childless or have only a single child. When values become personal rather than racial and social, when they take account, too exclusively, of personal desires and ambitions and leave out of account the needs of the race and the establishment of continuity in family and community living they are fundamentally destructive.

It seems senseless to continue to allow people to pile up in environments which are destructive to the race when economic progress no longer demands such concentration of population in cities as has taken place in the last century. We are now living in the age of the telephone, the electric motor, the automobile, and the airplane. It is time that we realized this and began to think how we might use these inventions to improve human living and to provide living conditions compatible with adequate reproduction.

One need not be gifted with any great imagination to think of many ways in which population might be redistributed so that most people could enjoy all the benefits which have come with city living and at the same time not be subjected to overwhelming social and economic pressures antagonistic to reproduction. It is quite possible that living in small communities is not of itself sufficient to insure that people will reproduce, once birth control has become universal, but it looks very much as though living in smaller communities might be one of the prerequisites for the development of a scale of values in which reproduction and the care of children are given equal weight with those amenities of living which are commonly associated with a high level of living in cities.

Today we have two additional reasons of the very highest importance for considering how we can take many millions of people out of our large cities—(1) the atomic bomb, and (2) biological warfare. (See the following chapter.)

CHAPTER 9

THE DISTRIBUTION OF POPULATION— MIGRATION

MASS MIGRATION SINCE 1820

The preceding chapter was devoted largely to the discussion of the rural-urban distribution of population as it was affected by the industrial and agricultural revolutions. These became potent factors in changing this distribution in England and Wales during the latter half of the eighteenth century and have gradually extended their influence throughout a large part of the world since that time.

As was pointed out, it was the changing productivity of agricultural labor which made possible this new rural-urban distribution of population. It is the same search for a place where one's labor can be used more effectively that produced the mass migration from nation to nation which began about 1820 and came to an end about a century later. Just as machine industry and the growth of commerce offered opportunities to the peasants of Europe to make a better living by moving from the small farms where the productivity of labor was very low to the towns and cities where labor productivity was higher, so the better economic opportunities of America, Australia, etc., attracted both peasants and workers from the older more settled countries where labor productivity was relatively low to foreign lands where a given amount of work would yield a better living.

In the 110 years from 1820 to 1930 approximately 38 million people came to the United States, almost all of them from Europe, and about 30 million of them remained here. Other millions went to Canada, Australia, South Africa, South and Central America, and smaller numbers to many other lands. It has been estimated that the total outward movement of Europeans during this period was probably in the neighborhood of 60 million and that the net outflow was 45 million or more. In addition, there have been many millions of migrants in other parts of the world, from China to Manchuria, to Malaysia, to Siam and to the islands of the Pacific; from India to Burma, Ceylon, South Africa, Malaysia, and the Pacific Islands; and from European Russia into Siberia. These as well as many other movements of people have affected not only the actual distribution of people over the earth but have determined the character of the culture of the regions into which they moved. Can anyone doubt, for instance, that the recent history of the Far East would have been different if the Russians had greatly outnumbered the Chinese in the settlement of Manchuria, or if the Japanese victory over Russia in 1905 had been followed by a great migration of Japanese peasants into this area instead of a mass movement of Chinese?

International mass migration did not really attain large proportions until about the middle of the nineteenth century. It culminated for the West in the decade before World War I when about 1.5 million migrants from Europe entered the Americas each year. Such a vast peaceful movement of peoples could not have taken place before the days of steam transportation although we should not forget that there was a considerable migration of Europeans to America in the seventeenth and eighteenth centuries and that movements like those of the Huns, the Mongols, and the Tartars have taken place ever since the dawn of history and no doubt long before man began to keep records.

Peaceful Migration to Unused Lands.—Before World War I a student of population would have been inclined to say that large-scale and peaceful migration would probably be one of the important sources of settlers for the almost unused islands of the Pacific (Borneo, New Guinea, and others) and the thinly settled areas of Africa and as well as those of Australia, Canada, and South America. But times change and the role of peaceful international migration in the settlement of the relatively unused portions of the world as well as in the more complete exploitation of the resources of nations like the United States and the Soviet Union, appears to be about played out.

Many countries no longer have vast areas of new land to settle and two World Wars have tended to make people everywhere acutely aware of national and racial differences so that immigrants are no longer welcomed in many countries as they were before 1914. Besides, in the interwar period (1919-1939) colonial areas were being closed more and more even to nationals of European origin other than those of the controlling colonial power, while the entrance of Asiatics was even more strictly controlled.

The net effect of these changes in attitudes towards international migration on a large scale has been to render it unlikely that peaceful migration will play any important role in determining the distribution of population in the foreseeable future. The only two types of international migration which may be of some importance in the near future are: (1) that associated with the forcible seizure of territory in war, and (2) that initiated by dominant national groups to "purify" their populations by ousting minority groups. Because of these conditions it seems rather useless to devote more than passing attention to free international mass migration such as took place before World War I.

Migration and Relief of Population Pressure.—At this point a word should be said about migration as a means of relieving population pressure in such countries as China, India, and Japan. It was noted above (Chapter 7) that there are still large areas of relatively unused land in Africa, in the Pacific Islands, and in South America, and lesser areas elsewhere. It would be quite natural to conclude that migration to these little used areas would be an important means of relieving the pressure of population in the densely settled lands of Asia. Although the writer believes that the resources of these thinly settled lands should be made available to the peoples of Asia as rapidly as is feasible yet he cannot believe that they will furnish any significant relief to the "teeming millions" of India or China. In the first place, the world does not have the facilities to transport millions of Chinese or Indians to the islands of the Pacific, or to Africa, or to South America. It would take some decades to organize such a movement on a large scale. In the second place, the populations needing relief from pressure are five or six times as great as the population of Europe in 1800 and live even nearer the subsistence level. Consequently any community in China or India which sent out enough emigrants to relieve the pressure of numbers would almost immediately experience a lower death rate and natural increase of its population would expand rapidly. Within a few years it would have just as many people as it did before emigration began and they would be living just as close to the subsistence level.

The writer made diligent inquiry in China to ascertain whether the migration to Manchuria from Shantung and Hopei had relieved population pressure in those provinces and the answer he received was that it had not. Some qualification was made in the case of particular small communities from which emigration had been relatively large. But even then it was said that the relief was only momentary; emigration had reduced the death rate but the birth rate remained high and population soon grew to its former level. Once more the death rate rose to an almost incredible height.

For this reason the writer is convinced that emigration can do little or nothing to mitigate the actual physical poverty of the densely settled lands of Asia. On the other hand, he believes that permitting these peoples to migrate even though relatively few could actually move would help greatly in creating a better atmosphere in which to discuss the problems of population pressure and the better distribution of the world's resources. This in itself would be a well worth-while achievement.

MIGRATION AND THE DISTRIBUTION OF POPULATION IN THE UNITED STATES

Just as economic forces produced the movement of people from farm to town and city and thus determined the rural-urban distribution of population, so economic forces set in motion a great movement of people into and across America and led to the present regional distribution of our population and our industry.

At the time the settlement of the United States began 80 percent or more of all people were farmers and were interested in getting land on which they could settle and care for their families. In large measure, the economic attraction of land explains the pattern of internal migration in the United States until the latter part of the nineteenth century, aside from the rural-urban movement described in the preceding chapter. The vast majority of the people involved in the great westward movement of our population were natives, although immigrants constituted a significant proportion of these westward migrants at certain times and in certain regions.

Westward Migration of Natives.—The Census of 1850, the first to distinguish the native born from the foreign born, showed that the East North Central States had only about 550,000 foreign born in a total population of 4,523,000. Since a large part of the foreign born who had settled there during the two preceding decades would still be living there, we know with reasonable certainty that the foreign born played only a minor role in the settlement of this region up to that time. We also know that a large part of the almost 4 million natives were migrants because at the extremely rapid rate of natural increase of 50 percent in each decade, the 51,000 of the census of 1800 would only have increased to about 115,000 by 1820

TABLE 13

NET ALIEN ARRIVALS OR DEPARTURES IN THE UNITED STATES, 1908-46
(*In thousands*)

Fiscal year	Net alien arrivals	Fiscal year	Net alien arrivals
1908	205	1928	228
1909	545	1929	228
1910	817	1930	175
1911	512	1931	*—10*
1912	398	1932	*—112*
1913	815	1933	*—91*
1914	768	1934	*—12*
1915	51	1935	*—6*
1916	126	1936	
1917	217	1937	9
1918	20	1938	31
1919	22	1939	69
1920	195	1940	43
1921	554	1941	63
1922	88	1942	37
1923	473	1943	46
1924	662	1944	58
1925	234	1945	109
1926	271	1946	108
1927	287		

and to about 387,000 by 1850. Actually there were 793,000 people in this region in 1820—about seven times as many as a high natural increase could account for. In addition, there were vastly more native born people in this region in 1850 than natural increase could possibly account for. Clearly, most of the population of these states in 1850 must have migrated from the East. Exactly the same process of settlement by natives migrating from the East went on in all the western states, with natives constituting an even larger proportion of settlers in the Southwestern and Far Western states.

The data on the state of birth of the native born, which became available in 1890, show that this westward migration of natives was still very great at that time. There were over 3 million fewer native whites of native parentage living east of the Mississippi River in 1890 than were born there. Clearly

TABLE 14

STANDARDIZED RATIO OF CHILDREN TO WOMEN, IN THE FARM AND NONFARM POPULATION OF THE UNITED STATES, BY REGIONS, FOR ECONOMIC GROUPS, 1940 *

	Northeast	North Center	South White	South Nonwhite	West
		Rural—farm			
Total	504	521	605	746	568
Group 1		⎫	867	770	914
2		⎬715	786	721	749
3		⎭	671	710	685
4		626	618	763	779
5		575	579		713
6	579	531	544	772	587
7	511	515	515		521
8	419	499	510		515
9		504	477		473
10			465		
		Rural—nonfarm			
Total	373	415	441	449	432
Group 1		648	591	477	698
2		600	553	424	634
3		525	522	396	584
4		487	471	386	537
5	574	433	452	⎫	490
6	511	416	411	⎬399	516
7	440	412	385	⎭	447
8	404	407	371		414
9	353	394	367		386
10	308	359	352		356

* Group 1 has lowest economic index. For the white population it takes 360 children 0-4 per 1,000 women 15-44 merely to maintain population; for the nonwhite population, about 378.

158 PLENTY OF PEOPLE

the internal movement of natives was much the dominant factor in the settlement of the West. We have tended to forget this fact because of the great numbers of foreign-born immigrants coming to us in the past. But since the foreign born are now only permitted to enter in relatively small numbers we are rapidly becoming aware of the importance of internal migration as the major factor affecting the growth and distribu-

TABLE 15

NUMBER OF CHILDREN IN THE FARM AND NONFARM POPULATION OF THE UNITED STATES (CORRECTED),* BY REGIONS, FOR ECONOMIC GROUPS, 1940

(*In thousands*)

	Northeast	North Center	South White	South Nonwhite	West
		Rural—farm			
Total	199.3	882.5	1,445.4	700.2	239.6
Group 1		⎫	23.9	387.1	18.9
2		⎬ 6.8	84.9	272.0	2.6
3		⎭	262.8	36.2	3.8
4		36.5	403.2	4.2	4.1
5		76.3	327.4		16.2
6	30.0	165.4	212.8	0.6	45.6
7	140.2	247.5	91.8		112.5
8	29.1	291.7	29.9		32.7
9		58.3	6.4		3.4
10			2.3		
		Rural—nonfarm			
Total	524.2	690.2	925.3	193.8	341.1
Group 1		3.5	40.9	116.1	15.2
2		4.7	62.1	51.2	3.5
3		9.6	130.8	20.0	6.3
4		45.4	143.0	4.1	12.1
5	7.1	67.1	162.4	⎫	18.2
6	30.2	99.0	146.1	⎬ 2.4	43.0
7	114.3	154.3	96.5		60.0
8	108.4	164.5	63.2		70.8
9	132.3	113.4	25.3		59.1
10	131.9	28.9	55.1		53.0

* For underenumeration.

tion of population in different regions and communities. It will therefore be of some interest to indicate as definitely as possible the regions and areas which are most likely to be affected by internal migration in the near future.

Regions of Probable Out-Migration in the Future.—The region of highest birth rate in the United States at the present time is the southern Appalachian-Ozark region, including the hilly country between these mountain groups. The second highest birth rate region is the remainder of the rural South, both white and nonwhite. This region has significantly higher fertility than either the rural North or West.[1] Table 16 shows that the white rural-farm population of the South had more children in 1940 than the white rural-farm population of the North and the West together, and about 37 percent of the white rural-nonfarm children. Clearly the South is still the largest reservoir of potential out-migrants in the nation. Whether it will continue to send them out as in the past will depend upon the expansion of industrial opportunity in the South as compared with that in the North and West. It appears quite probable that the South will be able to spare rather large numbers for several years at least.

The chances for the expansion of agriculture in the South are not large and the mechanization of cotton farming now proceeding quite rapidly is calculated to reduce the need for agricultural workers rather rapidly. Hence, for the next decade or more the South can spare for industry not only all its natural increase in the rural-farm population but a very considerable number of people from the present farm population. It seems rather unlikely that the industry of the South will expand fast enough to absorb all its rural surplus population. Hence the

---

[1] Exception should be made of the rural-farm population of Utah which has the highest birth rate in that group in any state. Utah's population is largely Mormon. However, the rural-farm population of Utah is small (less than 100,000) and although it can send out a relatively high proportion of its children, the total outward movement amounts to little compared with that of the areas discussed here.

belief that the South will continue to export men for some time yet. There is still a significant increase in the rural-farm populations of the North Center and West and although agriculture is much more mechanized in these regions than in the South, they too will be able to spare some rural youth although the number will be much smaller than in the South.

No mention of the cities as a source of net out-migration has been made because as already noted any net outward movement from them would mean actual loss of population since their fertility is already insufficient to maintain their numbers. But it should be noted that those few cities which have already lost population have done so (with possibly three or four exceptions) not because their death rates are higher than their birth rates but because people have moved from the central cities to the satellite areas surrounding them. The cities themselves and also their satellite areas are becoming more and more dependent on the rural areas for the mere maintenance of their numbers. Furthermore, since most of our large cities are in the North and West, where the increase of rural population is least, it seems reasonable to expect that these cities will become more and more dependent on the South for their population.

Areas of In-Migration.—Although we can tell in a general way where the major portion of the net out-migrants of the next two or three decades will originate we cannot tell with any precision where the net in-migrants will find a home. In other words, we know in a general way areas where the pressures pushing people out exist and we know that they largely coincide with the areas of highest fertility. We do not know with anything like the same exactness where attractions for migrants will develop. We do know, however, that the West Coast has exercised a strong attraction for migrants during the past several decades. It seems only reasonable to believe that it will continue to draw more than its share of migrants for some time yet. We also know that the larger cities of the South and

Southwest have been growing faster than those of the North and Northeast. Again, it seems reasonable to assume that there will be no startling departure from this general pattern of migration. However, we have probably passed the period in our national growth when we can take it for granted that all cities, states, or even all the major regions of the nation will grow steadily from decade to decade. Competition between cities and regions will probably increase and this will almost certainly result in more spotted and erratic population growth in many areas than in the past. There will be an increasing number of cities and areas which, for special reasons having little or nothing to do with their birth rates and death rates, will grow in numbers or will lose population. These special reasons will probably be chiefly economic and the gains or losses in population will be accomplished primarily through migration. Thus within the general pattern of migration outlined above there will be many particular movements and many local variations in growth which cannot be foreseen because they do not fit into any general pattern. Furthermore, even the general pattern of internal migration many change rather quickly and even violently under certain conditions, e.g., as a consequence of changes in the character of military weapons. This and some of the other factors which may significantly change the character of internal migration will be briefly discussed.

Migration Trends in the Future.—In any dynamic economy a number of significant changes in the location of industry and in the organization of commerce are certain to be taking place continually. At the time these take place we may scarcely be aware of them but this becomes less and less likely as more complete economic data are collected and as their dissemination is better organized. But we cannot know in advance whether the steel industry will move west or south and how much of it will move or whether it is only the new capacity which will be located in the new area. Such changes do take place, however, and they have a significant effect on the increase or decrease of population in a particular city or area. Likewise, the development of merchandising enterprises under energetic leadership may contribute materially to a rather rapid change in the proportion of the trade of a given area which comes to a particular city. Then, too, a given freight rate structure may determine the area over which a particular city or region can distribute goods economically, and a change in this rate structure which expands one trade area is likely to contract another trade area. At the same time this change in freight rates may effect changes in the cost of production detrimental to the present centers of production and thus encourage industry in new areas which have heretofore not been able to compete with the older centers.

Even where changes in the relative importance of industrial and commercial areas have been taking place for some time it is generally impossible to tell how far they will go and when any particular community will cease to grow, begin to decline, or commence to increase rapidly. Thus the movement of a significant portion of our textile manufacturing into the South, the development of the steel industry more intensively near the Great Lakes, and the expansion of mining in West Virginia and Kentucky at a faster rate than in Pennsylvania, are well known, but whether such shifts will result in net migration into or out of any given community is a matter of sheer guesswork. Changes in the relative economic importance of different localities may be considered a regular aspect of modern industry, but since they follow no known law they cannot be foretold. On the whole, however, it seems reasonable to expect that established trends, particularly regional trends, will not be suddenly changed.

As birth rates decline in the present areas of out-migration, the net migration from these areas to urban areas is likely to decline. This means that migration from rural areas to urban areas will probably become a smaller part of all internal migration. As this happens it would seem that the labor needs of particular urban communities would more and more be met by migration between these communities themselves. Thus, in the future, the net gain or loss of population by migration in most urban communities may tend to arise more largely from changes in their economic importance in relation to one another and particular cities cannot count on a general gain in the economic importance of all urban communities to insure them a large and constant gain of population.

Finally, if the changes in technology and the military considerations discussed above should lead to any considerable dispersion of industry and commerce, we might, conceivably, have a reversal of the present direction of migration to the extent that people would leave the large cities not only for their satellite areas but also for smaller cities and larger towns. However, there is no evidence which would lead one to anticipate any such change in the immediate future.

Migration in the Depression.—The chief net effect of the depression of the 1930's on internal migration appears to have been to reduce its amount rather than to produce any fundamental change in direction. The cities still continued to draw from the rural areas, and some of the older parts of the country still lost population to the more recently settled areas and to those having attractive climates. In only one of the nine geographic divisions did the depression speed up out-migration, viz., in the states of Arkansas, Oklahoma, and Texas, which contain a large part of the "dust bowl." In only two divisions was the direction of net migration reversed. In the East North Central States (Ohio, Indiana, Michigan, Illinois, and Wisconsin) a previous net *in* movement became a net *out* movement, while in the South Atlantic States (Delaware, Maryland, District of Columbia, Virginia, West Virginia, North Carolina, South Carolina, Georgia, and Florida) a net *out* movement became a net *in* movement. In both divisions, however, the net movement was so small that it can scarcely be regarded as a reversal of past trends; it was rather a quick fluctuation of short duration than a change in trend.

The slowing-up of the outward movement was sufficient, however, to result in a proportionally greater increase between 1930 and 1940 in the population of those regions normally having a net out movement than in those normally depending on in-migration for a part of their increase. Thus the South Atlantic and East South Central States (Kentucky, Alabama, Tennessee, and Mississippi) grew proportionally faster between 1930 and 1940 than any part of the country except the extreme West, which still remained the destination of a considerable portion of all our internal migrants. However, it should be noted that out-migrants still came largely from the areas indicated above and went to help swell the movement to the urban areas which had been gaining in the past. There was no significant reversal of the country-to-city movement during the depression. With the exception of the year 1932, when the farm population had a slight net gain due to in-migration, the farms lost population to the cities throughout the depression. The depression reduced the net number of migrants but did not greatly change the pattern of the movement to which we have become accustomed.

Migration in the War.—It is almost impossible to get any clear picture of war migration to compare with that of prewar years. The war created its own special needs and people flowed to areas which were already organized to produce war goods, or could readily convert their facilities to war production, or to new areas which undertook the new tasks such as shipyards, shell-loading plants, etc. The areas of opportunity were determined by military needs rather than by the economic forces customarily operating in peacetime. It may be said broadly that people moved in largest numbers into those cities where the products manufactured for war required relatively large amounts of labor in proportion to tonnage or volume rather

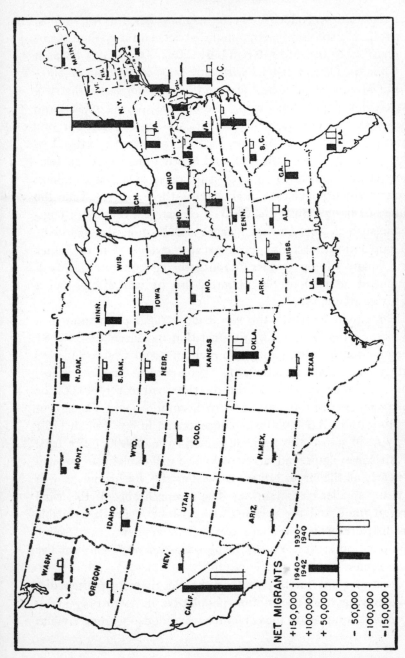

Figure 14. Average Yearly Number of Net Civilian Migrants, 1940-42 and 1930-40

Used by permission of Henry S. Shryock, Jr., author, "Internal Migration and the War," *Jour. Amer. Stat. Assoc.*, Vol. 38 (March, 1943) pp. 16-30, and Frank A. Ross, editor of the *Jour. Amer. Stat. Assoc.*

than into cities producing the basic materials for war goods. Thus the Pittsburgh metropolitan district with a civilian population of 2,127,000 in 1940 had only 2,082,000 in 1943 (March 1) while the Detroit district with 2,374,000 in 1940 had 2,566,-000 in March 1943. The Cleveland and Youngstown districts lost civilian population during these years, as did most large steel-producing centers, while the cities using the steel for war goods—Cincinnati, Baltimore, San Francisco, Seattle, Los Angeles, San Diego, Portland, and a few others—gained relatively large numbers in spite of a decrease of about 3 million in our civilian population during these three years. Like the centers of basic industry, several of our largest centers of commerce, such as New York, Chicago, and Boston, also lost civilian population but to an even greater extent. On the other hand, many of the smaller manufacturing communities with equipment adapted to the manufacture of war goods had a high rate of increase.

The extent to which the war concentrated population in a few large cities is shown by the fact that in March 1943 the 81 metropolitan districts gaining in civilian population after 1940 had gained a total of 3,060,000 or 10 percent in three years; while the other 56 metropolitan districts had lost 1,440,000 or 4 percent during this period. Furthermore, about 72 percent of this gain of 3,060,000 was concentrated in one fourth (21) of these 81 cities, all of which gained over 40,000. The need for airplanes, ships, and heavy ordnance will explain the growth of nearly all the larger centers as well as the mushroom growth of many smaller communities. The disappearance of the usual foreign trade and the decrease in consumer's goods available for distribution will account for the above-mentioned decline of population in New York, Chicago, Boston, and many smaller trade centers.

It is of some interest that of the eleven metropolitan districts having over one million population in 1940 only six—those best equipped to manufacture war goods—gained civilian population up to March 1943, while five—those depending more largely on trade and finance—lost population (see Figure 15). The total net gain of these eleven districts was only 123,000 but the six that did gain increased by 891,000. On the other hand, of the thirteen metropolitan districts having 500,000-1,000,000 in 1940 only four lost civilian population by 1943 (188,000) while nine gained (557,000) for a net gain in

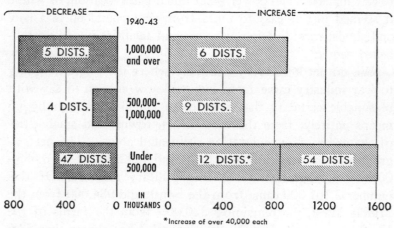

Figure 15. Growth of Metropolitan Districts in the United States, 1940-43

the group of 369,000. The most surprising fact in this whole war migration to the cities is that twelve metropolitan districts of less than 500,000 in 1940 gained in excess of 40,000 each by 1943 for a total of 850,000.

There is one other aspect of war migration that merits mention. This is the very rapid growth of a number of counties having a small, almost rural, population in 1940—counties not in any metropolitan district. There were 140 such counties that gained over 10 percent in civilian population between 1940 and 1943 and they had gained a total of 1,050,000 in these three years. This is about 160,000 more than the six metropolitan districts of over one million which showed a gain in the three years 1940-43. These small rapidly growing counties

were, for the most part, those in or near which military training centers had been located, or in which explosives factories
and shell-loading plants had been established, or in which
new industries, such as magnesium and aluminum, had been set
up. They were communities in which some kind of direct war
service was rendered which could be carried out better in a
thinly settled area than in a metropolitan center, where access
to raw materials and power determined plant location, or where
it seemed just as easy to build from the ground up in a new
and almost rural location as to expand facilities in some established center.

We do not know very definitely where the migrants going
to war industry came from but we know enough to say with
reasonable certainty that they came chiefly, although by no
means entirely, from the rural areas, towns, and small cities
of the areas of out-migration delineated above. The net migration from farms in 1940, 1941, and 1942 was about 3,655,-
000 (including men going into military service). Of this
number 2,161,000 came from the South and 984,000 from the
Middle West, the remaining 520,000 from the farms of the
Northeast and the Far West. Shryock[2] has shown that 52.6
percent of the counties of the United States lost over 5 percent
of their civilian population between 1940 and 1942. Most of
these are small rural or semi-rural counties. Hence we can
say with reasonable assurance that a large part of the war
migration came from rural areas with people from the farms
predominating.

Postwar Migration and the Distribution of Population.—
The information regarding what has happened to war migrants
since 1945 is so incomplete that not a great deal can be said.
It is well known that certain war plants have closed down and
the workers have scattered. Shell-loading and powder-making

---

[2] Henry S. Shryock, Jr., "Internal Migration and the War," *Journal of
the American Statistical Association,* Vol. 38 (March, 1943) pp. 16-30.

plants and ordnance testing grounds are good examples of plants for which there was no need as soon as the war was over. Many shipyards were also purely war enterprises and have been completely abandoned. Many others are working with greatly reduced staffs. The airplane factories are in much the same situation, although the expansion of commercial aviation and the development of new types of military aircraft have kept employment in them at a relatively higher level than in shipbuilding.

It appears that the net effect of postwar migration has been to reduce the populations in many of the counties where the sole reason for increase was a definite war service. The great demand for all kinds of consumers' goods following the war naturally increased operations in those factories which could be reconverted rather easily and quickly. Since these were for the most part the factories which had been producing such goods before the war and were located in or near large cities, it appears that a considerable portion of the migrants to war industries in the larger cities have remained and that the return of men from military service has further added to their population.

Metropolitan Districts Since 1940.—In August 1947 the Bureau of the Census issued data on the growth of population, April 1940 to April 1947, in 34 of the 140 metropolitan districts of 1940. These 34 districts, which were among the larger districts, gained 14.2 percent in seven years. The total national population increased only about 9 percent in the same period. Since the larger metropolitan districts have not been increasing quite as fast as all metropolitan districts in recent decades it is probably slightly underestimating the total metropolitan increase to assume the other 106 metropolitan districts increased at the same rate (14.2 percent) during this seven-year interval. Using this assumption, however, the total increase in metropolitan districts amounted to about 8,950,000 and they absorbed about 77 percent of the total national increase, leaving only about 2,700,000 (23 percent) for the increase of the nonmetropolitan population which then probably constituted just less than half (49.8 percent) of the total population. Hence, the rate of increase in the nonmetropolitan population was less than 4 percent as compared with 14.2 percent in the metropolitan population. If the metropolitan districts continue to draw such a large proportion of our natural increase for the remainder of the decade as they have for the past seven years, and this appears rather probable unless there is a serious depression before 1950, they will increase by almost 4 million more by that time and will probably contain over 51 percent of all our people. Thus it appears that the centralizing tendency which has long been manifest and which was greatly encouraged by war conditions is being carried over into the postwar period and is resulting in a renewed concentration of population in a few relatively large communities. This does not mean, of course, that the major part of the growth of metropolitan districts is in the central cities, for the trend toward the suburban areas (satellite areas) is no doubt continuing. It does mean that more and more of our people are crowding into our largest communities.

MILITARY CONSIDERATIONS IN THE DISTRIBUTION OF POPULATION

The one force which might counteract the continuing tendency to concentrate economic activity in large centers and large plants, and thus to keep on concentrating population in a few vast urban aggregations, is military necessity. There is no evidence, however, that military considerations are yet having any effect on the economic planning of large corporations or, indeed, even on governmental planning in this country as regards the distribution of population. Some general aspects of this problem have been mentioned in Chapter 5. But it will be in place here to give a few facts showing how vulnerable we are to attack by aerial weapons by reason of the heavy concentration of population and industry in a relatively few great centers.[3]

Population in the Largest Metropolitan Districts.—The eleven largest metropolitan districts in the United States contained 25.6 percent of our entire population in 1940 and the next eleven in size contained another 5.9 percent. Thus our twenty-two largest communities contained almost one third of our entire population and, as shown above, there is reason to believe that they contain a somewhat larger proportion now. The total area of the cities of over 25,000 in these 22 districts is only 3,535 square miles, or a little over 0.1 percent of the total area of the United States. In addition, in 1939 thirty-three industrial districts containing only ninety-seven counties and having only 1.7 percent of the area of the nation produced over 59 percent (in value) of all our industrial products. They contained over 35 percent of our population and 55 percent of all wage earners engaged in manufacturing.

Concentration of Certain Industries.—Our steel industry, certainly essential to national safety, employed 42.4 percent of all its workers in the Pittsburgh-Youngstown-Cleveland area in 1939. The Chicago area employed another 14.9 percent. Our motor car industry seems even more concentrated than our steel industry. In 1939, 62 percent of all its workers were found in the Detroit area and near-by Michigan cities. Finally, it may be pointed out that the 105 (1943) largest installations for the production of electricity had 51 percent of all generating capacity and 22 of these are found in or near our four largest cities.

Even the Ruhr did not offer better targets than we have built in the United States. It would be only elementary com-

[3] For more detailed discussion see the chapter by the author on "The Atomic Threat" in *Cities Are Abnormal*, Norman, Okla.: University of Oklahoma Press, 1946.

mon sense to begin to ask ourselves how we can redistribute
our population (and our industry) so that we shall at least have
a chance to survive if a sneak attack is made on us by very long
range bombers carrying not only atomic bombs but also the
weapons of biological warfare. In the present disorganized
state of the world it seems absurd not to consider how the
distribution of our population might be changed to render us
less vulnerable to the weapons which are almost certain to be
used if we have another World War.

Evacuation of Cities Not Sufficient.—As this is being written our Army has announced that it is making plans for the
evacuation of 75 million people or more from our cities in the
event they are attacked from the air. But their plans seem to
be confined to a study of the adequacy of transport facilities
to move people out of a given city or area when it is believed
to be in danger of attack. There is no intimation in the an-
nouncements thus far made that the Army is aware of what it
would mean to the evacuees or to the regular inhabitants to
dump 7 million New Yorkers on the surrounding countryside.
It is of little importance from a national standpoint to save the
people of any city from sudden death today only to have them
die of hunger and disease a few weeks later because the ability
of the surrounding country to produce food has been destroyed
by hungry evacuees searching for something to eat and because
of the disease which will inevitably ensue when vast numbers
of people are dropped into an area having meager public utili-
ties and no organized health service. If we wait to do anything
about the redistribution of population until our cities are in
imminent danger it will be too late to save them and their inhabitants from destruction and it will, in addition, make a large
measure of destruction in the countryside absolutely inevitable.
We should now be making careful studies of how industry can
be broken into smaller producing units so that it can be widely
scattered in many smaller communities.

SOME PROBLEMS OF INTERNAL MIGRATION

While it is of interest to know in a general way where our internal out-migrants are coming from and where they are likely to come from in the near future, as well as where they are now going, it is probably fully as important to indicate a few of the more significant social problems created by migration.

In many communities where in-migration is large the provision of adequate school facilities has proved to be quite beyond their means. This is particularly true of small satellite communities. This type of community often finds it quite impossible to provide adequate housing, water, gas, electricity, transportation, and health facilities out of local means. Under our present system of local taxation and control, these services remain highly unsatisfactory in many communities. There can be little doubt that the unhealthy, crowded, and generally unpleasant living conditions in many areas which have grown more rapidly than good living conditions could be provided are in part responsible for rapid rates of labor turnover, for large amounts of absenteeism, and even for high crime rates.

In some of the larger centers the mere physical difficulties of caring for increased numbers of incoming migrants at minimum standards have not been as serious as in many smaller places. But even if the actual physical plant in the larger places is more adequate to provide for the minimum physical care of their migrants, the great influx of migrants of highly diverse cultural backgrounds, and often of different races, creates insuperable problems of adjustment under the crowding and disorganization of community life which prevails. This very diversity of background in large bodies of migrants settling in city slums makes it extremely difficult to develop any community sentiment and control. The usual community restraints upon conduct do not operate as effectively on migrants who do not yet feel that they belong to the community as on older residents. This is one of the important reasons for the increase in crime and vice, for the undisciplined conduct of labor unions and their leaders, for delinquency among young boys and girls, and for many other unsocial types of conduct in communities having large numbers of migrants. The migrants are no more to blame, perhaps not as much, than the longer-time residents, for this breakdown of customary modes of conduct, but naturally they get into trouble more often and generally are made to appear as the most disintegrating influence in community life. The real difficulty is that migration breaks up customary ties and controlling habits and throws the individual (or family) on his own resources, with the inevitable result that much of his conduct becomes anarchic, i.e., without rule.

Social conduct needs to be organized by the community. On the other hand, vice can usually be organized by the individual for profit. Hence, the migrant finds an almost unlimited number of appeals being made to his appetites by people who can profit from their satisfaction, while the community too often does little to make him feel a member of it and to give him an opportunity to live decently. This problem of becoming assimilated into the life of a community is in essence always the same, but in times of unusual migration it becomes too much for the customary agencies of the community to handle and the result is widespread demoralization.

Migration certainly is not the only factor, or even the chief factor, in the breakdown of many of the established values of living which we are experiencing today, but it is a significant factor in many communities. Only time and real community effort will reestablish any effective community control over conduct. Too many people are moving rapidly from community to community and many of them are staying too short a time to become integrated into a community pattern of living. This is one of the prices we have to pay for a highly mobile population more and more of which is living in vast urban aggregations where the individual and family find it almost impossible to develop a feeling of *belonging*.

CHAPTER 10

SOCIAL AND ECONOMIC EFFECTS OF
AGE CHANGES

Frequent reference has been made in preceding chapters to the age changes taking place in our population but the consequences of these changes have not been dwelt on because they merit more detailed treatment than could be allotted them in other connections.

CAUSES OF AGE CHANGES

Barring extensive migration, the age structure of any population will be the natural result of its birth rates and death rates. If, as in India and China, birth rates and death rates are

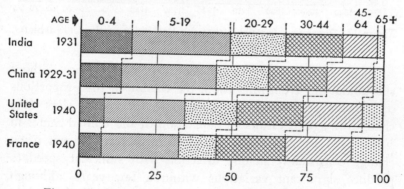

Figure 16. Percentage Distribution of Population by Age in
Selected Countries

very high at all ages, a large proportion of the total population will be found in the younger ages, in spite of the fact that one third or more of all children may die before they reach the age of five (see Figure 16). If on the other hand the birth rate is low and has been for some years, as in France, the crude death rate will probably be low, the exact level depending upon the effectiveness of public health work, and the proportion of young people will be low.

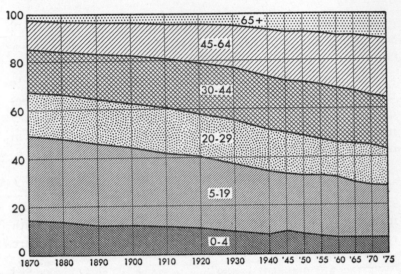

Figure 17. Percentage Distribution of the Population of the United States, by Selected Age Periods, 1870-1975

In actual life, where age changes are taking place without substantial aid from migration, the change in the proportions of persons at different ages is generally rather slow (see changes in age of estimated population of the United States in Figure 17) because death rates and birth rates do not often change consistently in one direction with sufficient speed to produce significant variations within a few years, although there are occasionally unusual developments which do produce rapid changes in certain age groups, such as the great decline in our birth rate during the depression and the equally great increase from 1941 to 1948, and the heavy loss of young men in the Soviet Union and Germany. We are concerned here, however, primarily with those longer secular changes in age composition arising from the fact that both birth rates and death rates have long been declining in Western countries.

Effects of a Decline in the Death Rate.—Experience has shown that the first large decline in the death rate will usually be in infant and child mortality and that this decline in the death rate of young children is practically certain to be greater than the decline in the birth rate for some years, perhaps for as much as three or four decades. At such a time the proportion of young children in the population will increase. The proportion of children will begin to decline as they pass into the older groups and as the birth rate begins to fall. Obviously, the death rate of children can fall rapidly for only a few decades while the first advances in public health are yielding large returns. Once the death rate has been reduced from *high* to *moderate* it costs more in time and effort to secure further proportional declines which are, of course, smaller in absolute amount. Some figures on age changes in our population will illustrate the general movement which has taken place in the West during the last century.

Effects of a Decline in the Birth Rate.—In 1820 we had an extremely young population; about 18.5 percent of our people were under five, and 39.4 percent were 5-19 years of age. Thus a total of 58 percent were under 20. The birth rate was high and the death rate was moderate for that day, although we would now consider it very high. With the decline in the birth rate and the aging of these large groups of children surviving from the period of high births, the proportion of the population under five declined almost steadily for 120 years until only 8.0 percent of our population was of this age in 1940. The proportion of young children has increased since 1940 to perhaps 9.5 percent, due to the recent increase in the birth rate, but it will soon begin to decline again. The age group 5-19 has also declined proportionally throughout most of this period. It, too, will increase temporarily as the children born during and following the war pass into it. The decline in the birth rate has probably been the most influential factor in this long decline in the proportion of children in the population but the decline in the death rate without doubt kept this proportion from falling faster at certain periods and may possibly have raised it somewhat in the years before a steady decline set in.

In Sweden the children 0-4 constituted 13.2 percent of the population in 1750 and varied between that and 11.1 percent during the next 60 years. Death rates and birth rates seem to have been about equally influential in determining the variations in the proportion of children in the Swedish population until about 1880. After that the decline in the birth rate was so much more rapid that the proportion of children declined steadily and even more rapidly in Sweden than in the United States, from 12.3 percent in 1880 to 7.0 percent in 1940. During the last 60 years the proportion of persons 60 and over in Sweden has risen from 9.4 percent to 13.8 precent, or by almost one half, in spite of a large emigration of young adults to the United States in the 30 years preceding World War I who would have added to the proportion of old people in 1940 if they had remained at home.

This relatively rapid change in the proportions of children and old people is a phenomenon which could scarcely have occurred until quite recently, when the birth rate was declining rapidly at the same time that the death rate was coming under more and more secure control, thus permitting a larger and larger proportion of all persons born to live out their normal life span (see Chapter 3).

The Extent and Speed of Age Changes

In all his history man has known only a young population: one in which perhaps one fourth or more was under 10 years of age and two fifths or more was under 15. Within the last few decades, since about 1880, in many industrialized countries these proportions have fallen as low as one sixth under 10 and one fourth under 15, while the proportion over 50 has risen from one tenth or one eighth to one fifth or more, and that over 65 has increased from one thirtieth to about one fourteenth in the United States and to one tenth in France. It is hardly to be expected that such age changes can take place without producing changes of far-reaching significance in our social and economic life. Older people do have different needs and interests than younger people; they develop different attitudes of mind toward the problems the community has to meet, and as they become more numerous they are going to demand more political and economic consideration. Since we are treating a new situation in human experience we cannot specify with any definiteness what most of the social and economic effects of these age changes will be, although a few of them are fairly obvious. We will first consider some of the consequences of a declining proportion of children.

The Decline in Children.—In the United States the largest number (2,956,000)[1] of births we ever had, prior to 1942, occurred in 1921. This number declined slowly for three or four years and then more rapidly until there were only 2,227,-000 births in 1933, a decline of about 680,000, or about 23 percent from the 1921 level. The number of births began to increase in 1934 with the beginning of recovery from the depression, but it was not until 1941 that the number of births again exceeded that of the lowest year between 1920 and 1930. Beginning with 1942 and continuing through 1947 the number of births has exceeded that of 1921 in every year except the last year of the war (1945).

Beginning in 1928 the children old enough to enter school—those born in 1922 and succeeding years—were fewer in number each succeeding year, with only insignificant exceptions, until 1940 (children born in 1934). Since 1940 the number

---

[1] In the following figures allowance has been made for nonregistration of births.

entering school has increased slowly up to the present but will soon increase much more rapidly as the children born in 1942 and later come of school age. With a total of about 3,910,000 births in 1947 the number of children entering school in 1953 will be over two thirds greater than the number which entered in 1939 (born in 1933). Beginning in 1948 elementary school enrollment will increase very rapidly for the next six or seven years, after which it will begin to decline again if the birth rate continues downward in 1948, as now seems probable from the data for the early months. In due time, high school enrollment will follow the pattern of the elementary schools. The decline in school attendance, when it does appear again, will probably be somewhat less than the decline in children of school age largely because of the increasing proportion of children 14-18 attending school.

No one can ponder the data on the changes in the proportion of children of school age which lie immediately ahead (see Table 16) without concluding that they raise very serious questions regarding our ability to provide adequate schools during the ensuing 12-15 years, although from the standpoint of the ratio of children of elementary school age (5-14) to males 15-59 (the most productive ages) there should be no particular economic difficulty in providing improved school facilities unless another great depression intervenes. The ratio of children 5-14 to males 15-59 has long been growing more favorable. In 1880 there was one child of this age to 1.2 males 15-59. By 1930 the ratio was one child to 1.53 males and by 1940 it was one child to 1.90 males. In 1945 the ratio was one child to 2.01 males and in 1950 and 1955 the ratio will be less favorable, hovering between one child to 1.75 males and one to 1.80 males. By 1960 it will be back to one child to almost two males (1.98). Thus, even the large increase in the birth rate after 1941 will leave the child-man ratio highly favorable as compared with 1930 (one child to 1.53 males) and any prior year. We should not have any great economic difficulty in providing good teachers and satisfactory school equipment for the prospective increase in school children even over the next few years. But the rather sudden fluctuations in births associated with the depression and the war do raise some very serious problems of adjustment for our schools, even when we can foresee quite clearly the extent of the increases (or declines) to be expected.

TABLE 16

Number of Children 5-14 and Males 15-59 in the Population of the United States and Ratio of Children to these Males, 1930-60

	Medium fertility, medium mortality, with immigration			High fertility *, low mortality, without immigration		
	Children 5-14	Males 15-59	Males to children 5-14	Children 5-14	Males 15-59	Males to children 5-14
1930.....	24,612	37,677	1.53	24,612	37,677	1.53
1940.....	22,431	42,545	1.90	22,431	42,545	1.90
1945.....	21,996	44,287	2.01	21,996	44,287	2.01
1950.....	25,254	45,257	1.79	25,197	45,058	1.79
1955.....	26,780	46,491	1.74	28,122	46,114	1.64
1960.....	24,752	49,039	1.98	27,203	48,502	1.78

* 15,000,000 births during 1945-50.

Consequences of Fluctuations in the School Population

In the decade before World War II both the decreasing school population and the economies forced on the schools by the depression discouraged many young people from entering the teaching profession. This was shown clearly in the declining enrollment in teachers' colleges. The coming of the war, coupled with a school population which was still declining, caused a veritable stampede from teaching. Not only did the draft take many young men from the profession, but better paying jobs attracted both men and women. Thus what appeared at the time to be a contraction of opportunity in teaching and an expansion of opportunity elsewhere created a serious teacher problem even during the war. The difficulty of getting proper equipment added to worries of school administrators.

Since the war the great demands of industry and commerce on the labor supply and the high cost of building have made it next to impossible to prepare for the coming influx of school children. Young men and women have been reluctant to enter teaching when it appeared that the demand would ease up considerably after a few years and they might find more permanent jobs elsewhere. Moreover, the reluctance of young men to enter the profession is considerably increased by the feeling that the school system is too frequently being run by the older men and women, and that young men do not have the same chance to get ahead as they did in the past. This is perhaps an inevitable consequence of a situation in which population is growing slowly. Slow growth comes first in the child population and is felt quickly by the schools. It is the unusually slow growth of the school population for a few years (depression) followed by an unusually rapid growth for a few years (war and immediate postwar) that makes the school situation so urgent now. There should be an opportunity for steady improvement, once the present emergency is past.

Expenditures on Children in the Home.—As families become smaller it seems reasonably certain that a smaller proportion of the family income will have to be spent on necessities for children. But it is almost equally certain that there will be a considerable increase in the total expenditure per child. Even though the mere necessities, clothing, food, housing, and medical care, require a smaller proportion of the family income, the better standards of child care will almost certainly demand better quality in the necessities and will keep adding many new items to the "must" list. Thus we may expect a considerable shift in the types of goods and services used by children. Whether there will be any decline in the proportion of the family income spent on the children will depend on how rapidly this "must" list increases. It seems not unlikely, however, that there will be a decrease in the proportion of the family income spent on children under high school age and an increase in the proportion spent on those of high school age and above, as the total length of the school period increases. This again will certainly involve a considerable shift in the types of goods and services bought for children. But we should not overlook the possibility that smaller families may very well result in a larger proportion of the family income being spent on the wants of the parents and in larger savings.

The decline in the number and proportion of children, although it will certainly make necessary considerable adjustments in the kinds and amounts of goods and services provided for children, should occasion no great economic difficulty, except in schools and a few other community services affected very quickly and directly by the increase in children just noted. But it is worth noting that the changes in the economic demands of children will inevitably result in more and more of our total expenditures going for the comforts and luxuries of life and thereby rendering economic activity less stable in times of stress. A proportional increase in nonnecessity expenditures will necessarily add to the probability of wide and perhaps violent fluctuations in the demand for such products and thus increase the range within which our economic activity is likely to fluctuate. This point will be enlarged upon in the following chapter.

THE EFFECTS OF MORE ADULTS ON OUR ECONOMY

Expenditures of Those in Prime of Life.—As already indicated, the decline in the proportion of children will probably leave more of the family income as well as of the national income to be spent on the needs and wants of adults in the prime of life. One might speculate at considerable length on how this will affect our business structure by increasing the demand of people 20-45 for better and faster automobiles, for travel, for expensive recreation, for small efficiency apartments, for luxury clothes, for more elaborate personal service, etc., etc., but it would remain only speculation. We can be reasonably sure that the general trend of larger adult expenditures will be to increase the proportion of the income spent on luxuries. Since these can be dispensed with when economic conditions are uncertain, this trend will still further enhance the probability of violent swings in economic activity. Whether this instability arising from an increasing luxury trade will be offset to any considerable extent by the greater ability to accumulate savings which can be spent to maintain normal living during periods of depression, cannot be told. It may work this way but we do know that in times of great uncertainty (insecurity) people are more than usually hesitant to make inroads on their "rainy day" accumulations.

The Middle-Aged in Our Economy.—Estimates of our future population show that in 1975 about 25 percent of our total population will be 45-64, compared with 20 percent today. There has long been much talk about the inability of industry to use the workers over 40 or 50 years of age. Consequently, we are facing an increasingly serious problem of how to use the middle-aged workers. The only way to prevent the demand for old-age pensions from creeping to younger and younger age groups and from becoming an intolerable burden on the national income would seem to be a reorganization of much factory and office work so that it can be carried on by workers past their most vigorous years but still in good health. There can be no doubt that most middle-aged people would rather have jobs than pensions, but if they cannot get the former they will certainly demand the latter and they are rapidly becoming numerous enough to put great force behind such a drive.

It is not certain, of course, how the decreasing size of the family will affect the personal expenditures of the middle-aged. It seems quite reasonable, however, to assume that more of their income will become available for their own use. Because of improving health they will also be able to work more steadily and hold better jobs if industry and business will make a real effort to employ them. Furthermore, if their incomes are larger they, too, will almost certainly spend more proportionally on nonnecessities and thus still further increase the likelihood of wide fluctuations of economic activity in a system which is so largely free as ours. Larger savings should, on the whole, work in the opposite direction and help to stabilize the demand for consumers' goods but it is by no means certain that they will do so. The very fact of increased family savings probably indicates that there are rather large reserves of certain necessities, e.g., clothing, housing, and household goods which can be drawn on in times of stress. Thus even the purchase of most necessities, except food and fuel, may be reduced to a very low level for some time when people feel highly insecure. We do not know that this will be the case but it certainly is a possibilty that cannot be ignored.

Effects of More Elders on Our Economy.—The war has shown that many types of work which were believed suited only to men in the prime of life, or at most to those of middle age who were in good health, can be done equally well, if not in equal quantity, by older men who are in good physical condition. In addition, there are changes taking place in the nature of industrial operations making it possible for older workers to operate many machines almost as effectively as younger workers. For instance, the use of automatic machines renders it unnecessary for the operator to have the agility, the strength, or the first-class vision that was needed when control and operation were manual. Moreover, many engineers now believe that most of the manufacturing of the future will de done on machines controlled by electronic devices. If this happens it will certainly mean that age will not be as great a handicap as it now is for many jobs.

Improving Health Among the Aged.—It is also realized now more clearly than ever before that health rather than age determines the kinds and amounts of work older people can do. Since about 1900-10 there has been an extremely significant decline in the incidence of children's diseases, measles, scarlet fever, diphtheria, enteritis, etc. A considerable part of the children born during the last 30 to 40 years have never had many of these diseases which, up to that time, were believed to be inevitable and which frequently had very serious after effects on the general health of the individual, often leaving him with a damaged heart, or impaired vision and hearing, or a weakening of the kidneys, or some other organic weakness which made him liable to wear out at a fairly early age. Besides, it appears that we may be close to the practical elimination of venereal disease as a sapper of the physical constitution, to a significant mitigation of the effects of pneumonia, and to the cure of many types of internal infections as sources of undermined health. The outlook, therefore, would seem bright for the arising of a generation of old people who are better able to carry on for five or ten years after 60 than were their parents and grandparents. This should certainly have a beneficial effect upon their employ-ability.

The stage would seem to be set, therefore, for people in the upper middle ages and early old age to do a somewhat larger part of the work of the world than in the past if their work is needed. Certainly there are going to be many more of them, and a much larger proportion of them, and it is essential both for the welfare of the community as a whole, and for their own happiness, that they be kept reasonably busy. Whether we will organize our economic life to take advantage of the work of these older people rests entirely on our willingness to do so; the techniques seem to be available, or soon will be, and the physical stamina of the people themselves seems likely to improve at the same time that the proportion of older people increases.

But while the outlook for an older population need not frighten us, we should not overlook the fact that their increased proportion in the population is almost certain to introduce many new elements into the organization of our economic, our social, and our political life. Some of the probable economic adjustments that will be needed have just been mentioned, but it may be added that almost certainly the kinds of goods and services demanded by older people will be different in many respects from those demanded by younger people. There should be no great difficulty in making the shifts in production necessary to meet their increased needs because they will not have to be made suddenly and their proportion in the population will fluctuate much less than that of children.

Increase in the Economic Power of Old People.—As the proportion of older people increases it seems altogether probable that a larger and larger part of the property of the nation will be concentrated in their hands. This will mean that they will have greater control over our economic life than in the past. We can only hope that it will not result in increasingly conservative business policies. There is just as much, if not more, need for pioneering in our economic life today, as there was 50 years ago. It is a matter of real concern whether the increasing control of older people over our economy will cause it to lose much of the initiative, the drive, and the adaptability it has shown in the past. There is some reason to think that this has been the case in France and England and that it explains, in part, the economic difficulties those countries are now experiencing. It remains to be seen whether, when wealth comes to be more concentrated in older hands, we will meet the need for initiative and new enterprise as well as we have in the past. Perhaps the answer is to be found in the age of the active managers of business rather than in that of the holders of securities, but this, too, is likely to increase as time goes on. The leadership displayed in many of our large business organizations, and by the older members of associations of business-men in recent years, does not inspire too much confidence in their willingness and ability to make the adjustments which must be made if our economic system is to be kept alert and ready to service community needs efficiently.

The Social Attitudes of Older People.—Finally, we cannot ignore the possibilty of a general change in outlook as a result of the decline in children and the increase in older people. Will we look more to the past and less to the future? Will the older people be powerful enough to forbid basic changes needed to adjust our life to the improving technologies being steadily developed? Will our social system become so crystal-lized that young people will feel it has no place for them, as one often hears young men from England and France say has happened there? If this should happen it will certainly be quite a different United States than we have known in the past.

CHAPTER 11

SOCIAL AND ECONOMIC EFFECTS OF THE SLOWER GROWTH OF POPULATION

THE EXPANSION OF OUR POPULATION AND OUR ECONOMY

When population is growing at a rate of 25-35 percent every decade, as was the case with us in the century from 1790-1890, it is clear that economic activities would have had to expand at least as fast merely to maintain the existing level of living. Since no one would question that there had been a large improvement in level of living during that century it is clear that the volume of goods produced per capita increased at a considerably more rapid rate. Since 1890 the level of living has probably risen at an even more rapid average rate than in the preceding century, in spite of the two great depressions, chiefly because of the decline in the birth rate. But even with the rapid decline in the birth rate during the last half century our population continued to grow fairly rapidly. Immigration remained high until World War I and even after that was moderately high for several years. From 1890 to 1910 our decennial increase slightly exceeded 20 percent and from 1910 to 1930 was somewhat over 15 percent. With the steady decline in the actual number of births after 1924 and the falling off in immigration after that date our population began to grow more slowly. In the quinquennium 1920-24 our total gain was probably a little over 9,500,000 and in the second quinquennium 1925-29 was probably a little less than 7,500,-000. Thus only about 43 percent of the gain took place in the second half of the decade, and the downward trend clearly evident at that time became much more rapid during the early 1930's.

Under the conditions that had so long prevailed it is not surprising that we had come to take it for granted that industry would automatically continue to expand at a rapid rate and that we did not inquire closely into the role which population growth played in this expansion. It appeared that our economy was expanding because of the forces it contained within itself, and hence required no general oversight or planning, except that by business itself, to insure its continued expansion. We did not seem to realize that just because rapid population growth had been an important element in the expansion of our economy its less rapid growth might create new conditions which would need to be "managed" if this expansion were to continue with only minor "setbacks," instead of contributing to the creation of serious social and economic problems.

This is not to say that the slower growth of population will inevitably result in a slower expansion of our economy. It does mean, however, the slower expansion of production for domestic use in many lines, particularly in those producing necessities. It means that if this slower growth in the volume of necessities is not offset by more rapid growth in other lines the net effect will be to reduce the rate of expansion of the system as a whole. It is obvious that when we had a population growth of only about 9 million (1930-40) we needed fewer new flour mills, or smaller additions to our existing mills, than when we had a growth of 17 million (1920-30). So it was with most of the other basic necessities of life. One need only envision the goods and services we would have needed to produce for an additional 8 million people—a population about the size of that of the Netherlands. We would have needed to construct the housing for about two and one half million more families, to grow the food they would consume, the fiber for the clothes they would wear, to provide the educational and medical services they would require, and so on through a long list of necessities, to say nothing of comforts and luxuries. Furthermore, we built and maintained the equivalent of two new Netherlands from a base population of about 105.7 million in 1920, while we built the equivalent of only one new Netherlands during the years 1930-40, from a base of about 122.8 million in 1930. Thinking in such concrete terms will help us to understand what this slower growth means to our economic life in reducing the rate of growth of the production of necessities and modest comforts assuming only the customary advance in level of living.

FUTURE ECONOMIC EXPANSION AND THE LEVEL OF LIVING

The above facts make it clear that unless the rate of improvement in the level of living of our more slowly growing population is accelerated enough to absorb the capital and labor which would have gone into providing a more rapidly growing population with its customary goods and services as well as its customary improvement in level of living, it is practically certain that economic expansion will be at a slower rate than heretofore. The writer is not predicting a slower rate of economic expansion as an accompaniment of slower population growth. So far as he can see, there need be no such consequence. The 131.7 million people in the United States in 1940 could easily have used goods and services equivalent to those which 140 million would have used at the living level of 1930 plus the customary improvement. They would not have been the same goods and services that the 140 million would have used. But the larger per capita volume of goods and services needed by 140 million people with a normally improving level of living could have only been bought by the actual population of 1940 (131.7 million) if they had had a per capita purchasing power which averaged about 6 percent greater than that of the 140 million. Furthermore, it would have been necessary for this smaller population not only to possess a larger average per capita purchasing power but to exercise this power if it were to consume the larger quantity of goods made by an economic system expanding at the same rate as in the preceding decade.

If these goods which constitute the national income, are allowed to accumulate either in the form of excess inventories of consumers' goods, as unused capacity of producers' goods, or if they are not produced because of uninvested savings, the economy will cease to work efficiently, with the result that production will be reduced and unemployment will accumulate.

DIFFICULTIES OF MAINTAINING AN EXPANDING ECONOMY

In an economy which has been expanding at a fairly uniform rate, with population growing rapidly, the division of the national income (generally thought of in terms of money) becomes somewhat stabilized into the two primary funds, (1) consumers' income, that which is spent currently for living, and (2) producers' income, that which is available for or used for producers' goods. The proportion of the national income allotted to consumers' and producers' incomes year by year will not vary greatly from an average established over a period of years, although these proportions may have a definite trend upward or downward. If for any reason something happens to change substantially the proportions of the national income which are available for the purchase of, or are actually used for the purchase of, either of these two classes of goods it will in a comparatively short time affect the ability of the nation as a whole to make effective use of all the national income until a new workable equilibrium has been established. The effects of this inability to use the entire national income may not be felt immediately if the proportion unused is not large. But, in the long run, these effects may be extremely serious when they do make themselves felt, because the accumulation of unused income will lead to heavy unemployment. Thus, if for several years a smaller share of the national income than is usual is spent for consumers' goods because population growth is declining and wages and salaries are not rising fast enough to take up the slack the time will soon come when fewer consumers' goods will be produced and smaller investments in producers' goods will be made. These conditions will soon lead to unemployment and the vicious circle of unemployment, decreased purchasing power for consumers, and still smaller investment in producers' goods, is closed. The severity of the setback to the economy will depend on how badly the distribution of the national income to consumers and producers is out of balance and how greatly the insecurity felt by both consumers and producers in this situation contributes to the contraction of spending.

A change in rate of population growth is certainly not the sole factor which may make it more difficult to use all the national income effectively at any given time and probably it is not the chief factor. It seems reasonable, however, to assume that when such a change in population growth comes on rather suddenly, as was the case in this country after 1925 and particularly after 1928, a new division of the national income between consumers' income and producers' income becomes more imperative than it would have been if population had continued to grow about as in the past. If there are fewer people than the economy is organized to care for in the customary manner with the balance it has achieved while population was growing rapidly, each person must be able to buy more goods than he had been buying in order to use the full production of the community. Purchasing the same amount per capita will not maintain the health of the economy. At any given moment, of course, any one of several other factors may have a more disturbing effect on the economic balance than the change in rate of population growth, e.g., technological progress or the development of monopolies, may rapidly increase the share of the goods in a particular industry, or in the entire economy, which goes to capital and management and thus becomes available for producers' goods. If this happens then the proportion of the national income available for consumers' goods will not be sufficient to keep the system operating at full, or near-full, capacity.

The difficulties in keeping a workable balance between consumers' incomes and producers' incomes in any highly dynamic economy are very great at all times, but if an economy is geared to allot to producers income sufficient to provide for an increase of about 2 million persons a year and then rather suddenly finds it needs producers' goods sufficient to provide for only one million it cannot immediately convert these producers' goods into consumers' goods and arrange for consumers' income to increase sufficiently to absorb these additional goods. Any new factor which adds to the difficulty of keeping a complex economy stabilized may, of course, become "the straw that breaks the camel's back" and the slower growth of population may be one such factor.

But even if a workable division of the national income between consumers' income and producers' income could be maintained at all times in spite of population changes, technological progress, the exhaustion of natural resources, etc., there would still remain difficulties in shifting from the production of consumer necessities to consumer comforts and luxuries at a time when population growth is decreasing fairly rapidly. No one would think of denying that if population is now growing only one half as fast as it was a few years ago the expansion of production in necessities need be only one half as great as formerly. Even if we assume that per capita consumption increases fast enough to keep the total volume of their production increasing as fast as in the past, although population growth is slower, it is obvious that the direction of the flow of capital must be changed. The nation will need smaller increases in wheat and other essential foods, in housing units, in clothing units, and in all other essentials. Capital which had been going into the necessity industries will be channeled into the production of comforts and luxuries. If, because of technological improvements, per capita productivity is increasing, the need for the rapid shift of capital from the production of necessities to comforts and luxuries becomes even more imperative. In the long run, no doubt, the shifts in production just noted will take place; in actual life, labor, capital, and management are not entirely fluid and cannot shift at once to new industries of quite a different character.

When much capital must be shifted from industry to industry there is inevitably much uncertainty on the part of businessmen as to their investment policies. This uncertainty is bound to increase as more and more of the products for which the market is expanding fall into the luxury class where personal tastes and choice and social attitudes rather than necessity determine where the consumers' dollars will go. In addition, it should not be forgotten that businessmen with capital are generally familiar with definite lines of business and naturally hesitate to embark on enterprises involving new productive operations and forays into new sales' fields about the stability of which little or nothing is known. Likewise the laborer is more or less reluctant to abandon a type of work which he knows for something quite different, especially if it involves moving to another locality. Then, too, the banker hesitates to make loans to individuals or corporations, not already well established, when they are embarking on new and untried enterprises. Thus the switch from enterprise which is no longer expanding, or expanding slowly, (necessities) to that which it is hoped is "coming" (luxuries) is not as easy in practice as in theory, although on the whole, it is much easier than organizing the shift in the proportions of consumers' and producers' incomes discussed above.

The difficulty of shifting capital from necessity to luxury industries is further enhanced as an increasing proportion of all consumption falls into the category of comforts or luxuries. The market for comforts and luxuries, while in the long run, limited only by income, is far more fickle as regards particular products and total volume at any given time, than is the

market for necessities. This makes investment in new enterprises, in a highly complex industrial system, far more uncertain than the expansion of necessity enterprises even when
population is growing rapidly and increases this uncertainty as
population growth becomes slower and thus decreases the proportion of consumers' income spent on necessities. Thus the
slower growth of population increases the likelihood of violent
fluctuations in economic activity. Only careful planning in
which the public shares is likely to prevent an expanding economy from becoming more and more unstable as population
ceases to grow while the level of living rises.

SLOWER POPULATION GROWTH AND MONOPOLY

Still another probable economic effect of slower population
growth is the strengthening of the trend towards monopoly so
manifest in this country in recent years. The increasing difficulties of doing business competitively in markets which are
not expanding as rapidly in the use of staple necessities as
in the past, and which are far more fickle because they are increasingly becoming luxury markets makes the limitation of
competition appear attractive to many businessmen. It is not
surprising, therefore, that many men feel that it will be easier
to insure the future of their particular businesses or to secure
stability in their industries by combining competitive enterprises or by controlling competition through gentlemen's agree-
ments or trade association activities than by leaving competition
unfettered. In this way they often obtain a firm control over
prices, in a smaller market to be sure, but they do not have to
make the effort required in a competitive economy to retain or
enlarge the share of their own enterprise in the market or to
expand the market by producing better products at lower prices.

The way of monopoly may insure the future of a given firm
or group of firms for a few years but it will certainly result in
weakened initiative and will injure the buying power of the
consumer in the long run. Unless monopoly is carefully reg-

ulated in the public interest and unless more effective inducements to efficient operation are developed within the monopoly framework than we have any reason to expect from past experience, the growth of monopoly will inevitably increase the demand for the public regulation of business or even for public ownership and operation of numerous types of business. Thus slower population growth may be considered a factor in strengthening the demand for public participation in economic planning. If, in the past, rapid population growth has acted as a fly-wheel to give momentum to our economy and to keep it from stalling too easily we must find a new stabilizer. There should be no insuperable obstacle to replacing the population flywheel with some other mechanism which will work just as effectively but none other has yet appeared which is so nearly automatic.

It seems probable that we must deliberately undertake to develop a mechanism to replace population growth if we would achieve any considerable measure of stability. Such planning is, of course, anathema to all "rugged individualists" but, clearly, our present economic system will not survive many such shocks as it received during the 1930's. If we want to preserve a large measure of freedom in our economy we shall have to do something to increase its stability. The conditions under which a *laissez-faire* system could be reasonably stable are passing. One of these conditions has been the steady and rapid increase of population and another was free land; neither of these can any longer be counted on to give stability to, or to insure the expansion of, our economy. We shall have to find new means to achieve these ends. These new means will almost certainly consist, in part, in more public control over the processes of allocating the national income as between consumers and producers to insure greater stability. Since the slower growth of population is one of the factors making for increased instability in our economy, it may very properly be regarded as a factor pushing us towards a larger participation by the public in the planning of economic activity.

CHAPTER 12

THE HEREDITARY FITNESS OF THE POPULATION

WHAT IS HEREDITARY FITNESS?

There are three possible assumptions regarding the trend in the hereditary fitness of a population: (1) that the hereditary quality of the population is improving; (2) that there is no measurable change taking place in its quality; and (3) that the hereditary quality of the population is deteriorating. In discussions of "fitness" the term "fit" is generally used to designate the ability of the individual to adjust himself, with at least a passable degree of adequacy, to the needs of living in his community. "Unfit," of course, is then used to indicate the inability to make such adjustments. The reader will notice at once that in the above sentences we have passed from statements about hereditary fitness to statements about fitness without such qualification. This is such a common error in discussions which undertake to deal with hereditary fitness that we must make clear at the outset exactly what we are talking about or the entire discussion will be so confused as to be valueless.

Hereditary Fitness vs. Social Fitness.—According to present biological usage, only traits or characteristics found in the genes and transmitted at conception are hereditary. We must keep this point in mind for the question discussed here is not whether there is any change in the proportion of the population which is socially inadequate or unfit but in the proportion which is hereditarily fit or unfit. These are two quite different matters. A population can only be said to be deteriorating hereditarily if the proportion of the people having genes which make impossible what the community would consider normal development is increasing and it can only be said to be improving hereditarily when the opposite is the case. Since most interest in hereditary fitness centers in the question: Is our population deteriorating hereditarily? the greater part of the discussion here will be confined to this point. Following the attempt to throw light on this question there will be a brief discussion of means which might be employed to improve the hereditary quality of the population and of some which might be used to increase the proportion of the people who are socially adequate.

Clearly, we cannot make much progress in answering the question whether there is a deterioration in the hereditary quality of a population until we find some way of distinguishing between the hereditarily fit and unfit. Certain groups of unfit which can be rather readily recognized are quite commonly thought of as being hereditarily unfit, i.e., as having hereditary traits which prevent them from living normal lives. Some of these, notably the lower types of the feeble-minded, also frequently manifest distinguishing physical stigmata which are often hereditary. But even these readily distinguishable types are not all hereditarily defective. A significant proportion of them have suffered accidents of one kind or another. Most members of this extremely defective group are also sterile, because of defective heredity, hence may be dismissed from consideration as transmitters of unfit heredity.

Another group readily identified as unfit is that of the mentally diseased who find their way into custodial institutions. But this identification cannot take place until there is a definite mental break and does not usually come in time to prevent reproduction. As a matter of fact, the mentally diseased, unlike the extreme mental defectives, are not usually sterile, but have families below the average size for the population at large. Moreover, most mental disease is not yet proved to be a gene-transmitted trait. It appears rather to be a combination of hereditary traits which "predispose" an individual to become abnormal if and when his environmental conditions become too complicated for him to cope with.

Intelligence Tests.—Unfortunately, the groups just referred to constitute only a small part of those who are quite generally assumed to be hereditarily unfit. Consequently, it is imperative to find some sure means of identifying this larger group of hereditarily unfit if any headway is to be made in improving the hereditary quality of our population. The proportion of any population which is hereditarily unfit obviously depends on the kind of scale by which such fitness is rated and the point on the scale below which people are considered unfit because of lack of ability to attain a higher rating. There have been many attempts to set up definite standards to separate the fit from the unfit on the basis of their heredity. The standard most used in recent years is the "intelligence test." It is quite commonly assumed that all persons having a rating below 70, when the average of all persons is 100, are mentally deficient and are biologically unfit. This group with a score below 70 is believed to constitute about 2 percent of the population.

It should be made clear at this point that this definition of "unfit" can only be thought of as the equivalent of *hereditarily* unfit on the assumption that intelligence tests measure hereditary traits quite accurately and exclusively. It is unfortunate that there has been altogether too great a readiness to assume that the "intelligence" measured by these tests is an hereditary trait. Hence the need to insist that not all members of a group stigmatized as unfit by intelligence tests are unfit because they lack the hereditary capacity to make a higher score in the tests; nor are they permanently unfit in the sense that they cannot make a fair adjustment to life in their communities if they have the right opportunities. Happily, it is increasingly realized that an intelligence test necessarily measures the complete personality, not merely traits transmitted at conception, that the person tested is an organism consisting of certain hereditary traits as they have been developed in the environment in which he has lived from conception to the time of the test. It is, therefore, quite impossible to say what proportion of the 2 percent of persons with low scores, who certainly have a great deal of difficulty in adjusting themselves to the life of the community, are unable to do so because of defective heredity and what proportion fails to score higher because of malnutrition, sickness, poor home surroundings, lack of educational opportunity, and the thousand and one other factors which constitute the total of their life experience up to the time of the test.

Those who are most convinced that the hereditary quality of the population is deteriorating quite generally accept these tests as measures of hereditary quality because they fail to realize how inextricably hereditary and environmental factors are woven together in the developed personality. It is quite logical therefore, for them to assume that the social inadequacy of these people with low scores is chiefly of hereditary origin. That they make this assumption is clearly manifest in the conclusions they draw from the facts showing differential fertility (see Chapter 2). They argue that since the poor, the uneducated, and the unskilled have larger families than the well-to-do, the better educated, and the more highly trained workers, the unfit are increasing faster than the fit and they mean the hereditarily unfit.

This argument begs the question. In the first place, we must realize that we have no conclusive proof that many of the unfit according to the intelligence tests could not make better scores if they had better opportunities to develop the qualities they have inherited. In the second place, it is often assumed that the unfit according to intelligence tests and the socially inadequate as shown by their poverty, their failure to get along in school, their carelessness in looking after their homes, their frequent unemployment, and their inability to hold good jobs, are the same people and that defective heredity lies at the base of both these types of inadequacy. No doubt many individuals will be found in both these groups and many are hereditarily defective but again this does not prove that either intelligence tests or social inadequacy are exact measures of hereditary fitness.

Survival of the Fittest.—Finally, the argument which is presumed to prove beyond peradventure of doubt that defective heredity is increasing in our population is that the "survival of the fittest" is no longer the chief selective agency among civilized men. It is said that the decreasing severity of the struggle for existence in modern times has made the survival of the unfit relatively much easier. As a matter of fact we do not know whether there was a differential rate of survival between classes in past times but the pat way in which this idea fits into the Spencerian interpretation of "survival of the fittest" and "natural selection" seems to many people to render further proof unnecessary. In judging the validity of this argument we must remember that the hardships of life have always borne more heavily on the lower classes than on the upper and that this is still the case as anyone familiar with our death rates knows. (See Chapter 4.) On the other hand, the upper classes have always suffered more from war and debauchery than the lower classes, thus tending to equalize their rates of reproduction. There is real doubt whether "natural selection" has ever worked as eugenically as many people assume. There is no doubt, however, that for the last two generations the lower economic classes in most Western countries have reproduced at a more rapid rate than the upper economic groups. But this does not prove that defective heredity is increasing relatively. Moreover, as already noted in Chapter 2, there is evidence that the birth differential between the upper and lower economic classes is declining and there is good reason to think that it may largely disappear in the course of the next generation or two.

In the light of the evidence we now have the most reasonable conclusion regarding the quality of our population is that the hereditarily unfit are not increasing much, if any, more rapidly than the remainder of the population. In any event, we do not yet have the means of identifying them with any precision. Consequently, we are not now justified in undertaking an extensive crusade aimed at preventing the propagation of the hereditarily unfit. On the other hand, we are justified in doing all within our power to provide social and economic conditions such that only the hereditarily unfit will remain in subnormal conditions.

STERILIZATION AND SEGREGATION OF THE UNFIT

The fact that we cannot undertake with assurance an effective program to eliminate more than a small proportion of the hereditarily unfit does not mean that the community should do nothing to discourage the biologically unfit from having children. It should do everything in its power to prevent the birth of hereditarily defective children. In addition, the community would be wise to discourage, by advice and persuasion, many of the people who are defective by accident, and presumably will not transmit an hereditary taint, from having children because the environment in which these children will be brought up will be such that it is almost certain to warp their development and make social degenerates of them. However, we should extend compulsory sterilization only as fast as we can positively identify the hereditarily unfit. In the meantime we can do much to reduce the socially "unfit" by removing the social conditions which make for degeneracy. We need to prevent the propagation of those who are hereditarily defective but we need even more to eliminate the social conditions which create inadequacy.

STERILIZATION VS. OPPORTUNITY

The surest way to improve the working quality of the population is to extend the opportunity to get a better education, to work steadily at more remunerative jobs, to live in better houses in less crowded and run-down neighborhoods, to secure better health service, and in other ways to insure good living conditions and social contacts. In spite of the growing realization that, at present, opportunity is not equally open to all, it will be well to note very briefly some of the chief ways in which opportunity might be enlarged with a reasonable prospect of improving the effective quality of our population. Only after we have done this can we be reasonably certain that the subnormals are also the hereditarily unfit.

Educational Opportunity.—The inequalities of educational opportunity due to the economic handicaps of both families and communities are now being widely discussed. There is a growing demand for state and Federal aid to education in communities which are economically handicapped. Many people are also beginning to ask why we should not have some form of scholarships which will make it possible for competent youngsters from poor families to secure such education as they can make use of instead of having to drop out of school at an early age to earn their living. We are gradually coming to realize that we have no basis, in fact, for saying that any social or racial group cannot make good use of better educational opportunity until such opportunity has existed for a time long enough to insure that it has become a customary factor in their lives. The real question is whether we want educational opportunity confined to those communities which can adequately support their own institutions, and to those families which can afford to support their children in prolonged educational endeavor, or whether we want it extended to all who are able to profit by it. Only after we have done the latter and have maintained open opportunity for several generations will we be able to tell much about the mental ability of the present disadvantaged classes.

Economic Opportunity.—It is highly probable, however, that the extension of educational opportunity to larger and larger groups, important as it is, will prove far less effective and much slower in raising people out of substandard groups into more normal ways of living than making moderate economic returns regularly available to them through steadier and better-paid jobs. It needs little proof to convince anyone that a plantation (cotton or sugar) laborer (white or Negro) receiving $2-$3 a day for 100-200 days a year cannot live decently and send his children to school after they are old enough to go to work. Nor can the miner living in a company house on company land, sending his children to a company-supported school, buying at a company commissary at greatly inflated prices and working 100-200 days a year be said to have reasonable opportunity, although his daily wage may be fairly high. One might continue almost indefinitely this enumeration of ways in which opportunity is denied the different groups because of the smallness and uncertainty of income, but there is no need. It will be generally admitted that where economic means for decent living are lacking it is highly probable that people will appear substandard, not only in level of living, but in the proportions of dependency and delinquency likely to be found among them. Again we must ask how we are to tell who is hereditarily unfit as long as such economic and social inequalities affect great numbers of our people. In all honesty we must answer: We cannot!

Health and Opportunity.—It is clear that in spite of all the public health work we now maintain, a great proportion of our people do not have opportunity to secure adequate health service. It needs no argument to convince anyone that the inability to get adequate health service is a handicap of the first order, economically, educationally, and in many other respects. Any community which does not provide for substantial equality in health opportunity can expect to pay for it by lowered economic efficiency, by increased dependency and custodial care, and by a general slackness in manner of living which will make the whole community appear substandard.

Opportunity and Identification of the Unfit.—This enumeration of ways in which unequal opportunity tends to keep many persons and groups in substandard conditions need not be continued. If we really want to improve the social quality of our population it is reasonably certain that we will accomplish far more within a decade or two by equalizing opportunity, economic, educational, health, etc., than by any program of eugenic sterilization we may be able to devise, and at the same time we will be making it easier to pick out the hereditary defectives. We know that poverty and bad housing make for juvenile delinquency. It is not so clear that any large proportion of the juvenile delinquents come from the biologically unfit. We know that poverty and uncertain work make for more poverty and dependency and poor health and a general incompetence, but we do not know that biological unfitness is responsible for any considerable proportion of the poverty-stricken. If we really want a more self-supporting, a more competent, a more self-respecting population the quickest way to secure it is to work for the extension of broader opportunity to all our people. After this has been done and after two or three generations have enjoyed this larger opportunity, we shall have better reason to assume that the socially substandard and the hereditarily unfit are the same groups. Even then we shall have to make selection for eugenic treatment on the basis of individual characteristics and not on the basis of mere membership in some group or class.

FAMILY EUGENICS

There is one other aspect of constructive action for improving the quality of the population which should not be overlooked, in addition to opening wider opportunity to the disadvantaged. It should be possible in the course of time to develop more interest on the part of the population at large in the biological quality of their children than has been customary in the past. Once it is understood that it is not only a personal but a community misfortune for a man or woman to mate with another who has basic hereditary defects which are likely to be transmitted to children, it should not be difficult to induce most people to guard against matings of this character to the best of their ability. This is quite a different matter from the definite public encouragement of matings which it is believed will, or might, result in superior quality children such as the nazis were said to encourage. At first, such endeavors should consist of nothing more than an educational campaign to show people the importance of exercising reasonable care in marriage and some public assistance in looking into family histories.[1] The building up of interest in the eugenic quality of one's family will involve developing a certain amount of pride of family. Public sentiment in this country has heretofore frowned on such pride because it has too often been associated with inherited wealth and a snobbish assumption of superiority. But it should not be considered snobbish to want to assure oneself as far as one reasonably can that one's children will start in life with a sound physical and mental equipment as well as that they will have opportunity to make use of such ability as they may possess.

The greatest difficulty in developing a reasonable interest in the hereditary quality of the family probably lies in the great mobility of our population. Most of us know but little of our ancestors and could not honestly assess their eugenic qualities if we would. The rapid movement of generation after generation from one part of the country to another has resulted in almost complete ignorance of one's family and has destroyed the natural interest always present when the family "stays put" for some generations. In time, however, the great mobility which has characterized us in the past may diminish and we will then naturally know more about our own families and the fam-

---

[1] I am not referring here to the so-called eugenic laws requiring examination for venereal disease before marriage. Such health measures are all to the good, but they are health measures rather than measures to improve the hereditary quality of the people.

ilies we are marrying into than has been the case heretofore. But we should not place any great hope on this change as a factor in improving the hereditary quality of our people in the near future.

Except for a small percentage of the population which we cannot yet identify with much assurance, there is good reason to believe that we have sound heredity, and that by far the greater proportion of our abnormal and problem individuals are the result of social conditions rather than of heredity. This is the reason for placing emphasis on making wider opportunity available to all our people and to urge caution in relying on sterilization, or segregation, or eugenic marriage laws, to effect any significant improvement in the biological or social quality of our people for some time to come. Many a "mute, inglorious Milton" may arise if opportunity is offered. But more important than the Miltons would be the lifting of the ill-fed, ill-housed, ill-clothed and one may add ill-schooled, ill-healthed, and ill-employed third of our people into a higher level where they could be reasonably sure of making good use of the qualities they were born with! This would do more to keep us a strong and virile people than the most rigidly enforced eugenic program that can be devised at the present time.

CHAPTER 13

MINORITIES

THE MEANING OF MINORITIES

In almost every nation and certainly in all large nations there are many smaller groups which differ in various respects from the larger and dominant group or groups. Fortunately in most cases these differences are small, or are differences in minor characteristics which do not arouse strong emotions and, hence, do not raise barriers of any consequence between these groups. Such minor differences do little to disturb the economic, political, and cultural unity of a nation. In the United States, for example, there is so little difference between most Protestant sects that their religious beliefs and practices do not separate them from one another to any significant degree on matters of national concern. In general this is also true of the differences between Protestants, Catholics, and Jews, although at times and under particular circumstances these differences in religious beliefs and practices may be great enough to arouse strong antagonisms and may result in efforts to place certain restrictions, more likely to be social than legal, on these minority groups.

Minority problems do not really arise, however, until minor groups are made to feel that their "way of life" and/or their "rights"—civil, political, religious, and cultural—are endangered by the type of conformity demanded by the majority, or that they are being kept as an inferior group subject to the will of the dominant group. The problems commonly associated with minorities—civil rights, religious freedom, freedom of movement within a country, freedom to work at any task for which one is fitted, freedom to attend public educational institutions, freedom to speak a language different from that of the majority, and perhaps other freedoms—do not arise in relation to dissident groups until they are made to feel that certain of their fundamental beliefs and rights are being suppressed or are in danger of being infringed upon.

There are as many causes leading to the development of minority problems as there are situations in which basic rights are felt to be at stake. It is never possible to know in advance when differences in belief or in behavior will lead to discrimination and persecution of the smaller dissident groups by the majority group, or by certain active elements in this group. Differences which at one time were considered fundamental and resulted in the most persistent efforts to secure conformity, even to the point of wholesale slaughter of the minority, are always disappearing as causes of friction because of changes in circumstances while other differences which mattered little at an earlier time come to be regarded as fundamental to national welfare by a new majority group.

In the Middle Ages differences in religious beliefs and practices were perhaps the greatest cause of the persecution of minorities. Today, when minorities are mentioned we tend to think first of groups whose political or economic rights are infringed or threatened although these are by no means the only bases on which discrimination takes place. Racial differences (in the United States) and ethnic differences (in Europe) create many of the minority problems which confront us today. They are no less troublesome than religious problems were in times past because they arouse no less bitterness of feeling. In addition, people seem no less ready to persecute or liquidate minorities holding dissident economic and political beliefs than the people of the Middle Ages were to persecute religious dissidents. In many parts of the world, of course, differences in religious beliefs and practices still arouse powerful emotions and lead to the most cruel persecution.

The Nature of Minority Problems.—The minority problems surveyed here are only a few of those which actually exist and little more will be attempted than a listing of them, with a bare statement of some of the more important social and economic difficulties arising in connection with them. There is no accepted solution for most of them, even in the minds of most majority groups, if we except the solutions of extremists like the nazis who believed either in complete extermination of relatively small groups like the Jews, or in forcing the mass migration of minorities and thus assembling into a compact body the different ethnic groups which largely constituted European minorities. Apparently the nazis did not consider the peoples they were conquering and intended to enslave as possible minorities. These peoples were to have no rights except as granted by the "master" race. Strange as it may seem, the nazis did not appear to realize that these enslaved peoples (Poles and Russians in particular) would become minorities which because of their great numbers would be far more troublesome than any minorities had ever been in the past. They seemed to believe that great cruelty and, if need be, wholesale slaughter would so cow these peoples that they would docilely accept complete German domination. The German experience with the Poles from the time of their division between Russia, Germany, and Austria (1795) had not taught them that persecution is the most certain way to insure unity in a conquered group, and that the more ruthless is the persecution, short of extermination, the more certain it is to turn the conquered people into an irreconcilable minority group.

The ideal solution of minority problems would consist not in bringing all minorities into complete conformity with the majority in beliefs, language, and habits of living, but in developing a broader tolerance of differences so that only a very few points of political, economic, and cultural conformity would be needed to assure the unity in national groups which is so essential to the achievement of national welfare. This is probably impossible as long as the national aims of large states are thought of so largely in terms of military power. But the fact remains that the necessary conformity of minorities must be secured, not by force, but by convincing all members of groups living within the boundaries of a nation that it is to their interest to respect those few beliefs regarding human rights essential to the pursuit of the common welfare. Short of this, the persecution of minorities will probably continue and may even become worse as differences in economic views become sharper. Economic heresy can arouse just as violent hatreds as religious heresy.

In real life it is often extremely difficult, and at times impossible, for all dissident groups within the boundaries of a nation to agree upon the few fundamentals needed to secure the degree of conformity demanded by the majority. People frequently become irritated by many differences which need not make for disunity if only they could learn to be reasonably tolerant of their neighbors. Unfortunately, molehills of difference are frequently made the basis for creating mountains of hate. When this happens nothing but complete conformity will satisfy the majority, or the people in power. Under such circumstances many mildly dissident groups become militantly suspicious minorities which are looking for discrimination and persecution in every act of the majority and the stage is set for greater or lesser civil strife. But these rather abstract considerations, while important, must not be allowed to monopolize our attention in this brief discussion. In real life minority problems are concrete and deal with particular situations.

MINORITY PROBLEMS IN THE UNITED STATES

The chief minority problem in the United States—why are they generally called minority problems rather than majority problems, since the responsibility for their solution must rest chiefly on the group or groups which have the power to change conditions?—is, of course, the Negro problem. We have 12 million Negroes who are largely excluded from the social, economic, and political opportunities which theoretically belong to every United States citizen. That this situation exists is generally admitted and yet very few of us even think of it as a minority problem.

The "Inferiority" of the Negro.—The chief reason for this exclusion of the Negro from equal participation in our nation's life is the belief, widespread among whites, that the Negro belongs to an inferior race. Those who have read the preceding chapters will realize that the writer believes there is no valid evidence supporting this view. As in the case of hereditary quality, we cannot *know* what any individual or minority group is capable of in the way of social and economic achievement until they have been given the chance to live as other groups and to share equally in the opportunities and responsibilities of the community for a considerable period of time. The differences between whites and Negroes commonly assumed by the whites to be racial differences can be accounted for in large measure by the differences in economic and social status which have prevailed ever since the Negro was first brought to this country. We do not *know* that they are racial differences. We only *assume* that they are because we first assume the general superiority of the white race to all others. We are slowly being forced to admit that the whites are not superior to the Chinese, Japanese, and Indians, but we do even this reluctantly and with many reservations. In the case of the Negro we are even slower and more reluctant to admit equality; we make more reservations because this brings a very difficult problem directly home to us. However, in spite of all our prejudices we are being forced little by little by facts to acknowledge that what we thought were evidences of racial inferiority are merely evidences of lack of opportunity. Only when the Negroes can live as the whites, can do the same kinds of work, can receive the same wages for like work, can enjoy as good health, can live in as good a neighborhood, and in a hundred other ways come under the same social and economic influences as the whites, can we really judge their ability to share fully in all aspects of our civilization. From what we know now it appears probable that if the Negro is allowed to share fully in our national life we shall find that differences in racial ability are of no importance. Our treatment of Negroes denies the basic theory underlying our democracy: that individual differences in ability and behavior must, in the long run, be allowed to determine a person's place in the community, that his membership in some minor racial or ethnic group or in some dissident group holding beliefs different from those of the majority must not be made the basis for discrimination unless his actions endanger the general welfare. It is not sufficient that they merely threaten the dominance of the majority or of some special group which claims to represent the majority.

The Solution of the Negro Problem.—There can be no simple *solution* of the Negro problem in the United States. We can hope gradually to improve the Negro's educational opportunities by providing schools equal to those of the whites, or better, by allowing him to share in the schools of the whites as is now possible in some parts of the country where there are but few Negroes. We can also increase his economic opportunity by removing many of the restrictions which prevent him from attaining an occupational status based on his ability to do the job, rather than on the fact that he is a Negro. With the improvement of his economic status which would follow on these changes in treatment there is no doubt that his general social status will improve. There is ample proof of this in the status attained by many Negroes in our northern cities. This, in turn, will make it easier to remove more of the social restrictions now imposed. Thus, gradually, the most degrading and

galling of the discriminations against the Negro could be relaxed without in any way interfering with the improvement of
living conditions among the whites. This would, of course,
involve the giving up of certain privileges and advantages by
some groups of whites. But this is always happening and, although always bitterly opposed by the group losing privileges,
must be regarded as a constant factor in social adjustment.
Such adjustments are, no doubt, opposed even more strenu-
ously when the group by whom the privileges are lost is a
majority racial group than when it is merely a different group
of the same race.

This slow relaxation of restrictions and improvement of
opportunities is not enough to satisfy many Negroes and we do
not argue here that it represents the *ideal*. Rather, it represents
the most that is *practicable* under the actual conditions that
now exist. To do less is a denial of the fundamentals of our
democratic belief; to do more, at once, will probably arouse
such fear and antagonism that there may well be a reaction
against the alleviations already made in the Negro's lot.

The Japanese.—The war has made the problems of the Japanese minority much more difficult. Some of the bitterness of
feeling manifested during the war will almost certainly disappear in the course of the next few years because of the
lessening of war tensions and because the Japanese appear likely
to be less concentrated on the West Coast than in the past. But
the Japanese, like the Negroes, are readily identifiable by their
physical characteristics, hence their complete assimilation into
the majority group is not to be looked for in the foreseeable
future. There is a rather strong probability that they will remain a small minority, suffering rather severe social and economic discriminations in areas where they are fairly numerous,
and denied participation in community life through neglect and
its accompanying isolation in communities where they are few
in numbers.

The Danger of Creating New Minorities.—Considering the fact that such large numbers of people from so many European nations have settled in this country it is perhaps surprising that we have so little discrimination against such groups. It is also somewhat surprising that there is so little antagonism between these groups themselves. Many of our immigrants have brought with them hatreds against other groups and, of course, speak different languages. They also have widely divergent cultural backgrounds. These differences have tended to promote a certain amount of segregation of immigrant groups and to arouse dislikes not only between the people already here and the immigrants, but also between different groups of immigrants.

Furthermore, it was to be expected that these different cultural backgrounds would lead different national groups to define "Americanism" differently. They came here for somewhat different reasons, even though economic reasons were dominant. It was, therefore, inevitable that we should have a considerable amount of social and economic discrimination against groups of immigrants. This is not said by way of excuse of such discrimination but only by way of explanation. If we of the majority group have been somewhat more tolerant of dissident groups than many other peoples it is probably because we have found it easier to make a living than most other peoples and have also had more opportunity to get acquainted with individuals from other national groups. But if we would prevent the creation of stubborn and militant minorities we must be careful not to attempt to force conformity of belief and action on dissident groups, except where it is absolutely essential to the general welfare and not merely to the welfare or dominance of other groups.

MINORITIES IN EUROPE

In Europe, with its long history of cultural differences between groups living in close proximity—differences which inevitably arose in a period when transportation was difficult and communication slow—there have been many minorities whose lives were made burdensome by the efforts of majorities to break up their established modes of living and thinking and to compel them to conform to those of the majority. Usually the most obvious feature of a minority in Europe is its language, which is different from that of the majority. But this difference is also associated, as a rule, with a manner of life based on different customs and traditions of long historical development. Then, too, there is frequently a different religious faith. Such a minority usually feels that all that is worth while in life is at stake when it is forbidden to have schools taught in its own language, or is asked to change its marriage rites, or submit to alterations in its system of land tenure, etc., etc., to conform to the ideas and modes of living of the majority. If it is also forbidden to participate on a basis of equality in the political life of the larger community, so that it seems to have only duties but no rights, it may very well become so antagonistic to the majority that it threatens the very existence of the political unit being cherished by the majority, especially if it can appeal for protection to a national group to which it is related by language or religion.

Language and Religious Minorities.—It is not possible to go into any detail here concerning the problems of any of these minorities. But, using language and religious affiliation as the basis of division between majority and minority, the data plotted in Figures 18 and 19 will give some idea of the size of the chief minority groups in several of the European countries in the interwar years.

Figures 18 and 19 are based on the census reports of the several countries. For this reason they may be assumed to understate the size of the minority groups to a certain extent, since during the interwar period every country was anxious to show that it was laying claim to as little population as possible which did not belong to the dominant group and that most of the territory it claimed was peopled by the dominant group.

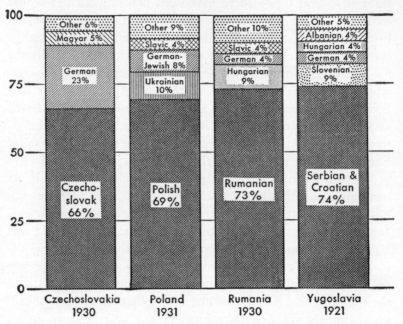

Figure 18. Language Distribution of the Population of Selected European Countries

Because of this desire, doubtful and unknown cases of mother tongue and religious affiliation were quite likely to be thrown in with the majority group. Where the minority problems of a country were particularly aggravating and attracted interest abroad there may even have been some deliberate falsification of records, although the writer knows of no evidence of such practices.

Primary Loyalties of Minorities.—In addition to differences in language and/or religion most European minorities have

quite a different pattern of daily habits and customs, such as
different farm practices, different types of houses, different
diets, different marriage customs, different forms of recreation,
etc., etc., which mark them off from their majority neighbors.
Under pressure from the majority the maintenance of all those
habits and customs which distinguish the minority from the

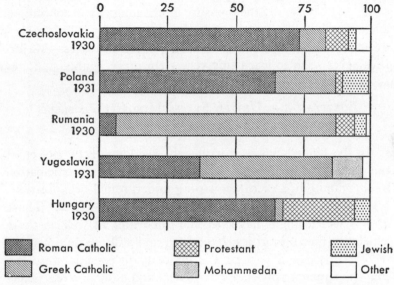

Figure 19. Religious Distribution of the Population of Selected
European Countries

majority has often come to be regarded as essential to group
survival. Even very trivial differences in customs are magni-
fied into basic differences, and loyalty to the minority in all
respects becomes the first law of life. Thus it is not uncommon
to find minorities adhering tenaciously to their own beliefs,
languages, and patterns of living even when it would be to
their distinct economic, political, and social advantage to as-
similate to the pattern of life of the majority. But, under pressure, acceptance of any belief or mode of behavior characteristic
of the majority comes to be regarded as a sign of betrayal of

their own group. It is easy to see that once such attitudes come to prevail it is almost impossible for these different groups to live together in amity. Usually such extreme differences in loyalties in groups living side by side in the same country are the result of force being used by the majority to compel the allegiance of the minority to the beliefs, ideals, and practices which the dominant group considers essential to the survival of its way of life. If the pressure on the minority is continuous and is harsh it usually drives people with minority beliefs underground, but does not eradicate the beliefs or practices. Majorities never seem to learn this very elementary truth.

EUROPEAN AND UNITED STATES MINORITY PROBLEMS CONTRASTED

In the United States, fortunately, we know little as yet of this deliberate withdrawal of the minority from participation in community life, or of the strong underground organizations formed to perpetuate minority ideals and practices. Those groups which might have become minorities as well as those which are now minorities, have been and still are anxious and ready to become a part of the majority in essential respects. The chief reason why they have social and economic character-istics (where they do have them) which distinguish them from the majority is that they are kept out of full participation in the life of the majority both by legislation (Jim Crow) and social discrimination. Racial differences in appearance (white and Negro), of course, cannot be eradicated. In Europe, on the other hand, many minorities have come to live to them-selves and to refuse to have more to do with the majority than is absolutely necessary. Probably because of discrimination against them in the first instance they want nothing but to be let alone to pursue their own lives in their own way.

In this country we have seen a little of this attitude in certain immigrant groups but it has seldom carried over into later generations, except in a few rural communities where there was a strong religious motive, and even then it has had little divisive influence. In the cities the children of immigrants have been unwilling to follow in the paths of their elders and have assimilated to the majority pattern of living at a pace as rapid as they knew how. The release from pressure by the majority, the manifest advantage of speaking English, the complete lack of any feeling that they are doing an honorable thing in refusing to adopt the habits of their neighbors, the relative mobility of people from community to community and many other factors have made most of our immigrants anxious to "become Americans." All this is so different from the attitudes of majorities and minorities in Europe that we have great difficulty in understanding that continent's minority problems, just as Europeans have great difficulty in understanding our greatest minority problem—the relations of whites and Negroes.

Before World War II.—The modern large nations of Europe grew by the welding together of small principalities and ethnic groups into larger units, generally under the leadership of one state which happened to be a little larger and more powerful or have more aggressive leadership than its immediate neighbors. Before this modern process of state building for many centuries there were no national boundaries and there was no common language extending over any considerable territory. In general one may say that during this prenationalistic era the barriers to the migration of any group were those due to the difficulty of moving, let us say from southern Austria to Rumania, or from Germany to Russia. These difficulties were very great. There were very few roads except local market roads, and such roads as existed were almost impassable most of the time. There was no way to secure reliable information regarding land which might be available for settlement and since probably 90 percent of the people were peasants, land was what was sought by most migrants. The mediums of exchange were all local so that travel for peasants was complicated by finding some way of supporting themselves by barter along the way. Furthermore, there were large numbers of local dialects so that it was often impossible for the uneducated peasant to communicate with other peasants only a few miles distant in the next valley or across the river.

On the other hand, there were no national boundaries and passports and many of the petty rulers were glad to have industrious and hardy peasants settle on their domains if unused land was available. Besides, during the ascendency of the Holy Roman Empire one could move over a good part of central Europe and still remain within its sphere of influence. But probably the most potent factors driving peasants to seek new homes although by no means the only factors, were the wars of religion and the accompanying persecution of dissenters which from time to time swept over many parts of Europe but were especially devastating in Central Europe. The people were driven from their homes rather than attracted to new lands.

But whatever the reasons for migrating, or whatever other conditions resulted in the existence of relatively small islands of people with different language, different culture, and perhaps different religion, most such groups became minorities as the feeling of nationalism developed when nations were established and when national boundaries were drawn. They became minority problems when the dominant group began to press for political and cultural unity and to regard allegiance to its aims and ways of life as the test of a desirable citizen.

Ever since the development of modern nationalism, therefore, a number of European nations, but particularly those of Central Europe, have been plagued by minority problems. These islands of alien peoples whose primary loyalties were to their small local community rather than to the nation became a festering sore in the body politic. If one will study Figure

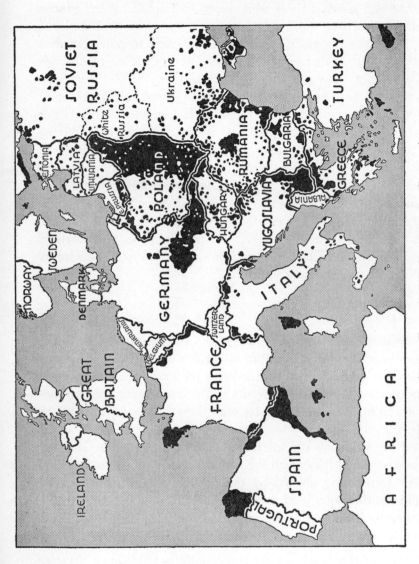

Figure 20. Where Europe's Principal Minority Groups Are

Reproduced from Headline Book, *Human Dynamite*, by permission of the Foreign Policy Association.

20 he will see that there were many such small "alien" groups in many parts of Europe.[1]

This was the situation when Hitler came to power, a situation almost made to order for one bent on creating trouble for the other nations of Central Europe. One of the theories on which nazism rested was that German blood was superior in quality to that of all other peoples. Hence, as soon as Hitler felt secure at home he began to agitate the return of all the "superior" German-speaking minorities to the Fatherland, in order to create a greater Germany. Where these Germans were living next to Germany, as in Czechoslovakia and Poland, their lands were to be annexed to Germany. Where they were to be "repatriated" (sometimes after hundreds of years of settlement in their then homes) they were to be settled on new German lands which were to be taken from such "inferior" peoples as the Poles and Russians.

MINORITIES SINCE 1938

It would take several chapters even to summarize briefly the data on what has happened to minorities since 1938. It will be necessary, therefore, to confine our remarks here to the mere mention of the principal events in the manipulation of minorities from the time the nazis went into Czechoslovakia up to the present.

Nazi Germany did all in its power to make the German-speaking minorities of all the Central European states feel that they were being abused by the Czechs, the Rumanians, the Italians, the Poles, and other peoples and to arouse in them a desire to be joined to Germany in one great German nation which would then have a population of about 80 million. The

---

[1] A word of caution is in order here. Not all the populations in the areas marked black on this map presented real minority problems. In Western Europe such problems were of little consequence but in Central Europe and reaching east into Western Russia minorities were numerous and in many cases the relations between majorities and minorities had become so embittered that national unity could not be counted on in times of stress.

nazis, of course, tended to exaggerate the number of German-speaking people living in other nations but even without Austria and the Sudetenland of Czechoslovakia there were probably

Figure 21. The Rumanians and Their Minorities

Reproduced from Headline Book, *Human Dynamite,* by permission of the Foreign Policy Association.

somewhere from 4 to 6 million Volksdeutsche (German-speaking people living in other nations) who could be brought "home" if land could be found for them.

The absorption of Austria and the Sudetenland were the first steps in the consolidation of all the German-speaking peoples of Europe. For all other homecoming Germans (Volksdeutsche), except a few in Poland, new land was needed and that part of Poland adjoining Germany on the east was the most desirable. Immediately after Poland was conquered the clearing of the Poles and Jews out of Western Poland was begun and by treaty with the Baltic states the Balts (Volksdeutsche) were evacuated from the Baltic states and moved into the former Western Poland. By treaty with Italy, Hungary, Rumania, and the Soviet Union in due course it was agreed to move other Volksdeutsche into the "incorporated provinces" of Poland and to exchange populations of certain areas in the German and Russian parts of Poland and Germans from the portion of Rumania conquered by the Russians. By the summer of 1942 it is believed that about 750,000 Volksdeutsche had been transferred to Greater Germany, but there were still far more to come.

By the summer of 1942, however, it appeared to the nazis that they would have land not only in Poland on which to settle the Volksdeutschen but plenty of room in the Ukraine and Bessarabia. Hence, the nazis changed their policy and began to use the Volksdeutschen in these areas to expand the German Empire into the conquered regions and indeed sent many residents from Germany proper (Reichsdeutsche) into them to assure full nazi control.

With the defeat of the Germans at Stalingrad and the retreat of their armies westward the whole scheme of German resettlement was upset. But it had gone far enough to displace a vast number of Poles and replace them with Germans and to start German settlement in a few other areas.

As the Russian armies moved westward these German settlers fled before them and, in addition, most of the Germans in East Prussia, the western part of Poland, and in the part of Germany east of the Elbe and the Neisse rivers were driven westward. Likewise, many of the Germans in the Balkans, who had, in general, welcomed the nazis, were also driven out. Poland and Czechoslovakia have been busy ever since the end of the war "repatriating" German minorities which did not flee with the German armies. Thus the German minorities in Central Europe have been "liquidated" by the war to a considerable extent.

The pattern of clearing out minorities by forced mass migration of which the nazis made so much use is apparently continuing. One reads of the exchange of populations between Czechoslovakia and Hungary, Hungary and Rumania, Hungary and Yugoslavia, etc., etc. There seems to be little doubt that minorities are being shifted about, much like pieces on a checkerboard, but just what is being done is not known in detail. One thing, however, seems reasonably certain; the people who think of themselves as Czechs, Hungarians, Rumanians, etc., will be more "pure" national groups than in the past. An ethnic map of Rumania as of today will certainly not look like Figure 21, which presents her pre-World War II ethnic composition. Nevertheless, preliminary results of her recent census indicate that Rumania has not yet succeeded in freeing herself entirely of minorities. Is this mass movement of minorities in Central Europe likely to continue until minorities disappear as political problems in Europe? No positive answer can be given to this question. We do know, however, that there is a minority problem in Trieste, that Yugoslavia, even after the expulsion of Germans, and its exchanges of population and territory with other Balkan powers, is made up of several ethnic groups which have heretofore been unable to get along together. We also know that if Greece should be broken up several minorities will be created, that there is still a German minority in Northern Italy, and that Rumania still has significant minorities of several nationalities. Even with considerable further mass migration of minority groups it does not seem likely that all minorities can be joined to majorities elsewhere by this process although the situation may be much ameliorated in the long run by this removal of minorities. It would be a great mistake, however, to suppose that the removal of minorities and the consolidation of ethnic groups will eliminate the causes of national frictions in Central Europe, since many of these causes were and are in no way connected with minorities. There will remain many causes for friction between Magyars and Rumanians although they may not be so embittered by the existence of minorities as in the past. Poles and Russians will not cease to dislike one another just because they are no longer intermixed and each is living on his own side of a given line, which the Poles at least think is in the wrong place.

Minorities in the Soviet Union.—Finally, attention should be called to the situation of ethnic minorities in the Soviet Union. It appears that much progress is being made in breaking down the barriers which have kept apart the Great Russians (the dominant group) and the scores of minor ethnic groups which are contained within the Soviet Union. The hostility of these groups in the past was no doubt in part the result of a deliberate Czarist policy to divide and rule but it also arose out of differences in language, culture, and religion. On the whole it seems no mean achievement to have drawn these many peoples together so that they could carry their part of a great war to a successful end.

The various measures taken to create a unified people out of the great number of ethnic groups found within the Union cannot even be enumerated here. The chief factor seems to be putting into practice the belief that though peoples may have different cultures they are equal, that only individuals are unequal and then largely because of different behavior based on different cultural patterns. The acceptance of this doctrine eliminates all reason for excluding anyone from any social or political position because of his racial or ethnic origin. Although it is scarcely to be expected that this belief is fully lived up to in practice there can be no doubt that progress is being made and that the outlook for the elimination of ethnic differences as a cause of internal strife is hopeful.

On the other hand, it must be recognized that dissident minority groups which might support a system of private property or believe in what we call democratic freedom are suppressed or even eliminated with utter ruthlessness by the Soviet authorities, supported by a relatively small minority. Thus, while the Soviet Union seems to have made a successful beginning in the elimination of ethnic and racial minorities by its sensible treatment of them it has developed no tolerance for economic and political minorities which believe in private enterprise and personal freedom. Nor does it appear to have any tolerance for them anywhere else. We in this country have far more tolerance for minorities holding dissident economic doctrines. Only occasionally have we persecuted such groups and never to the extent of driving them underground and making of them a compact and powerful revolutionary minority, although there are indications that we may now be moving in that direction.

Such considerations lead one to believe that, in the long run, only the development of a more enlightened justice and tolerance, along with a fundamental faith in democracy, interpreted as a belief in and respect for certain basic personal rights, will ever solve all of our minority problems. We certainly have a long way yet to go in learning to be tolerant of dissident groups —but we are accumulating a little experience here and there which shows us how they may be made to feel that they are a part of the community and that it is to their advantage to cooperate with the majority, even while retaining a large measure of personal freedom. Minority or dissident groups never learn this by force, but only by being given a real and equal share in the life of the community and by being shown that they do not have to give up anything fundamental to their integrity in thus becoming a participant group.

CHAPTER 14

POPULATION POLICIES

Current Interest in Population Policies

The greatly enhanced interest in population matters in recent years, particularly in population policies,[1] has arisen largely as a consequence of the emphasis put upon population questions by the fascists and nazis. In a world which is rapidly increasing in numbers, however, fascist and nazi concern with population matters was by no means the only stimulant to greater interest in such questions. Everywhere informed people were beginning to ask whether we had too many people, particularly in certain countries, whether differential birth rates were leading to undesirable results both within nations and between nations and whether there was any connection between war and man's growth in numbers. But even so, the population doctrines of the totalitarian governments aroused more interest in population than even those of the social scientists had and when these doctrines were put into operation they could no longer be ignored.

As early as 1924 Mussolini was talking about the fairly rapid growth of Italy's population and the difficulties of providing this population a decent living. But, quite contrary to his earlier position, taken when he was a socialist journalist, Mussolini opposed birth-control propaganda. By the end of 1926 birth-control propaganda and the display and sale of contraceptive devices were forbidden by decree and by 1927 Mussolini was talking about the need of an empire for a growing

---

[1] For an excellent detailed discussion of European population policies as they were before World War II see D. V. Glass, *Population Policies and Movements in Europe,* New York: Oxford University Press, 1940.

population and very clearly implied that Italy should become an empire. "With a falling population one does not create an empire but becomes a colony."

The nazis had clearly indicated their belief in the need of a large and growing population even before their advent to power. In fact, there was quite a school of thought in Germany antedating the nazis which deplored the declining birth rate as a danger to the power of Germany and the prestige of German culture. The nazis placed new emphasis on the importance of breeding from "pure" German stock and strengthening the power and prestige of the "master race."

It was probably the growing realization of the dangers of fascism and nazism to the peace of the world which called attention to their population policies and aroused many thinking people throughout the West to give consideration to population policies as a factor in the welfare of nations and of the world. Lest this opinion give the impression that other peoples had given no consideration to population policies it should be pointed out that many French people had long been concerned over the relative decline in France's population. After the Franco-Prussian War there was much discussion of France's need for a larger population, a discussion which was greatly intensified for a time after World War I. But this discussion in France aroused far less interest abroad than the more active implementation of population policies by the fascists and nazis. The fact is that very few people were even mildly interested in population matters before Mussolini and Hitler called them so forcibly to attention. This is unfortunate because the very term "population policy" has come to be associated in the minds of many people with authoritarian government, whereas there is no essential connection between them. In fact, efforts to control population growth so that it will contribute to community welfare are by no means of recent origin, nor have they been confined to peoples of Western Civilization.

Ever since the dawn of history there have been peoples who made more or less successful efforts to control their population growth. Some of these attempts have had qualitative aims (the exposure of weakling infants in Sparta) but for the most part they were concerned with the control of numbers. Furthermore, they were generally the result of local custom and tradition rather than the organized attempt of a government wielding power over a large population to secure the numbers it desired. Anthropologists also tell us that they find many tribal population policies among peoples who have no recorded history, the main purpose of which was to secure the survival of the tribe. Survival necessarily involves adaptation to environment and to the conditions created by the existence of competing tribes and peoples, hence these primitive population policies may be regarded as a part of the folklore developed to insure survival.

During the last two centuries Western peoples have, by and large, had comparatively little interest in population policies because population growth and changes, like other social changes, were supposed to work out to the greatest welfare of the nation or the community if no effort were made at public control, i.e., if a *laissez-faire* policy were followed. As a result the growth of population in the Western World has been almost incidental, a by-product, of the social, economic, and scientific development of this era in this region. Just because it has continued for so long and has been, in general, accompanied by increasing welfare, population growth has come to be regarded as natural, and talk of population policy is looked upon as something new and perhaps dangerous. But the operation of population policies is certainly not new and the establishment of such policies will be dangerous only if they are used for ends which are in themselves inimical to the general welfare.

The Population Policies of China

In order to indicate how population policies have generally operated in the past it may not be amiss to describe very briefly how China succeeded in maintaining and, perhaps, in slowly increasing her population throughout the centuries and how this policy is now creating serious problems.

Importance of the Family.—The whole system of ethical values in China as developed by Confucius and other ethical and religious leaders encouraged the maintenance of population. It placed supreme value on the continuity of the family and the duty of everyone to see that his family did not die out. If, because of accidents and personal deficiencies, either ethical or physical, a family seemed likely to die out, the customs provided not only for the taking of concubines but also for the adoption of children to insure its continuity. Since adoption of sons frequently involved breaking the blood line this practice constituted definite recognition that the continuity of family tradition was not necessarily dependent on biological continuity. But there should be no misunderstanding of the accepted policy, which demanded that if at all possible the family have male blood issue to carry on. Under the conditions determining the death rate this meant in effect that several sons should be born in order to insure the survival and reproduction of at least one.

The ethical values cherished by Chinese civilization were not thought of as constituting a population policy but they were such in fact, and have been highly effective both in accomplishing the ends aimed at by the ethical leaders of China and in securing the survival of the Chinese people. That they have also led to the growth of the Chinese over the centuries is probably just as incidental as our own growth in the West during the past two centuries or so has been to the pursuit of our personal and national welfare. With the high birth rate, insured by the great desire for family continuity, Chinese population was quite certain to grow whenever the food supply became a little easier and thus reduced the death rate, or when disease was a little less devastating than usual, also reducing the death rate.

The ethical values of the Chinese, which in effect determined their population policy, are still operating in a large part of the population which is now probably several times as large as it was some centuries ago. But the economic and social organization of China is undergoing changes which will, in the course of time, work changes in the actual habits and beliefs of the people and thus effect changes in population policy. But Western experience shows that effective changes in population policy will lag behind the economic changes which will, for a time at least, reduce the death rate. Hence, the age-old traditional population policy of China will almost certainly make much trouble for her in coming years because it will lead to an increase in numbers which cannot be supported except at an extremely low level of living, much as at present.

The main purpose in this brief mention of Chinese population policy is not to show how it is ill-adapted to present conditions, although it is very important for the Chinese to realize this, but to show how population policies are more or less unconsciously developed and become effective even though they are not thought of as population policies. This has probably been the usual procedure in past ages.

GROUP CONTROL OF REPRODUCTION

Many other examples of effective but unconscious community control over population growth might be cited. All would bear out the contention that many peoples have had population policies which more or less determined the birth rate or the death rate or both. In general, these policies have been effected through the development of a set of ethical values believed to be essential to group survival. The implication of these policies has always been that reproduction is not an individual matter to be left to individual whim but a matter for community concern because it affects the survival of the group and its relations to other groups. It is the treatment of reproduction as a purely individual matter of no concern to the community that is exceptional. It is our attitude in the West today which is "out of step" with history and with other peoples, rather than the other way about. We should realize this although we may think it better kept that way. We should also realize that we in the West have not been so completely without population policies as we commonly assume. Let us now turn briefly to the discussion of some of the population policies which have recently been promulgated and whose effectuation has actually been undertaken.

GERMANY'S POPULATION POLICIES

For some years (since 1933) the population policies of the nazis attracted a great deal of interest. The first feature of their policy to attract attention was their effort to increase numbers. Only later did the significance of the qualitative features of their policy become clear. The immediate source of the nazi desire to increase numbers, whatever its ultimate ideological base, was found in the fall of the German birth rate (see Chapter 2). The crude birth rate fell rather steadily in the late 1920's and was only 14.7 in 1933. When expressed in terms of its sufficiency for maintaining the population it was then only about 70 percent of that needed for mere maintenance.

BIRTH STIMULANTS

The nazis began to put their population policies into effect almost at once. The measures they took to increase the birth rate were of two general kinds which may be called negative and positive: (1) the negative measures were calculated to restrict the freedom of the individual to control births and consisted chiefly of efforts to reduce abortion and to make contraception more difficult, (2) the positive measures may be further divided into (a) economic assistance, consisting of measures intended to ease the economic burden of establishing and maintaining a family, and (b) psychological conditioning, consisting of measures aimed at developing attitudes of mind more favorable to the raising of larger families.

Negative Measures.—The measures against abortion consisted chiefly in more rigid enforcement of laws already enacted and definite police drives against abortion centers. This more rigid enforcement of the abortion laws was claimed to have had an almost immediate effect on the number of abortions. If this was the case, and it probably was, a reasonable assumption is that it would show up a few months later in an increase in births. The birth rate did rise early in 1934 before the other measures discussed below would have had time to show much effect.

A second type of repressive measure intended to raise the birth rate was to make contraceptive information and devices more difficult to secure. The sale of devices was not prohibited but their advertisment was stopped and all birth control clinics were closed. With birth control thus made more difficult to practice and more uncertain of effect, and with abortion made more dangerous, there was likely to be an even closer relation than usual between the number of marriages in one year and births in the following year.

Positive Measures: Economic

Marriage Loans.—The first of the economic measures adopted by the nazis was the marriage loan. All students of population recognize that an increase in the number of marriages is followed in due time by an increase in the number of births (see Chapter 2). Acting on this knowledge, the nazis arranged that any couple fulfilling certain conditions could get a marriage loan to help them set up housekeeping. The maximum amount of the loans was 1,000 marks but the average was probably not much more than half that amount. The chief conditions determining the granting of a loan were that the couple should be politically acceptable to the nazi authorities, of good stock (German), and that the bride-to-be had been working before marriage but would agree not to work outside the home unless the husband's income were unusually low or the marriage loan had been repaid. This last provision was relaxed after 1937, when labor became scarce.

The marriage loan was made in the form of coupons which could only be used for the purchase of certain specified types of household goods. Thus at the same time that it enabled couples to marry and set up housekeeping earlier than would have been possible otherwise, it also encouraged an increase in the production of household goods, and helped to reduce unemployment. In fact, the suggestion has been made that at first marriage loans were intended as a measure to reduce unemployment rather than as a measure to encourage marriage. But in the light of other nazis population policies this seems rather unlikely.

The marriage loan carried a low rate of interest and was largely repayable in children. No payment became due until a year after marriage and if a child was born during this period there was a cancellation of one fourth of the debt and a further postponement of any repayment for a year. If four children were born within four years the entire debt was cancelled and even if the four children were somewhat more widely spaced there would be only a few months in which one percent of the original loan need be paid.

Altogether, 1,770,775 couples had received marriage loans through December 1941, a period of almost eight and one half years, and there had been partial cancellation of loans on account of a total of 1,959,963 children, an average of only 1.1 children per marriage, although less than one eleventh had been married less than one year. That this number of couples availed themselves of marriage loans does not mean that the total number of marriages taking place 1933-1941 was increased by this number. Most of these marriages would have taken place in any event. But there can be little doubt that a good many marriages were hastened by the ability to secure a loan, and it seems probable that a considerable number of births were advanced somewhat because of the cancellation feature. There is much more doubt, however, as to whether the total number of births per couple was significantly increased by these marriage loans. A calculation by the writer shows that although the "loan" marriages entered into between August 1933 and October 1, 1940, had endured on the average about 4.7 years by January 1, 1942 (assuming no broken marriages), the average number of children born to these marriages was only 1.2. This certainly does not indicate any very high birth rate among the marriage-loan couples. Furthermore, our experience in the United States shows that the number of marriages began to rise here about the same time as in Germany and that the birth rate also rose in due course although not as rapidly as in Germany.

Family Allowances.—Another economic measure to encourage a higher birth rate was to grant parents, and especially parents of large families, certain allowances towards support of their children. These allowances were in cash, in goods, and services. Some consisted of a single payment and some were paid regularly, e.g., each month. In the former class were payments made and services rendered in connection with the birth of a child and the grant made to the father of a large family to enable him to buy a small plot of ground in the country, or on the edge of the city, where he could live more cheaply than in the city itself. In the latter class were payments and services more or less regular in character and intended to lighten the economic burden of children month by month. These regular payments increased somewhat more than proportionally with each child above four. Altogether, these aids were quite substantial in the case of large families but not substantial enough to offset the economic disadvantage of the large family when compared with the small family, the fathers of both having similar incomes from their work.

Remission of Taxes.—The abatement of taxes according to the number of dependent children was another means used to assist the larger families. The tax reduction on account of children was much more substantial in proportion to total income than our own income tax deductions for children. It continued until 25 years of age in the case of children taking advanced schooling. The taxes thus lost were recouped by heavier taxes on the unmarried and childless.

Miscellaneous Economic Measures.—In addition to the above there were a number of other less helpful measures but which in the aggregate rendered rather substantial economic assistance to families of four or more children. In some cities the children in the larger families were promised preferential treatment in city jobs when they grew up. The fathers of large families were often promised more steady work and promotion, and various bonuses and prizes were awarded to "child-rich" families. However, these bonuses not infrequently were important as psychological rather than economic stimulants of the birth rate.

Finally, not because the list of economic benefits has been exhausted but because space does not permit the enumeration of all the minor items, some of the professions were organized to collect contributions from those having larger incomes and from those with few or no children, the money thus "contributed" being allotted to those with larger families. Although this might be thought of as an additional income tax, it was said to be voluntary and was handled by the profession itself (e.g., doctors, dentists, etc.) and not through government channels. It was probably as voluntary as anything of this sort could be in a totalitarian state, which means that it was highly compulsory according to our standards.

The dominating motive back of this economic assistance to the family, with its emphasis on large families, was no doubt the desire of the nazi party to make Germany a great power able to rule Europe, and perhaps a great deal more, as well as a profound belief in the inherent superiority of the German people. The form of the assistance indicates that it was based on the conviction that in modern industrialized Germany children constituted such a definite economic liability that people could not be expected to raise families large enough to maintain the population, to say nothing of increasing it, if the community did not assume part of their cost.

POSITIVE MEASURES: PSYCHOLOGICAL

Spiritual Rebirth.—The psychological stimulants may be described very simply as progaganda aimed at building up an attitude of mind more favorable to raising larger families. The future of the Third Reich was pictured in glowing terms and one in which the position of the "master race" was to be highly exalted. To attain this exalted position and to maintain its dominance, the "master race" should grow rapidly in numbers. It would require present sacrifice of luxury and perhaps even of some comfort to raise more children, but this was well worth while in view of the glorious future which awaited this superior race. In addition, every possible appeal was made to the people to be loyal to the "Leader" by raising larger families in accordance with his wishes. The nazis explained the increase which took place in the birth rate as due chiefly to the rebirth of Germany caused by Hitler's leadership. He aroused the people from the lethargy of defeatism and infused them not only with a will to live but to expand and to take a place in the world consonant with their great natural superiority. Since they were also told that they could not be dominant long if they did not have more children they were supposed to have responded to this new atmosphere of hope and to have raised their birth rate. Some comments on the effects of this "psychological rebirth" will be made later.

In the very nature of the case there could be no clearly defined boundary between what was intended to help instill the whole nazi scale of values in the minds of the people, particularly in those of the youth, and what was designed to encourage a new attitude towards raising larger numbers of children. These two aims were inseparable. The propaganda for larger families was only part of the larger effort to indoctrinate the German people with a new philosophy of life, with a new faith in their great destiny and a strong desire to participate in this destiny through their children.

Finally, when any effort is made to evaluate the influence of this propaganda for larger families on the birth rate it must be remembered that the concrete economic measures noted above were operating at the same time and, at best, only a very rough approximation can be made of the separate influence of these several factors on the birth rate.

Hereditary Peasant Holdings.—The close relation between the economic and psychological measures is well illustrated in the effort to prevent the moving of rural people to the cities and to build up an hereditary peasantry on relatively small farms (40-50 acres). It will be recalled in this connection that everywhere farmers and other people living in definitely rural environments have larger families than city people. Two definite measures calculated to maintain this favorable rural attitude towards large families were adopted by the nazis. Despite the fact that they were not altogether new to Germany the nazis, as would be expected, claimed them for their own and gave them a definitely nazi twist. The first of these measures consisted in breaking up larger estates into relatively small family farms—a process long under way in Germany—to be purchased on easy terms by the proper persons (racially and politically) as family estates. A farm thus acquired had to remain in the family and could not be divided, although the son inheriting it had certain financial obligations to his brothers and sisters. The peasantry thus created was supposed to represent an elite group which would furnish a disproportionately large share of the soldiers and workers for a greater Germany. A second measure assisted farm laborers to purchase small plots of land for a home in rural communities. In this way it was hoped to prevent some of the rural exodus which had been as great in Germany as in the United States.

Such measures may be regarded as either primarily psychological or economic. If one is thinking chiefly of helping to maintain all those rural attitudes of mind which are favorable to relatively large families, then the psychological aspects will seem the more important. If, on the other hand, one is thinking of the practical measures needed to keep a large agricultural population on the land, then the economic aids to the peasants will seem the more important. These two aspects of the scheme were, of course, quite inseparable.

The Function of Women.—The nazis placed much emphasis on the function of women as the producers of the race and frowned upon careers for women. The girls, from the time they were eight or ten years old, were drilled in the belief that it was their duty to furnish children for the Greater Germany which was to come, just as it was the duty of the male to work and fight to achieve this dream.

The State and Children.—In addition, we are all familiar with the persistent effort of the nazis to break down the individual's allegiance to the family, to the church, to the local community, to the lodge, and to all existing institutions while building up a new allegiance to the *state* and to the *leader*. At all points this scale of nazi values emphasized the importance to Germany of more children and that the new Germany could not take its proper place in the world if the people did not raise bigger families.

It was inevitable, therefore, that the state should take over more and more of the training of children and should assume more of the economic cost of children even while they remained in the family. The logical conclusion from the nazi doctrine that all individuals belonged to the state and should eschew all action which the governing class deemed injurious to the state was that reproduction should be directed by the state. But, as we have seen, great effort was made to form the minds of the people so that they would willingly accept the dictates of the state regarding both the amount of their reproduction and the manner of bringing up their children.

SUCCESS OF THE GERMAN POLICIES

Changes in the Birth Rate.—Naturally we are much interested in measuring the success of the population policies described above. Unfortunately, we cannot say with any precision how effective they were, as a whole, or in any of their parts. But the data on births do show that there was an increase of about one fourth in the crude rate from the low point of the depression in 1933 up to 1936, and that from then until 1941 this higher rate was maintained or slightly increased. By 1936 the German birth rate had increased sufficiently to raise it from only about 70 percent of replacement to virtual replacement. After 1941, however, the birth rate declined and by the middle of 1942 had again fallen well below replacement level.

Population Policies and Economic Recovery.—In attempting to assess the effects of nazi population policies it must be recognized that the effects of the various economic measures adopted to encourage marriage and assist larger families cannot possibly be separated from the effects that would have followed the improvement in economic conditions, even had there been no definite effort to encourage a higher birth rate. The basis for this statement is found in the changes in marriage rates and birth rates in Sweden and the United States (see Chapter 2) as economic conditions improved, although no definite measures were taken in either country to encourage such increases. As was said above, it has been long known that marriage rates and birth rates respond rather quickly in the short run to the deterioration or improvement of economic conditions, and there is some reason to believe that the increase in these rates in Germany following the acquisition of power by the nazis was to a large extent the normal response to such improvement rather than the direct consequence of the pro-natal measures adopted.

Nazi Arithmetic of Births.—The nazis did not admit that economic recovery was of any importance in raising the birth rate. They figured the situation out about as follows: In the first place they assumed that without their definite measures to increase the *number* of births in Germany this number would have remained the same as it was at the bottom of the depression in 1933. Hence, all the increase after that time was the consequence of their policies. Of the increase of about 1.5 million in births during the six years from 1933-38 they held that about 600,000 took place on account of increased marriages, all of which they believed were due to marriage loans, and that an additional 900,000 births were due to increased fertility stimulated both by the economic measures taken and the psychological rebirth of the nation. Continuing this method of calculation up to 1942, a good nazi would have claimed a total of about 2.5 to 3.0 million additional births as the result of their population policy. This would just about make up for Germany's *direct* war losses (see Chapter 5).

It goes without saying that the unbiased demographer cannot accept the nazi view of the effectivness of their pro-natal policies. Let us see how this type of reasoning would work out for the United States. The total increase in births in the United States, 1934-42, above what it would have been at the 1933 level, was 2.17 million. If this were divided in the same proportion between increased marriages and increased fertility, as the nazis divided the German increase, we would get 860,000 additional births due to additional marriages and 1,310,000 due to increased fertility. This is a considerably smaller increase proportionally than took place in Germany but none of this increase of births in the United States was due to the stimulation of definite population policies. It came as the result of recovery from the depression, a recovery which was considerably slower in this country than in Germany.

Discount of Nazi Claims.—Thus it seems that we must largely discount the nazi claims of the effectiveness of their population policies as such, while recognizing that the widespread economic improvement following 1933, for which the nazis may properly claim some credit, did increase the marriage rate. This, in turn, led to an increase in the number of first and second births in due course of time, thus raising the general birth rate. It is by no means certain, however, that it led to larger average families even up to the time that Germany began to suffer military reverses, and if it did the increase was not large. Perhaps as much of this increase should be attributed to the suppression of birth control clinics and abortion and the greater difficulty of securing contraceptive devices as is attributed to the positive economic measures intended to induce the establishment of more families and the bearing of more children.

Effectiveness of Propaganda.—But though we must largely discount nazi claims for the effectiveness of their population policies in increasing the birth rate we should not conclude that these policies were without any effect. It is the opinion of the writer that they had some effect, that a good many people believing that a better day was dawning for Germany were encouraged to marry and start families who would not have done so without the stimulus of nazi propaganda and economic aid. The answer that will be made to this view is that the most effective propaganda for births among any people is better economic conditions and a more secure future. It may be so, but nazi propaganda was not entirely without effect. There is no good reason to deny that a belief in an ideal—in this case a future Greater Germany—and the conviction that children are essential to the realization of this ideal, would not be a sufficient motive to induce convinced devotees of this ideal to sacrifice present comfort and ease to its attainment. Such devotion to ideals has many times been effective in arousing people to great self-sacrifice and why should it not have operated in nazi Germany? No one denies that there were, perhaps are, many Germans, especially among the young, who are ardent believers in the nazi philosophy. Why would they not be as willing to have children to carry forward these aims as to make the many other personal sacrifices required of them in building up a nazi state? These are the reasons why the writer is disposed to give somewhat more credence to the nazi claims of having raised the German birth rate than a good many students of population. But again it should be said that these claims must be heavily discounted and the greater part of the credit for the increase in the birth rate from 1932-42 must go to the general improvement in economic conditions which continued up to about the end of 1940, and to the nazis' great military successes which continued almost to the end of 1942.

POPULATION POLICIES IN OTHER EUROPEAN COUNTRIES

Italy.—Little need be said about the population policies of Italy. They were adopted for the same basic reasons as those of Germany but, compared with the latter, they were fainthearted and do not seem to have aroused any considerable enthusiasm even among the fascists. The Italians, although urged incessantly by the fascists, did not increase their birth rate, probably because there was less economic improvement there than in a number of other countries and partly because, unlike most Western European countries, Italy still had a fair rate of natural increase. The Italian policies in effect at the time Italy entered the war (1940), although being continually strengthened, remained a rather feeble imitation of the German.

France.—The French population policy, until the decree issued on this matter in 1939, was a more or less haphazard affair. Up to that time most of the economic assistance had been administered by private agencies and funds. In the legal measures taken to encourage the birth rate, the prohibition of abortion and the forbidding of the display and sale of contraceptive devices had bulked large. The French policy was even weaker than the Italian as far as offering any real economic inducement to a higher birth rate was concerned, and there was no well-organized official propaganda for larger families as in Italy and Germany. Moreover, in spite of the evident fact that France's population had been growing more slowly for some decades than that of her European neighbors, there had never been a thorough official study of the entire population situation in France. The data on population, of course, came largely from official sources but they were publicized largely by private individuals and societies and the propaganda for a far-reaching population policy came from private sources. Up to the outbreak of World War II there is no proof whatever that French population policies had any effect on the birth rate. The most that might possibly be said about their accomplishment is that they may have somewhat retarded the decline of the birth rate. It may seem rather odd that this was the case, for a considerable number of individuals in France have been concerned over her low birth rate for a longer time than in any other country.

However, the population decree of 1939 was really the first determined official effort to set up a comprehensive population policy. Since it never became operative it furnishes no evidence as to how the French would respond to a rather thoroughgoing effort to increase the birth rate. In saying this it is understood that French attitudes toward reproduction are quite different from German attitudes and that even vigorous measures after the German pattern to encourage larger families might not have had the same effect in France. It should also be pointed out that without any well-organized population policy and without any substantial economic aid the French birth rate has risen significantly in the last four or five years. Indeed, it is quite possible that the economic difficulties of caring for a family have increased at the very time the birth rate has been rising. It began to rise even before the liberation and by 1947 had reached a crude rate of 20-21, which would not only replace France's population but add a little to it year by year if it were maintained. Up to this time French experience in encouraging larger families has little to tell us regarding the measures which might be effective for this purpose.

Sweden.—Sweden, too, became much concerned over the decline in her birth rate, which stood at about 73 percent of replacement level in 1933. In rather characteristic fashion the Swedes decided that if they were to do anything about raising their birth rate until it would maintain their numbers they should study the whole question very carefully and then act on well-established facts. A Commission was appointed to investigate Sweden's population question. It made a careful and thorough study of all aspects of the question and in due course Parliament adopted an official population program which it was hoped would not only raise the birth rate enough to maintain the population at its current numbers but would improve the quality of the people from the standpoint of health, education, and ability to participate in a democratic society.

The Swedish population policy is predicated on the belief that a democratic population policy must be based on the will of the people. It assumes that the voluntary control of births will and should become practically universal and that every child should be a *wanted* child. It aims to take a part of the burden of raising the next generation off the shoulders of the poorer people, who now have the larger families, and place it on the community which desires to maintain its numbers at a certain level. The hope is clearly present that the people as a whole will take an active interest in and participate in the raising of the next generation, that reproduction will not be left to chance. Furthermore, the measures taken show beyond doubt the intent that every child shall have a good start in life regardless of the social and economic position of his parents, and that he shall not be made to feel he is the recipient of charity when the community provides opportunities for a good start in life which his family cannot provide from its own means. The Swedes also consider their policy more fundamentally democratic because it will provide for the needs of children more in the form of goods and services—better housing and food, more complete health service and education, etc.—and less in the form of cash to the parents than the German, the French, or the Italian policies did.

A careful examination of the different policies, however, leads the author to think that this emphasis in the Swedish plan on assistance to children in kind, instead of to parents in money, is primarily a sugar-coating designed to make the increased cost to the community for the care of children more palatable to the well-to-do classes whose taxes are certain to be increased by any such reform. The basic democracy of the Swedish plan is shown in its recognition of the right of parents to decide on the size of their families, in the belief in the right of every child to have a good start in life, and in the clear statement that no child can have a good start in life if he or his family is assisted in such a way as to make him feel inferior, rather than by greater assistance in kind.

From this brief statement it is evident that the Swedish program places more emphasis on the right of children to a good home, to adequate medical care, to a healthy diet, and to proper education and training than on the need for more children, but believes that if parents can be assured of having their children well cared for in these respects they will be willing to have enough children to maintain their population at its present level. Whether this is true remains to be seen. The question of what is the best form in which to grant the increased aid for the improvement of living conditions for children which must come from the state, is unimportant from the standpoint of making the Swedish policy democratic. The form in which aid shall be granted is purely a matter of expediency which may very properly receive a different answer in each nation. It may be better for state aid to take one form in Sweden, let us say direct services to *all* children, but a somewhat different form in France, e.g., larger cash allowances to the family, because of the different structures of the two societies and the different attitudes towards various kinds of aid which prevail in them. There is no reason to think that one scheme is less democratic than the other, provided the aims of both are to provide the essentials of decent living to all citizens, and provided the people feel the measures used are consistent with what they believe to be their rights and their personal dignity.

Since only a small part of the Swedish program had been put into effect before the war interfered and since Sweden, like the United States, had a considerable increase in marriages and births as the depression passed and prosperity came with the war, there is probably less urgency now in putting the full program into effect. It may be several years, therefore, before we shall have any basis for judging how effective the Swedish program may be in raising the birth rate to maintenance level and keeping it there.

CHAPTER 15

A POPULATION POLICY FOR THE UNITED STATES

In this country we have never had a planned population policy. As yet, there is no appreciable demand for one although much the same general situation as regards present and probable future growth in numbers exists here as in Western Europe. Our population, except for a spurt during and following the war, has been growing slowly for some years (see Chapter 2) and the probability is that it will grow still more slowly until about 1975, then remain about stationary for a decade or a little more, after which it will begin to decline. That we have never had what could be called a population policy does not mean, however, that we have never followed national policies which influenced the growth of our population. Two such policies have undoubtedly had much influence on our national growth—our land policy and our immigration policy.

Our Land Policy and Population Growth

Making land readily procurable in family sized farms was undoubtedly a very potent factor in encouraging population growth in this country from the time of first settlement until near the end of the nineteenth century. During this period we were primarily an agricultural people and reasonably easy access to free or cheap land meant opportunity to most of our people. With an abundance of good land, easy to acquire, the size of the family had little effect upon the opportunity of the children to get a start in life and to attain at least as good a position as that of their parents. The chance to get land was enough. Furthermore, as long as there was a good chance to get land even the city workers, most of whom had had farm experience in their youth, did not have to worry much about their ability to take care of themselves and their families. If they did not like the conditions of their work in the city, they too could "go West" and take up land.

The land policy of the United States, in contrast to policies prevailing in much of South America, South Africa, and Australia, encouraged reasonably close settlement on family farms. Thus our land policy was, in effect, if not in intent, a population policy of the very greatest importance. That it attracted many people, both natives and foreigners, to the land admits of no doubt; nor is there any question that these farmers raised large families. From 1800 on the data show clearly that the people on or near the frontier had large families, much larger than those living in urban communities and in the older states. People on the frontier married young and the birth rate approached the physiological maximum, so that a land policy which kept attracting settlers to farms for over 200 years and kept farms relatively small was an extremely important factor in the rapid growth of population in our country. No more potent stimulus to population growth was ever devised, as the increase in our numbers amply testifies.

IMMIGRATION AND POPULATION GROWTH

A second policy which affected our population growth was the practically unrestricted entrance of immigrants during the period of great land settlement and for about 30 years thereafter—until after World War I. I have no hesitation in asserting that our immigration policy added materially to our numbers during the entire period prior to World War I, in spite of the oft-repeated dictum that immigrants only take the place of natives who would have been born had there been no immigrants. There may be conditions under which immigrants replace native births, but this seems highly doubtful when land is free, or nearly so, when industrial opportunity is ample, and when there is in general a dearth of labor available for the jobs open. The above conditions did prevail in the United States through most of the nineteenth century. The coming of vast numbers of immigrants may have hastened the development of urban industry and brought the end of free land earlier than it would have come otherwise, but that it added substantially to our population growth until about the middle of the 1920's seems to admit of little doubt.

CONDITIONS CREATING INTEREST IN A POPULATION POLICY

At the present time, as has been pointed out, the population of the United States is growing slowly, primarily because of the great decline in the birth rate. Assuming that the birth rate continues to decline but at a slower rate than heretofore, and that the decline in the death rate will also become slower, we shall probably attain a population of about 165 million by 1975; thereafter, save for a short period of relative stability, our numbers will diminish. This is the same demographic situation, with dates pushed forward 20-25 years, which has already called forth definite population policies in several European countries and is leading others to study their population problems carefully. It is not unlikely to lead the United States in the same direction in the not distant future. Our task here is to present some of the considerations which should be taken account of in developing a population policy for the United States. This necessarily involves making certain assumptions regarding the conditions which will prevail at the time we may be called upon to formulate a policy. Some of these can be foreseen without great difficulty, but others must remain obscure. Hence, some of the assumptions are certain to be open to serious question. Perhaps the best way to carry on will be to state explicitly the chief assumptions which it seems advisable to make at this time.

The Bases of a Population Policy

Since most population policies thus far developed do concern themselves to a large extent with controlling numbers, it will be assumed that this will be the dominating element in any policy we may adopt or encourage during the ensuing 25 years. Elements of a different character will be noted in their proper place. It will further be assumed that by 1975-80 we shall have a population of about 165 million, if in the meantime we make no concerted efforts at control. It is also assumed that the chief purpose of our policy will be to maintain our population at approximately this level. Alternatives to such an assumption would be (a) that we would desire to reduce our population to some lower figure, let us say to 140 or to 120 million, or (b) that we would desire to keep our population growing fairly rapidly, probably because of the desire to build up greater military strength.

Democracy.—Another assumption that will be made is that our present democratic system—as opposed to an authoritarian system—will continue to operate. This system will, of course, be modified in the future as it has been in the past, but it is assumed here that we will continue to rely on persuasion and the willingness of the individual to adapt his conduct to the rules laid down by the majority to secure a larger measure of general welfare. Hence, any population policy adopted must rely on the voluntary cooperation of the great majority of the people. This necessarily involves the belief that parenthood should be voluntary, but does not, of course, exclude the exercise of a certain amount of social pressure, exerted through public opinion, to secure a reasonable measure of conformity to the community's notion of what constitutes a desirable size of family. Furthermore, a democratic population policy must, like the Swedish, also assume that *every* child has the right to a good start in life—a good home, proper food and clothing,

good schools, and adequate training for work to which his ca-
pacities are suited. It is also assumed that the continuance of
a democratic system will be accompanied by a large measure of
private enterprise in economic life. Of course, where private
enterprise as understood at any given time comes into conflict
with democratic rights the latter must prevail.

Population Quality.—A third assumption is that we can do
very little at the present time to change the *hereditary* quality
of our people beyond forbidding reproduction to that small
class of people known definitely to transmit hereditary defects
(see Chapter 12), and discouraging reproduction by those who
have questionable heredity or physical defects which are reasonably certain to make them undesirable parents. This means
that the effort to improve hereditary quality by reducing the
size of families among the hereditarily unfit will constitute
only a minor part of any population policy adopted in the near
future. The real improvement in quality which we can actively
undertake is in social quality as represented in better health,
better education, better training, and wider opportunity to participate in all aspects of national life. Here the field is wide
open, and great improvement along these lines in the quality
of our citizens should be one of the important elements in any
population policy we adopt.

Better Distribution of Children.—Still another assumption
is that it is socially desirable for practically all people to participate in producing the next generation on as nearly an equal
basis as possible. Many people will regard such an assumption
as unnecessary and unwarranted because there is no clear evidence of the undesirability of having a large childless class in
the population. The reason for this assumption is the belief
that people will generally have a better balanced and more
humane outlook on the future if they have a fairly large biological stake in it than if they do not have any such stake, or

so small a stake that they have little in common with the mass of the population.[1]

It must be recognized, of course, that many couples cannot have all the children they want and that many will want more than the average number (about three) that would be needed to maintain the population, if it is assumed that only 15 percent of all women reaching childbearing age will never have a child and that only 15 percent can never have more than one child. Moreover, it should also be recognized that there are some people in the childless or one-child group whose contribution to society is worth far more than any number of children they might have brought into the world. But such people are few and it seems unfortunate to have as many men and women in positions of power and leadership, as we now do, who have no substantial biological stake in the future. It seems particularly unfortunate that we have developed such strenuous social and economic competition for the more important positions in the community that the three children needed by most fertile couples to insure maintenance of the population appear to so many people an insuperable handicap in attaining such positions.

Factors Controlling the Birth Rate.—A final assumption is that we now know enough about the causes of the decline in the birth rate (see Chapter 3) to formulate a policy which will lead to the size of population we may consider desirable. We do know that people who live in rural conditions have larger families than those who live in cities; that women who work outside the home have smaller families than those who do not, (even though there is a selective element here which probably exaggerates the real difference between these groups); that people

---

[1] It probably is not generally realized that about 20 percent of all women who reach 45 years of age are childless, that another 20-22 percent have only a single child, and that still another 20-22 percent have only two children. It would be necessary, therefore, for the two fifths with three or more children to have an average of about four children, merely to maintain the population. Obviously, at the present time, the burden of maintaining the population is falling on a relatively small proportion of the women—chiefly the rural-farm women and the poorer women in the nonfarm population.

in good economic and social position or hoping to get into such position have smaller families than those not so well off and not so ambitious; and that more and more people are becoming aware that the opportunities they can provide for their children are determined by how many children they have. Obviously, if a large proportion of the people living under urban conditions do not reproduce sufficiently to maintain their numbers, and we want to maintain numbers, then it is sheer stupidity to make no effort to disperse opportunity so that people will not need to move to large cities in order to find good jobs. It may be, of course, that the factors which really lead to the very low birth rates of cities are not peculiar to city life, but with our present knowledge the most reasonable assumption is that they are. If, however, it turns out that they are not, a more widespread dispersion of opportunity into smaller communities will probably have little effect on the birth rate.

Likewise, if more and more women work outside the home during the years they need to bear and raise enough children to maintain the population, and if these working women have very few children, we shall have to choose between their economic contribution as workers and their probable child contribution under changed conditions in which they are not compelled to work outside the home to obtain a decent living. It is scarcely reasonable to expect women to work for wages outside the home and to raise "normal" families at the same time.

No definite policy is being advocated on these points, but we cannot in all reason expect to control population growth intelligently if we do not squarely face the implications of the knowledge we possess about the factors affecting the birth rate.

Contraception has not been mentioned thus far as an important factor affecting the birth rate because it is not a cause in any true sense. It is merely a means of accomplishing an end. What we really need to know before we embark on any thoroughgoing population policy is the answer to the question:

Why do so many people want to limit the number of their children to so few that we cannot maintain our numbers? We certainly cannot answer this question satisfactorily at present, but I believe we are justified in assuming that we know enough about factors at work to formulate a tentative policy although we must hold ourselves ready to change this policy at all times as we secure better knowledge of the causes at work and of the means by which these causes can be eliminated or made to work towards the desired end.

The Economic Element in a Population Policy

The handicap about which people talk most (whether it really is the most important we are not fully certain at the present) is the economic; they say they cannot afford to raise more children than the one or two they have. What they really mean, in most cases, is that they cannot live at the level they deem necessary for their comfort and the maintenance of their social position and be able to give additional children the opportunities they would want them to have. No one who has examined this problem rather carefully can deny that there is much truth in this contention. The incomes of a large proportion of our people are inadequate to provide what we would generally consider a reasonable standard of comfort for a family of three or four children, if we include in this standard the assurance of being able to give them a fair opportunity to start in life. It seems probable therefore, that the community will have to assume some of the costs of providing larger opportunities to the children of a considerable part of our population if it wants enough of them to maintain numbers, and if the democratic ideal of equal opportunity is to be realized.

Certainly no one can be surprised to find that parents who must decide whether they will have another child or two and will accept the lower level of living this will entail, or whether they will remain content with the one or two they already have, more and more often decide in favor of the smaller family. The more comfortable classes have already made this choice in most cases (see Chapter 3), and in consequence have become the least prolific group in our population. The more prolific group in the population is rapidly learning that their best hope of improving their living conditions lies in the reduction of the size of their families rather than in securing enough income to maintain a good level of living and to give a larger family the opportunity desired. In a system where the income of most people depends entirely upon their contribution to the economy through their work there is no relation between the needs of the family and income.

This condition must be changed if the community (nation) wants any considerable proportion of the people to raise another child or two. Assisting parents with the expenses of raising children must, therefore, become an essential part of any population policy which is likely to be effective in maintaining our population. The exact form this assistance should take in order to be most effective probably cannot be determined without considerable experimentation. However, certain needs can be noted and they will, of course, suggest possible forms in which aid might be given.

Housing and Number of Children.—Better housing with better neighborhood conditions for the raising of children are coming to be recognized quite generally as an essential which must be provided if children are to be given a good start in life. It is also quite generally recognized that the incomes of a considerable proportion of our people are not sufficient to provide decent housing in neighborhoods where children will have opportunity for wholesome play and the development of healthy group activities. Consequently, low-cost housing in planned neighborhoods is probably one of the forms in which assistance should be given to parents. It will undoubtedly need to be subsidized housing. This will, of course, be called "un-American," perhaps even "communistic," but is it less "American" than to allow a large portion of our children to grow up in the slum conditions which now surround them? The answer seems obvious. Besides, we probably have no choice if we really want to maintain our numbers at about the level we shall reach by 1975.

Health and Number of Children.—In addition to some assistance to better housing in better neighborhoods there will probably also have to be assurance to parents of better health service for their children. This is so basic that there will be no argument as to the need. Nor will there be much argument regarding the inability of a large part of our population to provide this under the present system. Despite this acknowledged fact, many will maintain that more extensive community service for health will undermine the "rugged individualism" of American democracy and break down the independence of the family. Such arguments seem of doubtful sincerity when used to discourage the improvement in the public health service needed to assure all children a healthy body to start in life. Once the community accepts responsibility for health there will be no more danger of breaking down the desirable independence of the family than there has been in providing public education to those who could not afford family tutors and private schools.

Education and Number of Children.—Another aid to maintaining our population will be found in the extension of educational opportunity to the children of the less fortunate economic groups so that they will not have to quit school at an early age to take whatever job may be open to them as unskilled and untrained workers. Our school system should see to it that promising individuals among the lower income groups have the opportunity to go on to advanced work, on equal terms with children from more fortunate families. This is the only democratic way to insure against the development of a more or less closed class system.

Insecurity and Number of Children.—It must also be recognized that the uncertainty of one's ability to meet the usual obligations incurred in raising children is a powerful depressant of the birth rate. If we are to eliminate economic insecurity as an important factor in reducing the birth rate some way must be found to prevent the involuntary stoppages of work which render so uncertain the incomes of a considerable part of the city population, and to prevent the great price fluctuations which affect farmers in much the same way. Intelligent people will increasingly refuse to assume the obligations of raising a fair-sized family if they cannot be reasonably certain that they can fulfill their obligations in an acceptable manner. They will prefer childlessness, or at most, one or two children who can be given a good start in life to three or four brought up in semi-poverty and hence deprived of many opportunities that would otherwise be open to them. Let us not forget that if the number of births had remained at the level of 1933 there would now (1948) be 6.5-7.0 million fewer children under 10 in the United States than there actually are. Where births can be controlled it seems almost certain that people will reduce them when there is scant prospect of caring for children at standards commonly accepted as "decent."

The feeling of uncertainty regarding the future of one's children must also be a factor of some importance in the minds of many women because of the economic handicaps imposed on children by widowhood. Insofar as insecurity regarding the future is a factor of importance in reducing the size of the family it should be removed by assuring the husband that he can count on a fair-paying job at all times and that, in case of his death, the community will see that the widow has the means to raise her children in reasonable comfort and give them the customary opportunities.

FORMS OF FAMILY ASSISTANCE

Services or Cash?—In the judgment of the writer it would be better to render most of the economic aids to the family in the form of community services rather than in cash, where this is possible. It must be recognized, however, that some services would be better performed if cash were given directly to the parents, e.g., anything intended to assist in the adequate clothing of children, from layettes to school clothes, probably should be given in cash without any restriction as to the style, quality, etc. Since we have already become accustomed to a certain amount of public health service it would probably be better to expand this work and provide health facilities on much the same basis we now provide public education. The chief consideration in deciding upon the form of aid to the family for the benefit of the children should be to prevent the family from feeling that it is receiving charity, or is being in any way classed as abnormal in accepting such aid. We have come to look upon the public school as a proper community service because we need the type of citizen trained in such schools. Is good health one whit less important than good education? Is it less important to be brought up in a good home in a good neighborhood than to go to a good school?

Perhaps the best way to carry out the aid to families with children would be to make most of the services essential to health and a good preparation for life available to all, without any distinction between people of different economic and social status. They would then soon come to be considered a proper community service and the right of every citizen, just as the public school now is, and at the same time would greatly lighten the burden of those who have the larger families.

THE PSYCHOLOGICAL ELEMENT

But even if the economic handicaps are the most important of those now standing in the way of maintaining a birth rate at the level that may be desired, of providing good social opportunities, and of insuring economic and social security to the less fortunate classes it would be a serious mistake, probably a fatal mistake, to ignore the psychological factors in forming a population policy. The *climate of opinion* is undoubtedly a very important factor in determining the rate of reproduction. In the preceding chapter it was shown how this factor has operated in China and how it probably played some part in raising the German birth rate. Assuming that the voluntary control of births will become general, there is no reason to doubt that the community's attitude towards reproduction will become one of the most important factors in determining the number of children a couple will want to raise. If the community really wishes to do so it can build up an attitude which will encourage the desired size of the family; however, to accomplish this will require much determined effort. It is important to remember that the people who most need a favorable climate of opinion to induce them to raise larger families are in better-than-average economic circumstances and can be influenced less than the average citizen by any lightening of the economic burden imposed by having a fair-sized family.

In this class, ambition, desire for ease and luxury, and unwillingness to make any considerable personal sacrifice for children are the important, and probably decisive, factors. Only a change in the climate of opinion as it affects reproduction will have much effect on these people. There is some reason to believe, however, that if the community as a whole comes to place a higher value on reproduction than it now does most of these people will conform to the family pattern thus established. Those people who refuse to be influenced by such a change in social attitude towards reproduction, who persist in following modes of conduct peculiar to their own small group where reproduction is regarded as of little consequence in comparison with personal satisfactions, or who are not willing to assume the responsibilities of raising children, will inevitably die out. Although these people may have somewhat more than average intelligence as we now measure it, the very fact of their dying out, when this is voluntary, shows that their greater intelligence does not lead them to place much value on a future reaching beyond their own lives. We need not worry much over the extinction of such people. It has probably always been true that people who place personal values above biological and social values have had a low survival rate and there is no evidence that mankind is the worse because of this. It is when the community itself places a higher value, economically and socially, on doing most other types of work than it does on raising a fair-sized family that its survival it endangered. If the community does not create a greater interest in participating in the future through children, as well as ease the economic handicaps of those who want to raise children, we shall probably be unable to maintain our numbers.

How this new climate of opinion is to be created is by no means clear. However, it seems probable that many of our leaders will have to demonstrate their own faith in our future and their willingness to make personal sacrifices in raising children before we can develop an effective body of opinion not only sanctioning but encouraging fair-sized families. We shall have to substitute the ideals (values) and satisfactions of family life for the satisfaction of ever-higher levels of competitive consumption and the attainment of other forms of personal prestige, before we can hope to keep the birth rate at maintenance level. This is equivalent to saying that intangible social values are fully as basic in determining reproduction as the more tangible economic values. If this is true, then the neglect of these social values in the formulation of a population policy will doom it to failure. Unless people believe that the raising of a fair-sized family is highly desirable, and essential to the development of a rich personality, it seems unlikely that any economic inducements will be sufficient to keep us from dying out. On the other hand, even though many people do believe in the desirability of fair-sized families, and believe that raising three or four children will contribute materially to the achievement of very real and lasting personal values, the scales will not be tipped in the direction of raising more than one or two children if the economic and social disabilities involved in raising them remain as great as they now are.

POPULATION DISTRIBUTION AND POPULATION POLICY

As pointed out above, there has been a rapid and steady movement of people from farms and villages to cities ever since the Industrial Revolution began. This has resulted in increasing concentrations of population in the relatively few centers which are highly vulnerable to military attack and in which reproduction is too feeble to maintain numbers. In many cities in the United States the birth rate is already so low that numbers would decline from one fourth to one third in a generation if there was no immigration for some years. As was suggested above, an intelligent population policy will take these facts into account. Both from the standpoint of maintaining population and from the standpoint of military security it is desirable to prevent the increasing concentration of population in a few large cities.

The problem raised by inadequate reproduction in urban communities was recognized in the German, French, and Italian population policies but practically nothing was done to reconcile the need for an increasing proportion of nonagricultural workers with the need for a more rural type of life if the size of a population was to be maintained. The vital questions are whether people will reproduce under modern conditions of city life, whether modern industry and commerce can be so reorganized that more and more people need not be drawn into larger factories and offices in larger and larger cities, and whether military security can be obtained except through the dispersal of people and industry.

The author has no information on these points which is not available to everyone. It is altogether possible that failure of modern city populations to replace themselves is a passing phase of man's adaptation to a new type of civilization. To believe this indicates a faith in a *laissez-faire* population policy for which the author can find no justification. The older cities of Europe have as yet shown no signs of a rise in the birth rate as a result of a longer period of adaptation of their people to city life. It would be foolish to say that such a change in reproduction could not take place; it is equally foolish to rely on it in the light of such evidence on reproduction in cities as we now possess.

For reasons discussed in Chapter 8 it seems far more reasonable to assume that industry and commerce can be so reorganized that people need not be crowded together in cities than it is to believe that city dwellers will reproduce sufficiently to maintain themselves. In all the low birth rate countries rural people still have a replacement rate well above that needed for maintainence. It probably will decline farther, but at present it does not look as though the birth rate in the rural population would fall below the replacement level for a few decades at the earliest.

MILITARY CONSIDERATIONS

In addition to what was said in Chapter 5 about the effects of war on the distribution of population, the role of military considerations in the forming of a population policy deserves special mention. It can scarcely be expected that the statesmen of any of the great powers will look with favor upon policies which would lead to a decline of population in their countries as long as military considerations must bulk large in their national thinking, even though it should become quite clear that a good level of living could be attained only by actually reducing the population. It is one of the ironies of life that military considerations always seem to demand a larger population and the use of force to secure the larger resources and trade to support a continuing increase—a vicious circle from which there is no outlet as long as force is the prime factor in settling the disputes of nations. There can be no rational population policy in a nation (by "rational," I mean a policy intended to secure a high degree of social and economic welfare in peacetime) as long as military needs are pressing. This is a truism because in times of peace we define "welfare" largely in terms of *individual* welfare consisting of economic security, good health, leisure, good housing, etc., yet define it in terms of military security, in terms of what the community must do to survive, whenever survival is threatened by an outside force. Quite obviously, the individual plays a vastly different role in society when the dominant values in community life are determined by such different considerations. But military considerations are not limited to interest in the size of the population. As early as 1929, in her first five-year plan, the Soviet Union definitely undertook the dispersion of her industry, locating many of her new factories far to the east beyond the range of attack by air. This stood her in good stead in World War II and probably saved her from defeat. It is doubtful, however, if any location is now beyond the range of attack from the air and certainly will not long remain so. As pointed out in Chapter 9, the basic industries of the United States are highly vulnerable to air attack, and the possible destruction of human life by atomic bomb and biological weapons surpasses one's imagination.

Thus far the redistribution of population as a population policy does not seem to have been given serious consideration in any country except in the Soviet Union, and even there only the distribution of new cities in space has been attempted. There has been no attempt to organize production and the processes of commerce in smaller units, and to develop self-sufficiency within relatively small regions. However, the Soviet economic plans, even as they are, would probably result in more cities and metropolitan districts of 200,000-300,000 and fewer of · 1,000,000 or more than would be found in the West in a population of similar size. In the United States there is no indication whatever that military considerations have had any influence either on our thinking about numbers or about the future distribution of our population. If it turns out that the United States must give greater weight to military considerations, then most of the elements which we should like to see embodied in a population policy will have to go by the board. When military considerations become urgent they not only cannot be ignored but must be given first place in our plans. If our national survival is in jeopardy then the population policies needed would be substantially different from those suggested above. We would perforce think in terms of what is necessary to prevent our succumbing to a "blitzkrieg" in a world where the other great nations were planning such attacks. This would almost certainly lead to measures far less democratic than those discussed above. In critical situations there is not time to allow democratic procedures to take their regular course, nor can we rely on the sum of individual decisions to result in plans and organization adequate to insure the cooperation needed for national survival and the continuance of our way of life. But this line of thought need not be pursued now. A population policy suited to a democratic world in which each nation is more or less free to work out its own aims and ideals cannot be maintained in a world where national existence is constantly in jeopardy. This seems so obvious as to need no proof. Our recent experiences should have convinced us of the truth of this statement.

No matter how isolationist one may be, the fact remains that we live in a world where the political aims of one or two countries and the population policies calculated to support those aims will necessarily have to be taken into account in establishing a policy for ourselves. Only in a free world will we be free to set up a population policy for ourselves and to pursue aims which we believe will contribute most largely to our welfare as we now define that word.

Differences in the Population Policies of Nations

While the author believes that the maintenance of our population at about 165 million is a reasonable aim for the United States, he would like to have it clearly understood that this number is mentioned merely because it seems probable that we shall have about this number by 1975, if we do nothing to control our growth in the meantime. Furthermore, such a population can be maintained at a good level of living only if there is no significant decrease in the quantity or quality of our natural resources. The use of this number does not imply that 165 million represents an *optimum* population for the United States. The economic optimum may well be smaller while the optimum from certain other standpoints, e.g., strategic and cultural, might be larger. The size of population to be aimed at in any country should depend upon the resources available and the social values the nation desires to achieve. Even the maintenance of present numbers is undesirable in many countries. The writer believes that England, Germany, and Italy already have more people than is desirable from the standpoint of providing them with a good living while China, Japan, and India as well as other parts of Asia can only look forward to the most distressing poverty until they learn to control their population growth. On the other hand, a fairly rapid increase of population is probably desirable in Australia, New Zealand, and Brazil. The satisfactory adjustment of population to its resources should be a major factor in the population policy of any country. But since different peoples with like resources may prefer different numbers and different types of organization, they will have different ideas of how their resources should be used to yield the "good" life. In other words, national population policies should take account of the different values which give life its meaning among different peoples. However, the *satisfactory adjustment* of numbers to resources is by no means the only important element in a population policy, although discussions of policy often leave the impression that this is the case.

INDEX

Abortion in Germany, restrictions, 236
Adults, effect of increased number, 185
in our economy, 183-187
Aerial bombing and the large city, 99-102
Africa, death rate, 75
growth of population, 6, 26
land still available, 126, 154
Age changes, causes, 175-178
effect on health of country, 186-187
rapidity of, 178-181
social and economic effects, 175-188
United States, 176
Age, distribution, by countries, 175
in future, 184-185
Agricultural efficiency and urbanization, 139
Agricultural population, 134
Agricultural Revolution, death rate, 71-72
and distribution of population, 133-134
Aliens, United States, net arrivals and departures, 156
America, North and Central, growth of population, 6
Appalachian-Ozark region, growth of population in, 159
Argentina, density of population, 128
growth of population, 109-111
Arkansas, depression and migration, 163
Asia, growth of population, 6
Asiatics, migration of, 152
percentage increase, 7-8
Atomic bombs, 172
Atomic threat, Warren S. Thompson on, 171n
Australia, density of population, 128
future population, 106
S. H. Wolstenholme on, 106n
growth of population, 107-109
land available for settlement 126, 127, 269

Australia—*Continued*
population, Warren S. Thompson on, 129n
population carrying capacity, Griffith Taylor on, 129
sex ratios at birth, 95
stationary population, 129
Austria, growth of population, 107-109
sex ratios at birth, 95

Bacteria and disease, work of Pasteur, 65
Baltic countries, growth of population, 107-109
Belgium, growth of population, 107-109
sex ratios at birth, 95
Biological fitness, family eugenics, 206
(See also Hereditary fitness)
Biological warfare, 172
Birth control, Malthus' view on, 5
necessity of, 123-125
Birth rate, 28-47
as affected by age and sex, 29-31
divorce, 58-59
good and bad harvests, 55-56
proportion married, 29-31
in Appalachian-Ozark region, 159
in cities, 32
Class I, countries exercising control of, 107
control of, 54-55, 149
in early times, 31
countries with low and declining, 107-109
countries with medium, 109-111
crude, definition, 28
decline in, 149
history of, 33-34
psychological factors in, 59-60
in depression, 38-39
differential, 36
ambition, 51-53
in cities, 148
by economic classes, 51-55, 202
Germany during World War I, 84

DATE DUE

OCT 2 0 1988			